Innovation, Entrepreneurship, Geography and Growth

Edited by Philip McCann and Les Oxley

T0317369

WILEY-BLACKWELL

A John Wiley & Sons, Ltd., Publication

Library of Congress Cataloging-in-Publication Data

Innovation, entrepreneurship, geography, and growth / edited by Philip McCann and Les Oxley.
        p. cm.
    Includes index.
    ISBN 978-1-118-42728-6 (pbk.)
    1. Entrepreneurship.   2. Technological innovations.   3. Economic geography.   4. Small business–Growth.   I. McCann, Philip, 1964–   II. Oxley, Les.
    HB615.I5637 2013
    338.9–dc23

                                                                                        2012032711

A catalogue record for this book is available from the British Library.

Cover image: Global financial color charts and graphs illustration © Sergej Khakimullin/Shutterstock
Cover design by Workhaus

Typeset in 10/12pt Times by Aptara Inc., New Delhi, India

1   2013

CONTENTS

Notes on Contributors

Martijn J. Burger	Erasmus University Rotterdam
Tommaso Ciarli	Max Planck Institute of Economics, Jena
Riccardo Crescenzi	London School of Economics, London
Wenying Fu	School of Geography, South China Normal University
Shangqin Hong	University of Canterbury
Joris Knoben	Tilburg Universiy
Philip McCann	University of Groningen, Adjunct Professor of Economics at the University of Waikato
Valentina Meliciani	University of Teramo, Italy
Ernest Miguélez	Economics and Statistics Division, World Intellectual Property Organization and AQR-IREA, University of Barcelona
Rosina Moreno	AQR-IREA, Department of Econometrics, Statistics and Spanish Economy, University of Barcelona
Raquel Ortega-Argilés	University of Groningen
Les Oxley	University of Waikato
Simon C. Parker	University of Western Ontario, Canada
Otto Raspe	Netherlands Environmental Assessment Agency (PBL)
Javier Revilla Diez	Institute of Economic and Cultural Geography, Leibniz University of Hanover
Andrés Rodríguez-Pose	London School of Economics, London and IMDEA Social Sciences, Madrid
Maria Savona	SPRU, Science and Technology Policy Research, University of Sussex
Daniel Schiller	Institute of Economic and Cultural Geography, Leibniz University of Hanover
Frank G. van Oort	Utrecht University, Economic Geography

1

INNOVATION, ENTREPRENEURSHIP, GEOGRAPHY AND GROWTH

Philip McCann and Les Oxley

This special edition of the *Journal of Economic Surveys* provides a timely audit of the state of art regarding our understanding of the complex links between innovation, entrepreneurship, geography and growth. Until the 1980s these issues were all generally treated as being part of the Solow residual, and as such, were largely outside the domain of mainstream economic research work. Before this period, the assumed primary role of factor allocation mechanisms in driving growth relegated such issues to being topics of minor interest, and the situation only really started to change in the 1980s when a series of important theoretical and empirical publications first began to shift ideas and priorities after many decades of inertia. From the late 1980s onwards, the rate at which publications on these topics appeared accelerated rapidly. An early series of theoretical breakthroughs was followed shortly by a surge of empirical chapters, which increasingly opened up the debates to wider sets of issues. The debates first shifted from a focus almost solely on manufacturing and industrial arenas to services and other areas of the economy, and then secondly by emphasizing the role played by small as well as large firms in growth, followed by an increasing awareness of the non-technological and institutional aspects of innovation, and finally incorporating the role of geography. Over time, more commentators have taken on board something of a systems-type understanding of these phenomena, but econometrically such an approach poses great difficulties. Therefore, orthodox empirical approaches still dominate, but now the much improved availability of survey-based microeconometric data, as well as aggregate national and regional data, has provided for both more, and also for more nuanced, analyses. Overall, it is probably fair to say that our current understanding of innovation, and its relationships with entrepreneurship, geography and economic growth, is currently more advanced empirically than it is theoretically, although this is in marked contrast the situation pertaining three decades ago. However, what becomes clear from the chapters presented in this special issue is that there are still many aspects of these relationships that need both further theoretical as well as empirical analysis. A widespread acceptance of the centrality of technology, innovation, entrepreneurship and geography in driving economic growth means that these issues will no longer be treated as elements in

Innovation, Entrepreneurship, Geography and Growth, First Edition.
Edited by Philip McCann and Les Oxley. Chapters © 2013 The Authors.
Book compilation © 2013 Blackwell Publishing Ltd. Published 2013 by Blackwell Publishing Ltd.

an economic residual, but rather as the key issues on which public policy will seek to have a positive influence.

The chapters in this special issue all deal with different aspects of the relationships between technology, innovation, entrepreneurship and geography, which drive economic growth. They do so from a variety of theoretical, empirical and institutional angles, and importantly, each of the operate at the interface between at least two of these key aspects. Moreover, the ordering of the chapters also reflects the shifts in our understanding of these relationships, which initially operated at the interface between micro and macroeconomic theoretical models, were then developed econometrically using aggregate sectoral data, and since have rapidly been extended via the use of microeconometric and survey data to examine more disaggregated geographical and institutional aspects. As such, the aim of the special issue is to provide the reader with a comprehensive roadmap of the types of issues that research at the interface between these different aspects addresses, to reflect the developments in our understanding of these relationships, and to open up debates as to the most fruitful ways forward for enhancing our understanding of these issues.

The first chapter by *Simon Parker*, discusses the theoretical relationship between entrepreneurship, innovation and economic growth. It is clear that firm destruction, new firm formation and the ongoing inter-firm competition that this churning ensures, is an essential element of innovation and economic growth. Yet, the exact mechanisms by which these interrelationships operate are far from clear, and various theoretical arguments have been proposed. Parker distinguished three broad classes of theoretical approaches to understanding these relationships: models of creative destruction; models of innovation and implementation cycles; and models of production under asymmetric information. Despite their differences, these three models all share the property that entrepreneurship is potentially pro-cyclical, and one or two of them also admit the possibility that entrepreneurship trends may also exhibit acyclicality, whereas the major differences between the theories concern whether entrepreneurship is predicted to vary contemporaneously with the business cycle, or whether it lags or leads it. Taken together, these theories generate at least three major insights: first, personal assets are important for the occurrence and persistence of business cycles; second, expectations play an important role in the timing of innovations; and third, entrepreneurship continues even in recessions.

The second chapter by *Raquel Ortega-Argilés* discusses the huge econometric literature seeking to uncover the reasons for the transatlantic productivity gap, a productivity gap which rapidly began to emerge during mid-1990s. The emergence of this productivity gap was in marked contrast to the previous long-term trends. By the late 1980s the productivity performance of the two major macro-regions of Europe and North America had largely converged, after almost half a century of European economic restructuring and integration. However, this Transatlantic inter-regional convergence process was rapidly reversed some two decades ago, leading to a period of marked inter-regional divergence. The reasons for this divergence appear to be related to ways in which the United States reaped the benefits of the widespread adoption, and adaptation, of the new generation of general purpose technologies emerging, based on modern information and communications technologies (ICTs). The econometric evidence suggests that the productivity shock in favor of North America was related firstly, to production of ICTs, and then secondly to dissemination and use of ICTs in non-ICT producing sectors. Europe was much slower to realize either of these types of benefits, and the positive impacts of technological change have been lower than in the United States. However, from the empirical evidence it also becomes clear that within Europe there are large differences in these technology-productivity effects across sectors, firms and regions, and that a more nuanced understanding is called for.

The third chapter by *Shangqin Hong, Philip McCann and Les Oxley* considers the role played by the increasing availability of empirical surveys in shaping our understanding of innovation. An examination of the theoretical and conceptual arguments surrounding innovation, and the relationship between these arguments and empirical research, demonstrates that the evolution of our understanding of the nature of innovation, and also the role of innovation in economic growth and development, has in part been related to the evidence available. Early survey-based research tended to focus on manufacturing and science, reflecting a rather narrow understanding of innovation, and such surveys still dominate in some technology-science lead societies. However, over time in many countries there has been an increasing awareness of the role played by non-technical and institutional factors in driving innovation in service industries as well as manufacturing and engineering, and this shift in emphasis has also been reflected an increasing emphasis on the 'softer' influences on innovation. Most recently, the role of economic geography, and in particular the role played by the interactions between economic geography and institutions, in shaping, fostering and even inhibiting innovation, have come to the fore. These shifts both reflect, and have been reflected in, the contemporary nature of modern innovation surveys.

The fourth chapter by *Tommaso Ciarli, Valentina Meliciani and Maria Savona* discusses the literature and empirical evidence regarding the dynamics of the relationships between knowledge, structural change and the spatial concentration of economic activities in the case of business services. To do so, they explore how the role of knowledge has evolved in relation to the dimensions of: science, technology and structural change; the long-term processes of tertiarization of economies and in particular the growth of business services; and the spatial concentration of business services. This increasing spatial concentration is explained as an outcome of the increasing size and complexity of knowledge and the increasing need for managing this through spatial proximity. The argument is supported by empirical evidence on the spatial concentration of business services in the European regions.

The fifth chapter by *Frank van Oort, Martijn Burger, Joris Knoben and Otto Raspe* moves the discussion explicitly t a geographical level, and analyses very detailed Dutch data to examine the ambiguities evident in much of the empirical research regarding the role of agglomeration economies in fostering growth. Much of this ambiguity is related to measurement issues and heterogeneity in terms of the scale, time period, levels of aggregation, growth definitions and the functional form of the models applied. The authors argue that a powerful way forward for resolving many of these ambiguities lies in the application of hierarchical or multi-level modeling to firm-level datasets. Hierarchical or multi-level modeling, which allows micro levels and macro levels to be modeled simultaneously, is becoming an increasingly common practice in the social sciences. In economics, however, these techniques are still relatively under-used, but firm-level data, which is also geographically coded provides an ideal context for using such approaches to uncover the firm-specific roles in economic growth.

The sixth chapter by *Ernest Miguélez and Rosina Moreno* aims to devise a method for computing a composite indicator that measures the regional degree of exposure to external knowledge sources. Such methods are critical to allow comparisons between regions and to benchmark different places on the basis of their knowledge spillover characteristics. On the basis of this indicator the authors then propose a typology of regions according to their potential capacity to access non-local items of knowledge. It is this ability to access external knowledge sources, which helps them to overcome locally specific limits and to build on and recombine local and non-local complementary knowledge elements so as to produce a higher number of new ideas. Building on various research streams that have been relatively independent to date, they review recent key studies which motivates their approach and the construction of their composite indicator, which can then be used to appraise the extent to which each region is in an optimal position to access external innovative resources.

The seventh chapter by *Riccardo Crescenzi and Andrés Rodríguez-Pose* follows a similar approach to the previous chapter, although here the approach is primarily from a conceptual rather than an empirical angle. The authors discuss recent developments in the literature on local and regional innovative performance, with the aim of demonstrating how an integrated ad conceptual framework based on a combination and linking of different theories can serve as a foundation for comparing the relationships between innovation, geography and institutions in both developed and developing countries. Such relationships are often discussed in terms of 'regional innovation systems', and drawing on elements of endogenous growth theory, new economic geography and the innovation systems literatures, the chapter outlines an analytical framework for explaining the differences between innovation systems and their geography. This framework then forms the basis of an analysis of the differences in innovative capacity between the 'mature' technological leading regions of the European Union and the Unites States, and the 'emerging' technological catching-up regions of China and India. The systematic analysis of a large body of empirical literature shows that there are important differences between the spatial patterning of the regional innovation systems in the mature and emerging economies.

The eighth chapter by *Wenying Fu, Javier Revilla Diez and Daniel Schiller* adopts an evolutionary economic geography approach to examine the regional innovation system in two regions of China currently undergoing rapid transformation, namely Shenzhen and Dongguan. A comparison of the two regions demonstrates that the technological upgrading processes in the two regions are quire different, and in part depending on the different governance systems of the region. Indeed, the institutional development of the regions is seen to be a critical part of the evolutionary story of each region. In the case of Shenzhen, the production system of 1980s has gradually evolved to a higher level globalized system characterized by something of an interactive regional innovation system, in contrast to the grassroots-type globalized production system in Dongguan, where innovation activities are low and are still passively managed by global players. The review on the evolutionary path of electronics industry in Shenzhen and Dongguan reveals that the locational first-mover advantage in Shenzhen is further strengthened by the institutional first-mover advantage.

Taken together, these eight chapters succinctly capture the evolution of our understanding of the relationships between entrepreneurship, innovation, geography and economic growth. Although it is clear that research on these issues has made enormous strides over the last three decades, it is also clear that much remains to be explored. Reading these eight chapters sequentially suggests that a great deal of progress might be made from a theoretical perspective by finding ways to increasingly incorporate into growth models the types of insights discussed in these chapters regarding the interactions between technology, geography and institutions. Such theoretical approaches ought to be motivated by, and based on, the empirical evidence underlying most of the advances in our understanding of these issues, as it has been empirical research which has largely dominated the field over the last two decades.

2

THEORIES OF ENTREPRENEURSHIP, INNOVATION AND THE BUSINESS CYCLE

Simon C. Parker

The financial crisis of 2008 together with the Great Recession that followed it have refocused economists' attention on the determinants of business cycles and recessions. It seems that the need to understand the deep economic causes of business cycles is no less pressing now than it was at the time of the Great Depression. Arguably, what is different now is the importance that policy-makers attach to entrepreneurship as a source of growth and recovery (Lundström and Stevenson, 2005; Audretsch *et al.*, 2007).

Recent research has certainly demonstrated the important role entrepreneurs play in the economy. Entrepreneurs create jobs (Birch, 1979), commercialize and disseminate innovations (Acs and Audretsch, 1988), accumulate savings and wealth (Quadrini, 2000; Cagetti and de Nardi, 2006) and drive economic growth (van Stel *et al.*, 2005). However, we know less about how entrepreneurs affect and are affected by the business cycle (Parker, 2011).

This chapter aims to address this lacuna by reviewing several influential theories of innovation and the business cycle in which entrepreneurs play a prominent role. The chapter deliberately focuses on theory rather than evidence. Empirical research on entrepreneurship and business cycles is still in its infancy and research methodologies in this area remain under-developed at the time of writing. The interested reader can consult Parker *et al.* (2012) for recent overviews of the evidence. I have also chosen to focus on theories in which entrepreneurs play an important role, rather than attempting to review theories of business cycles in general. There are already several comprehensive reviews of the broader business cycle literature (e.g. King and Rebelo, 1999; Rebelo, 2005).

At the outset, it is important to clarify what I mean by 'entrepreneurship'. Reflecting the content of the chapters reviewed here, the term will be taken to have a dual meaning. In some contexts, it will refer specifically to entry, irrespective of whether this entails the creation of brand new firms or the creation of new plants by existing firms. In other chapters, it will refer to some productivity-enhancing effort by profit-seeking agents—often referred to as 'commercialization' or 'innovation'. This definition seems to have been favored by Schumpeter, who wrote that 'the function of entrepreneurs is to reform or revolutionize the pattern of production by exploiting an invention or, more generally, an untried

Innovation, Entrepreneurship, Geography and Growth, First Edition.
Edited by Philip McCann and Les Oxley. Chapters © 2013 The Authors.
Book compilation © 2013 Blackwell Publishing Ltd. Published 2013 by Blackwell Publishing Ltd.

technological possibility... this function does not essentially consist in either inventing anything or otherwise creating the conditions which the enterprise exploits. It consists in getting things done' (1942, 132).

The theories reviewed in this chapter can be classified into three categories. These categories are: creative destruction; implementation cycles and innovation; and production under asymmetric information. The first three sections of this chapter review theories under each of these headings in turn. The final section steps back and evaluates them in terms of what they teach us about entrepreneurship and the business cycle. The chapter closes with a brief discussion of limitations and opportunities for future research in this area.

1. Models of Creative Destruction and the Business Cycle

This section starts by briefly outlining Schumpeter's theory of innovation, creative destruction, and the business cycle. This theory has heavily influenced subsequent thinkers. Because of several major limitations of this theory, which will quickly become apparent, I will not dwell long on this material. Instead, it will be used as a platform for a formal model of creative destruction. The latter is less a model of business cycles than an investigation into the conditions under which creative destruction arises when demand drops exogenously, for example, in a recession.

1.1 Schumpeter's Theory of Business Cycles and Creative Destruction

Josef Schumpeter (1927, 1939) was one of the most influential early writers about business cycles, innovation, and entrepreneurship. In the words of one of the great economists of the twentieth century, Schumpeter argued that 'business cycles are the recurrent fluctuations in the rate at which innovations are introduced into the economy, in the intensity with which entrepreneurs exercise their *sui generis* function of overcoming obstacles to new combinations' (Kuznets, 1940, 259). According to Schumpeter, history contains a few unusual episodes in which groups of exceptionally able entrepreneurs introduce revolutionary innovations which transform existing technologies. During these episodes, economies grow strongly and experience booms. But the diffusion of these innovations eventually encourage imitators to swarm into the market and compete away the pioneering entrepreneurs' profits. Schumpeter argued that such imitators help to establish the new order as a new equilibrium for the economy. The economy slows down and stagnates, until another set of pioneering entrepreneurs disrupts the equilibrium again with a new set of revolutionary innovations which renders the previous ones obsolete. This precipitates the next boom, and the cycle repeats itself. Schumpeter suggested that this process of entrepreneurial innovation is responsible for the regular and commonly observed fluctuations in economic activity which he called the 'normal' business cycle.

The replacement of old technologies certainly benefits the entrepreneurs introducing the new ones, at the expense of incumbents whose production is tied to older technologies which now become obsolete. Schumpeter called this process 'creative destruction'. There are numerous examples of creative destruction, including the replacement of steam locomotives by diesel and electric trains; of the telegraph by the telephone; and of vinyl LP's by compact discs. Economists have recently begun to analyze disruptive Schumpeterian innovations and creative destruction in more formal settings (for a survey, see Aghion and Howitt, 1998).

Although the creative destruction concept has stood the test of time, numerous subsequent writers have criticized Schumpeter's account of business cycles. Simon Kuznets was an early critic, who pointed out that Schumpeter crucially fails to explain how unequal entrepreneurial abilities translate into 'bunching' of innovations through time which gives rise to booms and recessions (1940, 262–263). One possibility is the arrival of major technological breakthroughs that influence all sectors – a general purpose technology (GPT). But there is no scientific reason why GPTs should arrive in regular cycles; and there is no evidence that they do in practice either. That creates difficulties for Schumpeter's efforts to link regular business cycles to the arrival of irregular GPTs. As Kuznets pointed out, it is possible for GPTs to be associated with 'long wave' cycles, but it is hard to sustain this argument for short-term high-frequency cycles which are of primary interest to researchers and policy-makers.

Another problem with Schumpeter' theory is that, radical GPT advances apart, inventions tend to emerge continuously over time. Subsequent theorists have recognized this limitation and have developed more realistic models. One such model, of creative destruction in the context of a recessionary phase of the business cycle, is outlined next.

1.2 A Formal Model

An important theoretical question concerns the degree to which reduced demand during recessions leads to lower rates of new firm entry, rather than higher rates of exit among incumbents. To the extent that adjustment takes place on the new firm entry margin, the force of creative destruction may be mitigated. This is an especially important issue if new firms introduce new technologies while incumbents use less efficient, old-fashioned technologies.

A simple 'technology vintage' model of creative destruction is helpful to conceptualize the difference between entry and exit responses to recessionary drops in demand. Let $f(a, t)$ denote the density of production units aged a at time t, where a varies between 0 (new entrants) and some endogenous maximum age $\bar{a}(t)$ at which point a firm's technology is obsolete and the firm exits. Both $f(a, t)$ and $\bar{a}(t)$ are assumed to be continuous functions. With an exogenous firm failure rate of $\delta > 0$, the number of units which have survived for a years by time t is therefore

$$f(a, t) = f(0, t - a)e^{-\delta a} \qquad 0 \leq a \leq \bar{a}(t) \tag{1}$$

where $f(0, t - a)$ indexes entries of firms that were new a years ago. Hence the rate of change in the number of firms, $N(t)$, at time t is

$$\dot{N}(t) = \frac{d}{dt} \int_0^{\bar{a}(t)} f(a, t) \, da$$
$$= f(0, t) - \{f(\bar{a}(t), t)[1 - \dot{\bar{a}}(t)] + \delta N(t)\} \tag{2}$$

The first term of (2), that is, $f(0, t)$, measures the rate of creation of new firms. The second term measures the rate of destruction of existing firms. The technical conditions $f(0, t) \geq 0$ and $\dot{\bar{a}}(t) < 1 \; \forall t$ ensure that (endogenous) rates of firm creation and destruction are always non-negative.

Caballero and Hammour (1994) use this framework to identify the conditions under which either entry and/or exit will accommodate a decline in consumer demand. Those conditions turn out to hinge on whether costs of firm entry are either constant, c [referred to as case (a)] or an increasing function of the firm creation rate in the industry as a whole [referred to as case (b): cost $= c(f(0,t))$ with $c'(\cdot) > 0$]. Case (b) is consistent with industry-wide adjustment costs, which are convex in the amount of resource reallocation taking place.

Entry occurs until the net present value of profit flows $\Pi(a,t)$, discounted at rate $r > 0$, just covers firm entry costs c. Instantaneous profits are $\Pi(a,t) = P(t)\kappa(t-a) - 1$, where $P(t)$ is the endogenous industry price at t; $\kappa(t-a)$ is the output of a firm aged a at t; and operational costs are normalized at 1. For simplicity, Caballero and Hammour assume that a firm entering at time t produces fixed output $\kappa(t)$ over its lifetime $[0, \bar{a}(t)]$. They further assume that newer firms have higher productivity, owing to exogenous technical progress, which grows at rate $\gamma > 0$. If $T(t)$ denotes the maximum lifetime of a firm created at t, perfect foresight implies

$$\bar{a}[t + T(t)] = T(t). \tag{3}$$

Hence we can write, in its most general form, the free-entry condition as

$$c(f(0,t)) = \int_{t}^{t+T(t)} [P(s)\kappa(t) - 1]e^{-(r+\delta)(s-t)}ds. \tag{4}$$

Equation (4) implictly nests case (a) as a special case: this arises if $c(f(0,t)) = c$.

Exit occurs the instant profits $\Pi(a,t)$ hit zero. Ongoing technical progress means that the oldest firms exit first: hence $\bar{a}(t)$ satisfies

$$P(t)\kappa(t - \bar{a}(t)) = 1. \tag{5}$$

Finally, the model is closed by specifying the demand side. Total spending on the industry, $D(t)$, varies exogenously. We have

$$P(t)Q(t) = D(t) \tag{6}$$

$$Q(t) = \int_{0}^{\bar{a}(t)} \kappa(t-a)f(a,t)\,da \tag{7}$$

where $Q(t)$ denotes industry output.

This completes the set-up of the model, which comprises the system of equations (1), (3), (4), (5), (6) and (7). The key to solving this system is to recognize that the path $\{f(0,t), \bar{a}(t)\}$ (i.e., the trajectories of firm creation and destruction) determines the path of $T(t)$, $P(t)$ and $Q(t)$, given exogenous $D(t)$. This point is useful for establishing the model's key result:

Proposition 1 (Caballero and Hammour (1994): Industry adjustments to recessionary demand shocks). *If entry adjustment costs are such that $c'(f(0,t)) = 0$ [i.e., case (a) above], a reduction in firm creation can fully accommodate a reduction in demand – without the need for any firm destruction. But if $c'(f(0,t)) > 0$ [case (b) above], firm creation does not generally fully accommodate reduced demand and some firm destruction must also take place.*

Proof. *Use (3) and (5) in (4) to solve $\bar{a}(t)$. In case (a), the solution $\bar{a}^*(t)$ does not depend on $D(t)$ or $f(0,t)$, so is independent of time: $\bar{a}^*(t) = \bar{a}^*$. Hence no creative destruction occurs, since that would entail a reduction in $\bar{a}^*(t)$. Instead, $f(0,t)$, the rate of new entry,* *adjusts completely. To see the full implications of this, note that a fixed $\bar{a}^*$ implies that $P(t)$ in (5) falls continuously at rate γ, which is the rate at which $\kappa(t)$ grows. Then $f(0, t)$ can be solved from (6), (1), and (7). Provided $f^*(0, t) \geq 0$ [a sufficient condition for which is $\dot{D}(t)/D(t) > -(\delta + \gamma)$] a reduction in demand is therefore accommodated entirely by a reduction in $f(0, t)$.*

For case (b), analytic solutions to the system are unavailable. But simulations (Caballero and Hammour, 1994, Sec. II. B) can be used to demonstrate that a fall in demand will in general be accommodated partly by a decrease in the creation rate $f(0, t)$ and partly by an increase in the destruction rate, $\bar{\dot{a}}(t) < 1$ (see (2)).

Thus Caballero and Hammour established that if costs of adjusting entry rates are constant [case (a)], reductions in aggregate demand can be accommodated entirely by reductions in rates of entrepreneurial entry. Although outdated firms are the most likely to turn unprofitable and be scrapped in a recession, in case (a) zero marginal costs of reducing entry mean that they can be 'insulated' from a drop in demand, and continue to survive (though only until they reach the maximum age $\bar{a}^*$ associated with technological obsolescence, which in case (a) is independent of demand). On the other hand, if entry costs increase with the number of entrants [case (b)], then it does not pay to accommodate reductions in aggregate demand entirely by reductions in the rates of entry. As Caballero and Hammour put it: 'Reducing the rate of technology adoption to a near standstill in a recession may require firms to catch up at prohibitively expensive rates in the ensuing expansion' (1994, p. 1357). Then part of the demand contraction must be accommodated by firm destruction. This outcome of outdated technologies being continually pruned out of the productive system implies that recessions have a 'cleansing' effect on overall industrial productivity.

Cabellero and Hammour (1994) went on to analyze employment and output data from US manufacturing plants over 1972–1986, in order to determine which of entry or exit is most responsive to changes in demand. Their results showed that the rate of job destruction is considerably more responsive than the rate of job creation, to changes in industrial production. This suggests that case (b) is more empirically relevant than case (a): the 'insulating effect' of job creation is far from complete. It is noteworthy that a calibration exercise by the authors revealed that only a small elasticity of creation costs $c(f(0, t))$ is sufficient to explain observed industry dynamics. Furthermore, whereas job creation rates appear to respond relatively smoothly and symmetrically to changes in demand, job destruction responds asymmetrically, being more accentuated in recessions. This mirrors the evidence which shows that recessions tend to be characterized by short and sharp reductions in employment, while upturns entail a smoother, more protracted process of employment growth.

Case (b) of Caballero and Hammour's model can also explain why recessions typically witness *both* plant creation and plant destruction. For example, simultaneous firm creation and destruction was observed in the US auto industry following the onset of the Great Depression. Plant shutdown, which accounted for one-third of the change in industry employment during the Depression, removed smaller and older craft-production car plants, *at the same time as* entries of more efficient mass production-based plants occurred (Bresnahan and Raff, 1991). Broader cross-industry evidence from the postwar period also reveals simultaneous high rates of job creation and destruction in a swathe of narrowly defined industry sectors (Blanchard and Diamond, 1990).

2. Innovation and Implementation Cycles

As noted earlier, Schumpeter's (1939) theory of business cycles suffers from two major drawbacks. First, it generates cycles almost by assumption: breakthrough inventions are assumed to occur irregularly and to be bunched together in time. Moreover, these cycles are entirely supply driven and exogenous; neither demand, nor demand expectations, play a role. Second, Schumpeter's theory relates to long-wave cycles, rather than to the short-wave business cycles which tend to be of greater economic, practical, and policy interest.

Shleifer (1986) proposed a simple model which addresses both of these concerns. In his model, N firms produce consumption goods which consumers demand in equal proportions. In period 1, firms in sectors $1, \ldots, n$ generate inventions. In the second period, firms in sectors $n + 1, \ldots, 2n$ generate inventions, and so on. In period $\Upsilon := N/n$ (taken to be an integer for simplicity), firms in the last n sectors generate inventions. In period $\Upsilon + 1$, the next round of inventions begins with sectors $1, \ldots, n$—and the process repeats itself.

Invention is not the same as innovation. Although a firm generates an invention, it may choose to delay its commercialization (i.e., innovation) until a later date. It is assumed that innovations can be delayed without the risk that another firm will implement it first (though only until the next idea arrives to the sector Υ periods later). The ensuing analysis will show why delay can be optimal, and how it can give rise to business cycles, even though the flow of inventions is, as just described earlier, uniform over time.

In the absence of innovation, firms within a sector are Bertrand competitors. Hence price is driven down to marginal cost, which is the wage rate, normalized to unity. All firms make zero profits: $\Pi = 0$. Aggregate income is $D = \sum_N \Pi + L = L$, where L is the size of the (fixed) workforce. Prior to innovations, aggregate income is therefore fixed.

Innovating firms gain the benefit of producing output with $1/\mu$ the labor needed previously, where $\mu > 1$ across all sectors and in all periods. This allows that firm to reduce prices infinitesimally and so capture the entire market for its good for the duration of one period. The period after, every competitor firm imitates the innovation, prices are competed down to the lower marginal cost, and profits for all firms in the sector are once again driven to zero.

In a period t when an innovator controls the market, it makes profits of $\Pi_t = (D_t/N)(1 - 1/\mu)$. Here, D_t/N is total demand for its good, which it captures in full. The output of each firm is assumed to be equal to labor input, so the total cost of producing this output for an innovating firm is the labor input (= output) times the price $(1/\mu)$, namely $(D_t/N)(1/\mu)$. Thus we can write $\Pi_t = mD_t$, where

$$m := (\mu - 1)/N\mu \tag{8}$$

is a positive constant.

Every firm's decision problem is that of timing: each firm wishes to choose the period, T, at which it turns its invention into an innovation and captures the innovation's (temporary) value. Shleifer's key contribution is to show that firms in different sectors, receiving inventions at different times, may all nevertheless choose to innovate at the same moment – which is when demand is highest. To see why, suppose every inventing firm from $t = 1, \ldots, T$ innovates in the same period, T say. Then aggregate profits are $\sum_N \Pi = nT\Pi_T = nTmD_T$. Because $D_T = \sum_N \Pi + L$ it follows that

$$\Pi_T = mD_T = \frac{mL}{1 - nTm}.$$

Letting $\beta < 1$ be firms' discount factor (which Shleifer endogenizes), inventing firms in period 1 face the NPV maximization problem

$$\max_{T}\{\beta^T m D_T\} = \max_{T}\left\{\beta^T \frac{mL}{1 - nTm}\right\} \qquad (9)$$

Denote the solution to (9) by T^*. Note that we can rule out $T^* \geq \Upsilon$ since inventing firms will not risk excessive delay which allows a competitor to appropriate the entire benefits of an invention. But, in general, there are multiple possible solutions to (9). One possible solution is $T^* = 1$. This is a steady-growth acyclical equilibrium in which inventions are implemented immediately. More interesting is a solution where $1 < T^* < \Upsilon$ – the case that will be considered hereafter. In this case, a firm generating an invention in period 1 is willing to wait until T^* to commercialize it. But then all other firms inventing subsequently (up to T^*) must be willing to wait too, since their discount rate is lower. Thus different firms obtaining inventions at different times all choose to commercialize at the same time. This triggers a temporary boom at T^* (high output and demand, D_T) which fulfils the expectations of the boom. That expectation of high future value is what convinces firms in periods 1, 2 and onwards to wait until T^*. Expecting a profitable boom in the distant future, firms optimally delay innovations, thereby keeping the economy in a no-growth slump. It is precisely because firm profits in one sector are spent on the output of firms in all other sectors [captured in the maximand of (9)] that every firm benefits from waiting for the prosperity of a boom.

The full cyclical process is as follows. Prior to a T^*-boom, the economy is in stasis. The boom at T^* lasts one period during which output rises. The following period, $T^* + 1$, output remains high while prices fall under Betrand competition to the new lower marginal costs. The economy remains in this state until the next boom at time $2T^*$, when output rises once again and prices once more fall the period after. And so the process continues, in a series of 'implementation cycles'. By inspection of (8) and (9), a large value of T^* is positively associated with a large cost reduction (technological progress) μ. Larger cost reductions are associated with higher demand because the profits from innovation are redistributed to households in the form of higher income. Every firm has an incentive to wait until demand is high before implementing their inventions. The higher is T^*, the longer the economy is stuck in stasis, but the bigger the boom that ultimately follows.

Unlike Schumpeter (1939), Shleifer links innovations to demand. Unlike Schmookler (1966), this link is not a response to actual demand conditions, but rather is a response to forward-looking demand expectations. Shleifer's model can give rise to multiple cyclical equilibria. Entrepreneurs' self-fulfiling expectations determine which particular equilibrium obtains and therefore how long a recession lasts. The different equilibria are Pareto ranked; the most profitable equilibrium, which one might expect entrepreneurs to choose, need not be the most efficient one. Shleifer went on to show that an informed stabilization policy, financed by a progressive tax on returns in the boom, can sometimes raise welfare; but if large booms are necessary to compensate entrepreneurs for high fixed innovation costs, such a policy can have the perverse effect of discouraging any implementation and so stopping all technological progress.

The indeterminacy of the various equilibria suggests an incompleteness in Shleifer's model. Another drawback of that model is its strong assumptions of drastic but costless imitation, exogenous invention, and the impossibility of storage. As Francois and Lloyd-Ellis (2003) point out, if entrepreneurs can store their output, they should hire labor, produce and then store output when costs are low (i.e., during recessions) – and sell the output when demand is high (i.e., during booms). Obviously, this would undermine the existence of implementation cycles as Shleifer conceived of them.

The model of Francois and Lloyd-Ellis (2003) generalizes Shleifer's in several important respects, relaxing the assumptions about drastic and costless imitation and non-storage. But from our perspective, perhaps the most important feature of Francois and Lloyd-Ellis (2003) is that their entrepreneurs actively choose to devote effort towards developing new innovations (which detracts one-for-one from production time). This makes entrepreneurs central actors in Francois and Lloyd-Ellis' model – in contrast to their role as merely passive recipients of inventions in Shleifer's. To see their active role in Francois and Lloyd-Ellis, let T_v denote the time of boom v, and T_{v+1} denote the time of the next boom, where $v = 1, 2, \ldots$. As in Shleifer's model, it turns out that all successful inventors choose to implement their inventions at the next boom at T_{v+1}. Hence worker productivity, and so also the wage w_v, is fixed within cycles, i.e., for all $t \in [T_v, T_{v+1})$, $\forall v$. Let $\Pi_{v+1} > 0$ be entrepreneurs' expected benefit from commercializing at $v + 1$ given that their invention efforts succeeds only probabilistically. For small $t \in [T_v, T_{v+1})$, $\beta^{T_{v+1}-t} \Pi_{v+1} < w_v$; but at some finite time $T_E \in [T_v, T_{v+1})$ this inequality begins to reverse:

$$\beta^{(T_{v+1}-T_E)} \Pi_{v+1} = w_v . \tag{10}$$

Thus in the interval $(T_v, T_E]$, the economy does not grow and no effort goes into invention-seeking. At T_E, effort begins to be directed away from production and toward the entrepreneurial endeavor of seeking productivity-enhancing inventions. As in Schleifer's model, production output is equal to labor input, so reduced production effort lowers output directly. Taken literally, this implies that entrepreneurs (or less literally, entrepreneurial managers and workers) are 'responsible' for economic downturns; or, at least, entrepreneurship is a leading indicator of a subsequent boom. But at the same time entrepreneurs are also responsible for the inventions that jump the economy out of recession and create the next boom at the completion of the implementation cycle at T_{v+1}. With the introduction of more productive technology at T_{v+1}, wages jump upwards to a new, higher equilibrium level w_{v+1}, which persists until T_{v+2}. At $t = T_{v+1}$, $\beta^{T_{v+2}-T_{v+1}} \Pi_{v+2} < w_{v+1}$ analogous to before. But eventually, the next-boom version of (10) holds: entrepreneurs once again divert effort away from production and towards invention. And so the mechanics of the new boom get underway again.

Elegant though the Francois-Lloyd-Ellis model is, it controversially predicts that more invention activity takes place in recessions than in booms. In fact, Barlevy (2007) cites evidence showing that R&D spending is strongly pro-cyclical: most R&D funds are spent during booms. That might appear surprising given that the opportunity cost of resources such as R&D effort are lower during recessions, when production labor receives a lower payoff. As Barlevy (2007) explains, this benefit of intertemporal smoothing can be overwhelmed by an offsetting expected cost of delay, leading to pro-cyclicality. This expected cost reflects the risk of appropriation of the entrepreneur's innovation by rivals if the entrepreneur does the R&D in recessions and delays the release of the innovation to the boom.

Space does not permit me to reproduce Barlevy's complex model here. But to get a flavor of how this argument works, consider the following *highly* simplified account of a labor market. Similar to Francois and Lloyd-Ellis (2003), entrepreneurs can allocate resources between R&D and production. Labor in production receives a wage of $w/(1 + \Delta)$, where $\Delta \in \{0, 1\}$ is the (exogenous) time agents must wait before the economy finds itself in the next boom. If $\Delta = 0$ the boom is taking place now; if $\Delta = 1$ the economy is in recession and the expected time to the next boom is one period. Hence wages are lower in bad times than in good times.

All entrepreneurs are endowed with one unit of effort which is perfectly divisible: let $e \in [0, 1]$ denote the amount devoted to R&D and $1 - e$ the amount devoted to production. While an extra unit of effort increases total returns in production one-for-one, it merely increases the probability of a successful innovation from R&D, denoted by $p(e) \in [0, 1]$, where $p'' < 0 < p'$. If an innovation is successful and there is no negative knowledge spillover externality (i.e., appropriation risk), the innovation generates a discounted return in entrepreneurship of $\beta^{\Delta}\Pi$, where $\beta > \frac{1}{2}$. Note that Δ appears here to replicate the property of the Shleifer and Francois-Lloyd-Ellis models, namely that entrepreneurs do best releasing their innovation in the boom. [This property is not shared by Barlevy's model, but it is convenient to assume it here to illustrate the result.] If on the other hand there is a knowledge spillover externality, a future imitator can appropriate some of the benefits. This is not a problem if the entrepreneur releases her innovation straightaway (i.e., if $\Delta = 0$) but it is a problem if $\Delta = 1$ and the entrepreneur has to wait until the next boom. Then possible imitation reduces the expected return by some factor $\lambda \in (0, 1)$.

In the absence of a knowledge spillover externality, entrepreneurs face the problem

$$\max_{e} \left\{ \frac{(1 - e)w}{1 + \Delta} + p(e)\beta^{\Delta}\Pi \right\} \tag{11}$$

The solutions to this problem are denoted by e_{Δ}^*,

$$e_1^* = \Gamma\left(\frac{w}{2\beta\Pi}\right) > e_0^* = \Gamma\left(\frac{w}{\Pi}\right) \tag{12}$$

where Γ is the inverse function of p'. This ranking states that more R&D is done in recessions because the opportunity cost of allocating labor to production is lower. That is the inter-temporal smoothing result which Barlevy (2007) seeks to overturn by introducing externalities.

The result can be overturned because the first-order condition for e in the presence of externalities is

$$p'(e) - \frac{w}{(1 + \Delta)(\beta\lambda)^{\Delta}\Pi} = 0$$

Hence we obtain the solutions $e_{\Delta}^{\dagger}$, where

$$e_1^{\dagger} = \Gamma\left(\frac{w}{2\beta\lambda\Pi}\right) < e_1^* \tag{13}$$

Furthermore, if $\beta\lambda < \frac{1}{2}$, we have

$$p'(e_1^{\dagger}) > p'(e_0^*) = p'(e_0^{\dagger}) \tag{14}$$
$$\Rightarrow e_1^{\dagger} < e_0^*$$

The ordering in (14) gives us the desired result. If the perceived danger of losing an innovative advantage through knowledge spillovers is high enough (i.e., λ is small enough), entrepreneurs choose to concentrate R&D in the boom state rather than the recession state, despite the higher opportunity cost that entails. Barlevy (2007) identified this as a source of inefficiency, and went on to argue that procyclicality of R&D is likely to increase the welfare costs of macroeconomic shocks. It does so because growth becomes more costly and the shocks become more persistent. A suitable corrective policy instrument is countercyclical R&D subsidies.

3. Models of Production Under Asymmetric Information

Several models show that asymmetric information problems can induce entrepreneurs to take actions which create or exaggerate business cycles at the aggregate level. This section reviews three models which isolate different channels through which asymmetric information affects entrepreneurial behavior in this way: (1) costly state verification, when lenders have to incur costs to observe entrepreneurs' project returns; (2) moral hazard, when lenders run the risk that entrepreneurs divert effort away from their mandated investment projects; and (3) adverse selection, when lenders cannot distinguish between hidden entrepreneurial types.

3.1 Costly State Verification

Bernanke and Gertler (1989) analyze a simple overlapping generations model comprising agents who live for two periods. In the first period, agents earn income which they save to finance consumption in the second period. The greater is income (e.g. in boom times) the greater are savings, S: this will drive capital accumulation and thereby output in the analysis later.

There are two goods: a capital good and a final good. There are separate production functions for each good. Entrepreneurs produce capital goods: each entrepreneur is endowed with a capital good investment project. There is a fixed fraction of entrepreneurs, N, in a population of unit size. Entrepreneurs differ in their ability, ω, to produce the capital good, which requires $x(\omega)$ inputs to produce. Ability is observable to entrepreneurs and lenders. The function $x(\cdot)$ is increasing in its argument: hence low-ω types are the most efficient. The distribution of ω is uniform over $\omega \in [0, 1]$. The total supply of capital at time t is denoted by k_t and is derived later. The capital good is used to produce the final good, output of which at time t is denoted by y_t. The final good has the stochastic production function

$$y_t = \theta_t f(k_t) \tag{15}$$

where θ_t is a random shock with mean θ, and $f(\cdot)$ is a concave function. Capital goods sell in $t + 1$ for an expected price q_{t+1}.

The output of the capital good is also random, being 'low', κ_1, with probability π_1 and 'high', $\kappa_2 > \kappa_1$, with probability $\pi_2 = 1 - \pi_1$. Expected capital good output, κ, lies inbetween. Entrepreneurs can observe their own output perfectly, but lenders have to pay a fraction ζ of the total value of the capital good in auditing costs to (perfectly) reveal the outcome. Obviously, lenders only audit when entrepreneurs declare the bad outcome κ_1.

Consider an entrepreneur who wants to maximize her expected next-period consumption, but whose required project input $x(\omega)$ exceeds her savings, S – necessitating borrowing from a lender. Suppose the entrepreneur is audited with probability p if she declares the bad state. Let c_1 and c_2 denote her consumption payoffs in the two states when she is not audited. Also, let c_1^a be her consumption payoff in the bad state if she is audited and found to be telling the truth; if she is found to be lying, she is punished with consumption of zero.

The optimal contract devised by lenders solves the following problem:

$$\max_{\{p,c_1,c_2,c_1^a\}} \pi_1\left(pc_1^a + (1-p)c_1\right) + \pi_2 c_2$$

subject to

$$\rho(x-S) = \pi_1\left[q\kappa_1 - p\left(c_1^a + q\zeta\right) - (1-p)c_1\right] + \pi_2(q\kappa_2 - c_2) \tag{16}$$

$$c_2 \geq (1-p)\left[q(\kappa_2 - \kappa_1) + c_1\right] \tag{17}$$

$$c_1, c_1^a \geq 0 \tag{18}$$

$$0 \leq p \leq 1 \tag{19}$$

Constraint (16) ensures that competitive lenders receive their required expected gross rate of return of ρ on their loans. Constraint (17) ensures that entrepreneurs have no incentives to misreport the good state as the bad state; it binds if $p > 0$. Constraints (18) are limited liability constraints ensuring non-negative consumption, while (19) is a feasibility constraint on p.

The optimal contract takes a simple form. First, note that if S were sufficiently high so that all entrepreneurs could always repay lenders, even in the worst state, then

$$q\kappa_1 \geq \rho(x(\omega) - S)). \tag{20}$$

In this case no monitoring is needed: the optimal $p^* = 0$. Second, suppose now that (20) does not hold. Then constraints (17) and (18) must all bind. This implies that the lender should ensure that entrepreneurs enjoy no consumption in the bad state ($c_1^* = c_1^{a*} = 0$), to discourage them from under-reporting their project outcomes. Using these equalities together with (16), we obtain

$$p(\omega) = \frac{\rho(x(\omega) - S) - q\kappa_1}{\pi_2 q(\kappa_2 - \kappa_1) - \pi_1 q\zeta}. \tag{21}$$

This $p(\omega)$ is just sufficient to ensure that entrepreneurs report honestly when the good state occurs. An implication of (21) is that the expected agency cost, that is $\pi_1 p(\omega)q\zeta$, is decreasing in entrepreneurial savings, S.

Agency costs can reduce the number of entrepreneurs willing to implement their projects. Some entrepreneurs, called 'good', are willing to implement even if they are audited with probability one in the bad state. All entrepreneurs with $\omega < \underline{\omega}$ are defined as 'good', where $\underline{\omega}$ marks indifference between getting expected payoff $q\kappa$ minus expected auditing costs $q\pi_1\zeta$ and repayments $\rho x(\omega)$ in the bad state: that is, $\underline{\omega}$ solves $q\kappa - \rho x(\underline{\omega}) - q\pi_1\zeta = 0$. 'Fair' entrepreneurs on the other hand are only guaranteed to get positive expected net returns if $p = 0$: all entrepreneurs with $\underline{\omega} \leq \omega \leq \overline{\omega}$ fall into this range, where $\overline{\omega}$ solves $q\kappa - \rho x(\overline{\omega}) = 0$. Finally, 'poor' entrepreneurs (with $\omega > \overline{\omega}$) have negative expected net returns even if agency costs are zero.

It follows immediately that all good (poor) entrepreneurs will (will not) undertake their projects. In contrast, only a fraction $g(\omega) = \min\{1, S/S^*(\omega)\}$ of fair entrepreneurs invest, where $S^*(\omega)$ solves (20) as an equality.[1] We can now state the main result:

Proposition 2 (Bernanke and Gertler (1989): Dynamics of capital and output). *Total capital formation is decreasing in agency costs and increasing in entrepreneurs' savings. In good times, when savings are high, capital formation and output remain high; this persistence would not arise in the absence of agency costs.*

Proof. *Define $p^*(\omega)$ as the maximum of the RHS of (21) and zero. Then by the foregoing arguments,*

$$k_{t+1} = N\left[\kappa\underline{\omega} - \pi_1\zeta \int_0^{\overline{\omega}} p^*(\omega)\,d\omega\right] + N\left[\kappa \int_{\underline{\omega}}^{\overline{\omega}} g(\omega)\,d\omega\right] \qquad (22)$$

Agency costs reduce capital formation directly in (22) (i.e., via ζ) as well as indirectly through $p^*(\omega)$ (q.v. (21)). Higher savings, S, on the other hand increase capital formation via both $p^*(\omega)$ and $g(\omega)$. In a boom, savings are higher and therefore so is capital next period, k_{t+1}. This in turn increases expected output next period, y_{t+1}, via (15), thereby perpetuating the boom. Precisely the opposite process occurs in a recession, which is perpetuated for the same reason.

Finally, note that absent agency costs we would have $\zeta = 0$ and $g(\omega) = 1$. The latter equality holds because all fair entrepreneurs, with $\omega < \overline{\omega}$, optimally invest when there are no agency costs: $q\kappa = \rho\,x(\overline{\omega})$. Then (22) reduces to

$$k_{t+1} = N\kappa\left(\underline{\omega} + \int_{\underline{\omega}}^{\overline{\omega}} d\omega\right) = N\kappa\overline{\omega}$$

In which case, capital and output are independent of entrepreneurs' personal wealth (savings), and are fixed in expected value terms. Therefore agency costs are necessary to introduce persistence into business fluctuations.

Hence personal wealth can be a source of output dynamics when agency costs are present. Upturns increase savings, which reduce the agency costs of financing real capital investments, which amplifies the upturn. Conversely, in times of financial distress, agency costs are higher, which reduces capital formation and hence output. Furthermore, shocks to borrower net worth which occur independently of aggregate output can trigger a recession. So too can redistributions from borrowers to lenders, such as happens during debt deflation. Arguably we have seen the former at work in the 2008 US financial crisis and 'Great Recession', while both the former and the latter seem to have occurred in Japan in the 'lost decade' of the 1990s.

Another noteworthy feature of Bernanke and Gertler's model is that the dynamic effects of shocks can be asymmetric. In good times, when the capital stock is high and the economy is functioning at a high level similar to what would apply without agency costs, a wealth-induced reduction in agency costs can have little additional effect on output. In contrast, a downturn associated with an adverse productivity shock θ_t, for example, can generate large negative effects from agency costs. This implies that sharp investment downturns will be more likely than sharp upturns – which appears to be broadly consistent with the business cycle patterns observed in practice.

3.2 Moral Hazard

A different version of the Bernanke-Gertler model, which incorporates moral hazard rather than costly state verification, generates similar results. The exposition below presents a simplified treatment of a moral hazard problem loosely based on Rampini (2004).

Whereas Bernanke-Gertler has a fixed supply of entrepreneurs, only a variable fraction of which chooses to undertake investment projects, Rampini has a variable number of entrepreneurs, N – all of which undertake projects should they choose to enter entrepreneurship. Entrepreneurs invest all of their savings, S, in an investment project in return for a financial contract. Agents enter entrepreneurship if their expected utility from doing so, namely

$$EV(S) := \pi U(c_1 - e_1) + (1 - \pi)U(c_0 - e_1) \tag{23}$$

exceeds the safe return in paid employment, which is $U(S + w)$. Here π is the probability the entrepreneur gets a good return, κ, which financiers reward with high consumption c_1. $1 - \pi$ is the probability of a bad return, associated with consumption $c_0 < c_1$ (and, for simplicity in my exposition though not Rampini's, output of zero). Financiers have to choose $(c_1, c_0) \in \mathbb{R}^2$ in order to elicit high levels of unobservable entrepreneurial effort, e_1; low effort $e_0 < e_1$ results in zero output with certainty. The form of (23) implies that effort costs utility measured in terms of consumption. As in Bernanke and Gertler (1989), S is savings or wealth. Paid employment yields a wage $w > 0$: $w + S$ is fully consumed in that occupation. Unlike Bernanke and Gertler, individuals are taken to have homogeneous abilities but heterogeneous S endowments, whose distribution function is $G(S)$. Rampini assumed that $U(\cdot)$ exhibits decreasing absolute risk aversion (DARA). Hence wealthier agents are less risk averse than poor agents.

In Rampini's model, entrepreneurs' incentive to supply high effort e_1 is shaped by the agency cost $c_1 - c_0$. This difference in consumption is an agency cost because risk-averse entrepreneurs would prefer smooth consumption. An unwelcome intertemporal difference in consumption galvanizes entrepreneurs to supply privately costly effort. Under conditions of competition, investors choose (c_1, c_0) to maximize (23) subject to the following resource and incentive compatibility constraints:

$$\pi c_1 + (1 - \pi)c_0 \leq S + \pi \kappa \tag{24}$$

$$\pi U(c_1 - e_1) + (1 - \pi)U(c_0 - e_1) \geq U(c_0 - e_0) \tag{25}$$

Rampini showed that the agency cost $c_1 - c_0$ is decreasing in S. To see why, denote the solution of (23) subject to (24) and (25) by (c_0^*, c_1^*), and consider a positive macroeconomic shock at t which shifts the distribution $G(S)$ to $F(S)$, where $F(\cdot)$ first-order stochastically dominates $G(\cdot)$. Let $(\hat{c}_0, \hat{c}_1)$ be the new solution for $F(S)$. If Rampini is wrong, $\hat{c}_1 - \hat{c}_0 > c_1^* - c_0^*$. But this requires a lower c_0 since (24) must bind at the optimum. But this in turn entails a reduction in the RHS of (25), which cannot be because (25) must bind at the optimum as well. This is a contradiction – so $c_1 - c_0$ must be decreasing in S.

Note a similarity here with Bernanke and Gertler: when wealth increases, for example, in booms, agency costs decrease – that is, agency costs are counter-cyclical.

Denote the S values which solve the occupational choice problem $EV(S) = U(S + w)$ for G and F by S_g and S_f, respectively. By the above arguments, $S_f < S_g$, from which both of Rampini's main results follow. First, DARA implies that if $EV(S_g) \geq U(S_g + w)$

then $EV(S) \geq U(S + w)$, $\forall S \geq S_g$. In other words, everyone with wealth greater than the marginal entrepreneur S_g will become an entrepreneur; and, following a positive shock causing $G \to F$, the number of entrepreneurs increases: $N(S_f) = 1 - F(S_f) > N(S_g) = 1 - G(S_g)$. Thus by increasing wealth, a boom increases the willingness of people to bear risks in entrepreneurship. Second, in a boom the lower agency costs (i.e., $\hat{c}_1 - \hat{c}_0 < c_1^* - c_0^*$) further increase incentives to turn entrepreneur. The reason is that agents bear lower risk (i.e., smoother consumption) in entrepreneurship under F than under G, thereby making entrepreneurship more attractive.

Although Rampini (2004) did not do this, it is easy to trace out the implications for business cycle variations. The equivalent expression to (22) in this model is $k_{t+1} = N(S_f)\pi\kappa$. Higher savings increase the number of entrepreneurs $N(S_f)$ as just explained, which in turn promotes capital formation and output y_{t+1} next period [via (15)]. Thus risk aversion can have first-order impacts on capital and output, by changing the level of entrepreneurial activity. In this model, entrepreneurial activity is procyclical, amplifying productivity shocks.

3.3 Adverse Selection

Hidden entrepreneurial types embody another form of information asymmetry, which can generate a different form of inefficiency, namely adverse selection. This section shows how adverse selection can exacerbate (exogenously determined) productivity shocks. In the model below, which is a (considerably) simplified version of Ghatak et al. (2007), the Bernanke-Gertler mechanism of endogenous cycles is set to one side; adverse selection does not *cause* but instead *exaggerates* cyclical variations whose origin derives from some external, unexplained, source.

Suppose entrepreneurs know their probability of success ('ability') with certainty, but lenders do not. The distribution function of ability is $G(\pi)$. As should now be familiar, there is a marginal entrepreneur $\hat{\pi}$ such that everyone with ability $\pi \geq \hat{\pi}$ becomes an entrepreneur while everyone else with lower ability becomes a worker. The value of $\hat{\pi}$ that solves the occupational choice problem is derived below, under the assumptions of costless entry and exit. The average ability of all active entrepreneurs $\bar{\pi}$ conditional on $\hat{\pi}$ is

$$\bar{\pi} := \frac{1}{1 - G(\hat{\pi})} \int_{\hat{\pi}}^{\infty} \pi \, dG(\pi). \tag{26}$$

Lenders cannot observe individual π values but do observe $G(\pi)$. The best they can do is to extend a single pooled loan contract to all active entrepreneurs, who total $1 - G(\hat{\pi})$ in number. Let r be the competitive interest rate on entrepreneurs' loans. Expected bank returns per loan are $\bar{\pi}r$ which in a large population of entrepreneurs and under conditions of perfect competition in the credit market exactly covers the return to depositors of ρ. That is, $r = \rho/\bar{\pi}$.

Entrepreneurs start with no funds and require no capital, but they do have to borrow in order to cover their labor operating costs. These costs are the product of the amount of labor they hire, l, and the exogenous wage rate per worker, w. Let $f(l)$ be the concave production function generating output if the entrepreneur is successful; there is no output if the project fails. Setting aside issues of limited liability, the expected profit of an entrepreneur with ability π is $\Pi(\pi) = \pi f(l) - wl(1 + r)$. Hence $\hat{\pi}$ solves

$$\hat{\pi} f(l(\hat{\pi})) - wl(\hat{\pi})(1 + r) - w = 0. \tag{27}$$

The labor demand of an entrepreneur of type π, namely $l(\pi)$, solves the first-order condition

$$\pi f'(l(\pi)) = w(1+r) \qquad \forall \pi \geq \hat{\pi} \,. \tag{28}$$

Differentiation of (27) and (26), respectively, yields

$$\frac{\partial \hat{\pi}}{\partial w} = \frac{(1+r)l(\hat{\pi})+1}{f(l(\hat{\pi}))} > 0 \tag{29}$$

$$\frac{\partial \bar{\pi}}{\partial \hat{\pi}} = \frac{(\bar{\pi}-\hat{\pi})g(\hat{\pi})}{1-G(\hat{\pi})} > 0 \tag{30}$$

Equation (29) implies that a positive productivity shock which increases w increases the ability of the marginal entrepreneur. Wage work becomes more attractive to previously marginal entrepreneurs, who quit entrepreneurship. By (30), the average quality of a smaller pool of entrepreneurs is higher, reflecting the fact that the marginal entrepreneur is of low ability.

The key result below hinges on the responsiveness of the demand for labor to the wage, w. Implicit differentiation of (28) yields

$$\frac{\partial l(\pi)}{\partial w} = \frac{(1+r)+w(\partial r/\partial w)}{\pi f''(l(\pi))} \tag{31}$$

where

$$\frac{\partial r}{\partial w} = \frac{\partial r}{\partial \hat{\pi}}\frac{\partial \hat{\pi}}{\partial w} = -\left[\frac{1+(1+r)l(\hat{\pi})}{f(l(\hat{\pi}))}\right]\frac{\rho g(\hat{\pi})(\bar{\pi}-\hat{\pi})}{\bar{\pi}^2[1-G(\hat{\pi})]} < 0 \tag{32}$$

The sign of the all-important derivative (31) is ambiguous in general. The denominator is certainly negative, but the numerator can take either sign. The special contribution of the model centers on the magnitude of the negative (by (32)) derivative $\partial r/\partial w$ in the numerator of (31). To see why, consider the first-best case without asymmetric information. Then entrepreneurs would face individual-specific interest rates which would not depend on w. Consequently $\partial r/\partial w = 0$, and the sign of (31) would certainly be negative – the standard neoclassical result of a downward sloping labor demand curve. However, if adverse selection makes the value of (32) so large in absolute terms that (31) turns positive, labor demand curves can be upward-sloping. Hence adverse selection is a necessary (though not a sufficient) condition to generate the following result:

Proposition 3 (Ghatak *et al.* (2007): Entrepreneurs' optimal hiring decisions can exaggerate business cycles). *When adverse selection is present, and is sufficiently strong that the demand for labor slopes upwards, then it is possible (though not guaranteed) that the hiring decisions of entrepreneurs can exaggerate upswings in output when wages are high, and exaggerate downswings in output when wages are low. These effects are absent when information is perfect and there is no adverse selection.*

Proof. *Aggregate output is*

$$Q = \int_{\hat{\pi}}^{\infty} \pi f(l(\pi)) \, dG(\pi) \tag{33}$$

Differentiate (33) to obtain

$$\frac{\partial Q}{\partial w} = -\frac{\partial \hat{\pi}}{\partial w}\hat{\pi} f(l(\hat{\pi}))g(\hat{\pi}) + \int_{\hat{\pi}}^{\infty} \pi f'(l(\pi))\frac{\partial l(\pi)}{\partial w} \, dG(\pi) \tag{34}$$

The first term of (34) is certainly negative, by (29). The second term of (34) is negative (positive) if the labor demand curve slopes downwards (upwards). Adverse selection that is strong enough to make the second term of (34) positive is necessary but not sufficient to make the sign of (34) positive overall. Then positive shocks that increase w have the following effects: the number of entrepreneurs decreases [by (29) and the monotonicity of $G(\cdot)$]; these entrepreneurs hire more workers in aggregate than before [by (31)]; and overall output increases [by (34)]. Negative shocks have the opposite effects if (34) is positive: output falls even further in recessions, since the quality of the entrepreneur pool worsens (adverse selection).

In the absence of adverse selection, $\partial r / \partial w = 0$ so the second term of (34) is certainly negative. Then the sign of (34) is certainly negative too. In this case, the hiring decisions of entrepreneurs do not exaggerate cycles, but rather moderate them.

The central mechanism in Ghatak *et al.* (2007) model is the quality of the entrepreneur pool, which can improve sufficiently when wages increase that the demand for labor increases even more, further fueling wages and the boom. Ghatak *et al.* went on to show that in this case policies which favor workers relative to entrepreneurs – for example, a worker minimum wage, a tax on entrepreneurs, or a subsidy to expand employment in incumbent firms – can improve the quality of the entrepreneurial pool so much that they can be self-financing, and moreover generate benefits which 'trickle up' to the remaining entrepreneurs. Everyone would become better-off and so support for these policies would be unanimous.

Ghatak *et al.* (2007) also went on to extend their model by allowing wealthy entrepreneurs to post collateral and so obtain separating contracts. They showed that a wage increase in this setting can again generate upward-sloping labor demand curves, but for a different reason: with fewer low-quality types in the entrepreneurial pool, less collateral is needed to separate types. That enables more high-quality but low-wealth entrepreneurs to obtain favorable loan terms and hire more labor, driving up wages, and fueling the boom. But in this case, wealthy entrepreneurs do not support policies which raise the wage, as they do best paying lower wages.

4. Concluding Remarks

This chapter reviewed several prominent economic theories of entrepreneurship, innovation and the business cycle. The theories fall into roughly three categories: models of creative destruction; models of innovation and implementation cycles; and models of production under asymmetric information. Despite their differences, they all share the property that entrepreneurship is potentially pro-cyclical; one or two of them also admit the possibility of acyclicality (notably, Shleifer, 1986, and Caballero and Hammour, 1994). Time series evidence (Parker *et al.*, 2011) suggests that pro-cyclicality of entrepreneurship – at least if entrepreneurship is measured in terms of the number of self-employed – is consistent with data from the UK and Spain, but not with data from the US.

The major predictive differences between the theories concern whether entrepreneurship varies contemporaneously with the business cycle, or whether it lags or leads it. Caballero and Hammour (1994) study adjustments by entrants at the time when recessions strike: there is no role for lags or leads. Neither are there in Shleifer's (1986) model of implementation cycles, which takes entrepreneurship to be contemporaneous with booms. This prediction is relaxed in the model of Francois and Lloyd-Ellis (2003), in which entrepreneurs build up to a boom by systematically investing in discovery opportunities beforehand. In that model, entrepreneurship leads the cycle. In contrast, Bernanke and Gertler (1989) model has variations in the cycle leading entrepreneurship, which in turn perpetuates the state of the cycle the economy finds itself in. The other asymmetric information models, of Rampini (2004) and Ghatak et al. (2007), are essentially atemporal, though both can be shoe-horned into a Bernanke-Gertler-type framework, in which entrepreneurship is a lagging indicator.

These theories generate at least three major insights. First, the Bernanke-Gertler model stresses the importance of personal assets for the occurrence and persistence of business cycles. In particular, the bursting of an asset bubble or the dilution of the quality of balance sheets can precipitate a recession in the real economy, as a reduction in wealth worsens agency costs in the credit markets and thereby makes entrepreneurship less attractive. This seems to gain at least some face value from the experience of the US in 2007–2008, where a housing bubble deflated and lenders began writing off debt containing subprime loans. The ensuing recession might well have had 'real economy' causes too, including sharply rising commodity prices; but it remains likely that restricted credit was an important factor.

Second, and related to this point, expectations play an important role. As Shleifer argued, to the extent that entrepreneurs control the timing of their innovations, business cycles can arise as a result of co-ordinated entrepreneurial choices. More generally, expectations drive asset prices and bubbles, which as just noted can have real effects, magnifying and even creating upswings and downturns.

Third, as Caballero and Hammour point out, entrepreneurs continue to enter markets even in recessions, introducing superior technologies which eventually replace those of incumbents. This suggests that even in recessions the seeds of future growth are present, with productivity improvements driving increases in future living standards. However, this analysis shows that entrepreneurs need sharp incentives to innovate. Thus a policy of levying procyclical taxes on entrepreneurs – as was envisaged by Shleifer (1986), Barlevy (2007) and Ghatak et al. (2007), for example, – must only be undertaken with the greatest caution. As Shleifer observed, if a stabilization policy is too accentuated, entrepreneurs will not anticipate sufficient future benefits to make costly innovation worthwhile.

Despite the impressive nature of the contributions reviewed here, there would seem to be abundant opportunities for further theoretical research on entrepreneurship and the business cycle. Arguably, one line of research which could be developed further relates to the origin and impact of bank lending requirements. For instance, asset-based lending practices can lead banks to lend more to entrepreneurs in good times and less in bad times when balance sheets weaken. Hence bank lending restrictions could be an important channel through which financial shocks become transmitted to the real sector of the economy. More generally, bank regulations, including mandatory reserve ratios, carry potentially far-reaching implications for access to finance amongst entrepreneurs and hence the ability of entrepreneurs to start new ventures (Evans and Jovanovic, 1989; Parker and van Praag, 2006). At the time of writing, governments the world over are seeking to tighten banking regulations. Yet only a few years earlier, pressure for financial deregulation was no less strong. Could the demand for financial regulation be counter-cyclical, perhaps operating with a time lag? Researchers could usefully endogenize financial regulation in future analyses of entrepreneurship and the business cycle.

One way of endogenizing bank regulation could be via a formal political – economy model in the presence of lobbying by the banking sector. An alternative approach would be to model a game between banks and regulators, where the former have an incentive to adopt excessively risky lending practices since their downside will be covered by a public sector bail-out if they are 'too big to fail'. Periodic crises with restricted lending to entrepreneurs in bad times could emerge endogenously from such a model.

In fact, entrepreneurship might play a counter-cyclical role in stablizing the economy, rather than a pro-cyclical propagation role as proposed by most of the theories reviewed earlier. For instance, entrepreneurship could enable workers laid off in a recession to continue to use their human capital, thereby avoiding a more prolonged downturn later on owing to deterioration of human capital and unemployment 'scarring' (Arulampalam *et al.*, 2001). Admittedly, this counterfactual might be hard to identify empirically. Also, people pushed into entrepreneurship from layoffs, who had never tried entrepreneurship before and were unaware of their talent there, might come to find it a more productive occupation than wage employment (*cf*. Jovanovic, 1982). These and other possibilities deserve to be explored in future research.

Arguably, any model of entrepreneurship and the business cycle which seeks to draw lessons from the recent financial crisis needs to incorporate asset bubbles. The inflation of the US housing bubble, for example, helped underpin lending to entrepreneurs given the widespread nature of collateral-based bank learning rules; while the puncturing of the bubble withdrew liquidity, denying credit even to many viable businesses. In fact, the US did not experience a national housing bubble in the first decade of this century, but rather a diverse set of regional bubbles – with some regions experiencing no meaningful house price appreciation at all. Regional aspects of entrepreneurship-induced business cycles seem to have attracted little or no research to date.

In fact, one can ask whether entrepreneurs could actually help to create asset bubbles. Here a broad definition of entrepreneurship might be warranted. For example, one could argue that securitization of sub-prime lending was an 'entrepreneurial opportunity' pursued by venturesome investment bankers. Exploiting these opportunities generated huge private gain at the price of injecting systemic risk into the financial system. In this respect, it resembled the 'destructive' entrepreneurship highlighted by Baumol (1990).

Finally, some of the models reviewed in this chapter generate conflicting predictions. It should be possible, at least in principle, to identify the most empirically relevant theories by confronting them with suitable data. For example, just as Barlevy (2007) adduced evidence in favor of his view of R&D being pro-cyclical (in contrast to Francois and Lloyd-Ellis, 2003), so it should be possible to eventually pronounce on whether the quality of entrepreneurship increases in recessions (as argued by Caballero and Hammour, 1994) or in booms (as argued by Ghatak *et al.*, 2007). However, empirical testing of the theories could be difficult to perform in practice. Few of the theories define 'entrepreneurship' explicitly, implicitly regarding entrepreneurship as an activity which involves production and innovation. While this convention is unobjectionable in and of itself, it does not match most available data sets in which entrepreneurship is usually measured as the number of business owners or self-employed. There is clearly a pronounced disjunction between theoretical and empirical constructs in this respect, a problem which is compounded by the fact that many of the theories also allow entrepreneurship to involve *de alio* rather than purely *de novo* entry. Special data sets will likely be needed to match theory with empirics.

A full history of the 2008 financial crisis and Great Recession remains to be written. When it is, one hopes that it will inspire researchers to delve more deeply into the entrepreneurial origins of this, and the next, crisis.

Note

1. Bernanke and Gertler (1989) show that fair entrepreneurs optimize by gambling on a lottery in which $g(\omega)$ winners get full self-finance (requiring no auditing, as noted above for (20)) while $[1 - g(\omega)]$ losers do not invest at all. (In fact, Bernanke and Gertler's qualitative results continue to hold even if lotteries are not available.)

References

Acs, Z.J. and Audretsch, D.B. (1988) Innovation in large and small firms: an empirical analysis. *American Economic Review* 78: 678–690.

Aghion, P. and Howitt, P. (1998) Market structure and the growth process. *Review of Economic Dynamics* 1(1): 276–305.

Arulampalam, W., Gregg, P. and Gregory, M. (2001) Unemployment scarring. *Economic Journal* 111: F577–F584.

Audretsch, D.B., Grilo, I. and Thurik, A.R. (eds.) (2007) *Handbook of Research on Entrepreneurship Policy*. Cheltenham, UK: Edward Elgar.

Barlevy, G. (2007) On the cyclicality of research and development. *American Economic Review* 97(4): 1131–1164.

Baumol, W.J. (1990) Entrepreneurship: productive, unproductive, and destructive. *Journal of Political Economy* 98: 893–921.

Bernanke, B. and Gertler, M. (1989) Agency costs, net worth, and business fluctuations. *American Economic Review* 79(1): 14–31.

Birch, D.L. (1979) *The Job Generation Process*, Cambridge, MA: MIT Programme on Neighbourhood and Regional Change.

Blanchard, O.J. and Diamond, P. (1990) The cyclical behavior of the gross flows of US workers. *Brookings Papers on Economic Activity* 2: 85–155.

Bresnahan, T.F. and Raff, D.M. (1991) Intra-industry heterogeneity and the Great Depression: the American motor vehicles industry, 1929–1935. *Journal of Economic History* 51(2): 317–331.

Caballero, R.J. and Hammour, M.L. (1994) The cleansing effect of recessions. *American Economic Review* 84(5): 1350–1368.

Cagetti, M. and de Nardi, M. (2006) Entrepreneurship, frictions, and wealth. *Journal of Political Economy* 114(5): 835–870.

Evans, D.S. and Jovanovic, B. (1989). An estimated model of entrepreneurial choice under liquidity constraints. *Journal of Political Economy* 97: 808–827.

Francois, P. and Lloyd-Ellis, H. (2003) Animal spirits through creative destruction. *American Economic Review* 93(3): 530–550.

Ghatak, M., Morelli, M. and Sjöström, T. (2007) Entrepreneurial income, occupational choice, and trickle up policies. *Journal of Economic Theory* 137: 27–48.

Jovanovic, B. (1982) Selection and the evolution of industry. *Econometrica*. 50: 649–670.

King, R.G. and Rebelo, S.T. (1999) Resuscitating real business cycles. In J.B. Taylor and M. Woodford (eds.), *Handbook of Macroeconomics* (pp. 927–1007). Amsterdam: Elsevier North-Holland.

Kuznets, S. (1940) Schumpeter's business cycles. *American Economic Review* 30: 257–271.

Lundström, A. and Stevenson, L.A. (2005) *Entrepreneurship Policy: Theory and Pracrtice*. New York: Springer.

Parker, S.C. (Ed.) (2011) *Entrepreneurship in Recession*. Cheltenham, UK: Edward Elgar.

Parker, S.C. and van Praag, C.M. (2006) Schooling, capital constraints and entrepreneurial performance: the endogenous triangle. *Journal of Business & Economic Statistics* 24: 416–431.

Parker, S.C., Congregado, E. and Golpe, A. (2011) Is entrepreneurship a leading or lagging indiactor of the business cycle? Evidence from the UK, Forthcoming in *International Small Business Journal*.

Quadrini, V. (2000) Entrepreneurship, saving, and social mobility. *Review of Economic Dynamics* 3: 1–40.

Rampini, A. (2004) Entrepreneur activity, risk and the business cycle. *Journal of Monetary Economics* 5: 555–573.

Rebelo, S. (2005) Real business cycle models: past, present and future. *Scandinavian Journal of Economics* 107(2): 217–238.

Schmookler, J. (1966). *Invention and Economic Growth*. Cambridge, MA: Harvard University Press.

Schumpeter, J.A. (1927) The explanation of the business cycle. *Economica* 21: 286–311.

Schumpeter, J.A. (1939) *Business Cycles: A Theoretical, Historical and Statistical Analysis of the Capitalist Process*. NY: McGraw-Hill.

Schumpeter, J.A. (1942) *Capitalism, Socialism and Democracy*. NY: Harper.

Shleifer, A. (1986) Implementation cycles. *Journal of Political Economy* 94(6): 1163–1190.

van Stel, A., Carree, M. and Thurik, A.R. (2005) The effect of entrepreneurial activity on national economic growth. *Small Business Economics* 24: 311–321.

3

THE TRANSATLANTIC PRODUCTIVITY GAP: A SURVEY OF THE MAIN CAUSES

Raquel Ortega-Argilés

1. Introduction

The productivity performance of an economy can be explained by the contribution of employment to certain sectors and by the contribution of this employment to productivity in general. In the 1980s, the United States (US) economy seemed to be in danger of losing its competitive edge to other nations such as Germany or Japan. Indeed, by the early 1990s the European economy appeared to almost catch the US economy, but since then a significant transatlantic productivity gap emerged at precisely the time when European Union (EU) was embarking its most fundamental period of deregulation and integration. At the start of the second decade of the 21st century, and even after the financial crisis and the ensuing recession, the US economy was still ranked fourth in global economic competitiveness by the World Economic Forum. The observed transatlantic productivity gap, which was evident by the late 1990s, suggests that there are important differences in these mechanisms between the US and EU, but the reasons for this are not clear-cut and important debates have emerged. Disparities in the contribution of particular sectors of activity in the economy due to differences in the number of firms or employees in them are known as the *structural effect*, whereas disparities in the contribution to productivity by individuals located in the economy can be called *intrinsic effect*. However, which of these two effects primarily accounts for the productivity differences also needs to be considered in the light of other possible factors that might have influenced the EU–US productivity divergence.

There is much evidence to suggest that in comparison to the EU economy, the US economy is still characterized by higher levels of investments in information and communication technologies (ICTs), today's most important General Purposes Technologies. These differences in such investments, and the so-called 'new economy' effect they induce, are argued to be one of the main explanatory factors behind the transatlantic productivity gap (Jorgenson and Stiroh, 1999; Oliner and Sichel, 2000; van Ark *et al.*, 2002, 2003; Stiroh, 2002; O'Mahony and van Ark, 2003; Stiroh, 2005; Bloom *et al.*, 2007; Rogerson, 2008). The argument broadly is that the 'new economy', as it was called, provided US economy with a high presence of firms in many new growth sectors such as information technology,

Innovation, Entrepreneurship, Geography and Growth, First Edition.
Edited by Philip McCann and Les Oxley. Chapters © 2013 The Authors.
Book compilation © 2013 Blackwell Publishing Ltd. Published 2013 by Blackwell Publishing Ltd.

biotechnology and nanotechnology. However, even with this US dominance in the production of information technologies, the ICT-using sectors such as retailing and many other
manufacturing and service industries played a very important role in the productivity gap.
In particular, the entrepreneurial culture of the US, the flexible labour markets and the upskilling labour force are argued to have fostered a greater adoption and adaptation of ICTs
in other sectors than in EU, and the effects on these other sectors are at least as important
as the effects on the ICT-producing sectors themselves. Yet, whether this is the case, and
the arguments as to exactly why this might be the case, is the topic of this chapter.

The chapter is organized as follows. Section 2 summarizes the historical analyses of the
evolution of the productivity levels in the US and EU economies. Section 3 discusses the
relationship between R&D, ICTs and productivity, and section 4 discusses the role played
by other specific sectors on the observed productivity differences. Section 5 examines the
role of other issues in determining productivity gap, such as product and labour market
regulations, firm organizational issues and the entrepreneurial culture. Section 6 discusses
the argument that the transatlantic productivity gap may be statistical artefact based on
the differences in data construction and also inadequate measurement techniques. Finally,
section 7 provides some conclusions.

2. Historical Evolution of the EU-US Productivity Growth Differentials

There are many pieces of research which try to analyse the historical evolution of the
differentials of growth the EU and the US economies in different periods of the history.
However, the studies analysing these issues differ in many aspects, such as in terms of the
variables used to analyse growth, the methodologies employed and the periods and sectors
under examination. It is therefore necessary to build up an overall picture so as to identify
the issues on which there is much agreement and the issues on which there are still areas
for further investigation.

As can be seen in Figure 1, average labour productivity growth, proxied by GDP per
hour worked, in the US accelerated from 1.2% in the 1990–1995 period to 2.5% in the
period 1996–2006 (see van Ark, 2002; van Ark *et al.*, 2008); conversely, labour productivity
growth in the EU15 that had experienced a catching up with the US at the beginning of the
1990s, experienced a productivity growth decline from 2.4% before 1995 to 1.5% in the
later period.

2.1 *Productivity Differences between the US and EU as a Whole*

van Ark (2002) analyses growth rates in the labour productivity and per capita income as
a proxy for living standards for a set of OECD countries for the periods 1990–1995 and
1995–2001. The description of the growth rates shows that Canada, US and the EU (EU15
without Luxembourg) experienced a substantial improvement in terms of per capita income
in the last period under analysis. With respect to labour productivity growth, the results
also present greater differences across countries. In particular, as regards the comparison
between US and EU, the results show a strong acceleration in the EU at the beginning of
the 1990s (2.5% labour productivity growth rate) and a slowdown in the mid-1990s (1.3%),
whereas the opposite is shown for the US (from a 1.1% growth rate in the beginning of the
1990s to 2.0% growth rate at the end of the decade). Amongst other causes, van Ark (2002)

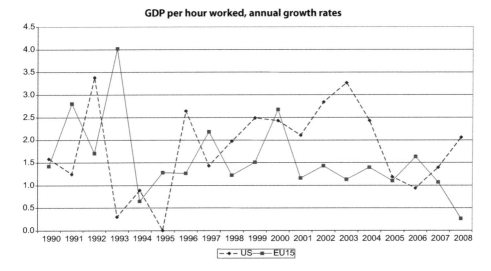

Figure 1. Labour Productivity Growth in the US and the EU15: 1990–2008.
Source: OECD (OECD Statistical Extracts: *http://stats.oecd.org*).

attributes these disparities mainly to the differences in the volume of annual working hours per person employed and the share of the population at work.

Gordon (2004) showed that for the periods (1870–1990) and (1990–2003), the private sector of Europe was falling behind from 1870 to 1950, experienced a catch up after 1950 and then fell behind again after 1995. Europe has almost closed the gap in productivity *levels* by 1995, but its slow growth since then has caused its relative productivity levels to drop from 94% to 85% of the US level. The data used in this analysis comes from Maddison (2001) and refers to the total economy of 12 countries (namely the EU15 minus Greece, Portugal and Spain) weighted by their relative GDP for period 1870–1990. For the 1990–2003 period of analysis, the data was updated with OECD data on all of the EU15 member states, and over the decade between the mid-1990s and the mid-2000s that the GDP growth gap between the EU and the US was almost entirely driven by differences in total factor productivity (TFP) (van Ark *et al.*, 2008; Jorgenson *et al.*, 2008; McMorrow *et al.*, 2010).

Several subperiods on the evolution of labour productivity growth in the 20th century have been analysed in Erken (2004). The growth of labour productivity in the EU15 shows a downward trend over time (3.1 average annual percentage change between 1970 and 1980; 2.4 between 1980 and 1990; 2.0 between 1990 and 2000 and 1.2 between 2000 and 2005) whereas the US exhibits the reverse. The US shows a rapid acceleration in the rate of productivity growth over time (1.4 average annual percentage rates between the years 1980 and 1990, 1.6 between 1990 and 2000 and 2.5 between 2000 and 2005). For a selection of OECD countries Erken provided a decomposition of labour productivity growth per hour worked for the period 1995–2005 in two periods, 1995–2000 and 2000–2005. The analysis provides more evidence on productivity causes be showing that more heterogeneity could be found in the overall productivity growth within the European countries in the period of 1995–2000 compared to the 2000–2005 period. Erken's results are in line with previous literature in which the decrease in growth was due to two effects: ICT-capital deepening playing a less prominent role as a source of productivity growth after 2000 and the decrease in TFP in many countries, in particular in the Mediterranean countries (Italy, Spain and Portugal).

McGuckin and van Ark (2004) compared the periods 1990–1995 to 1995–2003 and provided a uniform treatment of the total economy. The 1995–2003 difference between US and European productivity growth is less severe compared with previous analysis based only on the private economy. However, the initial European breakdown evident in the data for 1995–2000 worsened with data for 2000–2003, where the US sustained its productivity growth revival.

Rather than aggregate productivity, Bourlès and Cette (2007) consider the trends in US and other industrialized country in hourly labour productivity. It emerges that two-thirds of the slowdown of 'observed' productivity at the time of the first oil shock is attributable to an increase in employment rates and to a smaller decrease in working time. Between the first and second half of the 1970s, annual productivity growth decreased by about one point for the 'observed' indicator and one-third of a point for the 'structural' hourly productivity indicator (the one calculated controlling for differences in hours worked and the employment rate). For the 2000–2004 time period, structural productivity slowed down and its trend growth (about 2% a year) was between that which was evident in the second half of the 1990s (2.6%) and that of the 1980–1995 time period (1.6%). There is no such slowdown for 'observed' productivity, because it was offset by the effects of decreases in the employment rate and average working time. Therefore, since 2000, US productivity gains seem to have been structurally less significant than those of the second half of the 1990s. The very high levels of observed productivity in some European countries in recent years compared with the US are generally attributable to lower hours worked and employment rates. Therefore, in 2004, in all the countries, relative structural productivity was lower than observed productivity, with the gap being all the greater when the observed relative productivity level was also high. While the observed productivity level in Germany, France, Ireland, Norway and the Netherlands is similar to (over 95%) or even higher than the US level, the structural level is also very high in only two small countries, namely Ireland and Norway. For these two countries, observed productivity is artificially raised by specific features, namely, the impact of profit transfers stemming from very atypical corporate tax incentives in the case of Ireland and a highly capital-intensive structure with the focus on three industries – oil, timber and fisheries – in the case of Norway. Apart from those two special cases, the fact that structural hourly productivity levels are higher in the US than elsewhere shows that US is indeed setting the technical frontier in terms of productive efficiency and that other countries are lagging behind to varying degrees. From the beginning, or the middle of the 1990s, depending on the country being considered, observed and structural productivity declined in all countries relative to the US, apart from Norway and Sweden. This relative deterioration was attributable not only to the acceleration in productivity in the US, but also to the slowdown in productivity in almost all the other countries.

In Timmer et al. (2010), the description of the long-term pattern of convergence experienced since 1950 between the European and US productivity growth is presented. To illustrate the growth evolution in these countries several indicators are used: GDP per capita, GDP per hour and hours worked per capita. The GDP measures are compared to the US levels and are adjusted for differences in relative price levels using the GDP-based purchasing power parities for 2002 from the OECD. During the 1950s and the 1960s, European growth rates converged to the US rates by means of higher investments, along with the adaptation of foreign technologies accompanied with higher levels of supporting institutions. In the 1970s and the 1980s, the productivity gap between the EU and the US continued to narrow as a consequence of the higher labour productivity growth in the EU-15 and an unchanged gap in per capita income. Several arguments are provided explaining why the EU working hours per person employed declined from similar levels in the 1970s to three quarters of the US level in the 1995. Amongst them are the increase in income taxes, labour costs, the preference for leisure time, the high payroll rates that increase the structural unemployment and the high levels of unionization experienced in some European countries. In the 1990s, average annual labour productivity growth in the market economy accelerated from 1.9% (1973–1995) to 2.9% (1995–2006) in US, whereas in the EU it fell from 2.5% to 1.5%. Timmer *et al.* (2010) argue that the slowdown in labour productivity is connected *in the short run* with these labour restructuring issues in several European economies during this period (Blanchard, 2004; Dew-Becker and Gordon, 2008). In the long run, however, the continuous disparities in the growth patterns of both economies can be associated with the endogenous development in investment rates (in different input factors) and the adoption of technical change. In the mid 1990s, the US economy experienced a boost in the productivity of ICT-producing industries and a capital-deepening effect from investments in ICTs in different sectors of the economy. US ICT-using industries, and principally in market services, experienced an increase of productivity, albeit after a certain delay due to the reorganizations required in adopting the new technologies. In Europe, however, a continuous lag in the adoption of ICTs clearly contributed negatively to the catching process achieved during previous decades.

Uppenberg (2011) chapter illustrates the composition of GDP growth in the US, the EU and its member countries for the periods 1980–1995, 1995–2001 and 2001–2008 based on the OECD-STAN data, presenting a breakdown of average GDP growth rates into the contributions of employment and labour productivity. The results for different subperiods show that different sectors in different countries have grown at different speeds. The results of the Maudos *et al.* (2008) shift-share analysis of the productivity slowdown of the EU15 with respect to the US since 1995 show that the difference in the intrasectoral effect is the main cause behind the growing productivity gap between both economies. The slowdown in growth in the EU15 is above all caused by modest pure gains of productivity within European countries and is not due to sectoral re-allocation of employment.

2.2 Productivity Differences US and Different Parts of Europe

The literature that analyses the productivity gap between Europe and the US (especially in the 1990s) has mainly focused on the comparison between the productivity performance of Europe as a whole and the US (Jorgenson *et al.*, 2005; Timmer and van Ark, 2005). However, during that period some European countries (e.g. Ireland, Finland and Sweden) as well as the US appeared to perform in terms of productivity. This implies that in some cases the overall aggregate EU underperformance hid the positive performance of some European countries as a consequence of the aggregation procedure. A stream of literature has therefore also recognized that the heterogeneity amongst European countries appears to be more pronounced than the differences between the overall EU and the US (Gordon, 2004; Gordon and Dew-Becker, 2005; Timmer *et al.*, 2010).

Gordon (2004) recognizes that the heterogeneity amongst European countries is more pronounced than the difference between the EU and the US. Numerous studies have shown a relatively strong positive correlation between MFP growth and measures of ICT use, for example, the ratio of ICT expenditure to GDP or the change in PC use per 100 inhabitants over the 1990s. In such comparisons, numerous countries achieve higher MFP growth rates than the US over the 1990s, including Ireland, Finland, Sweden, Denmark, Norway, Canada and Australia. Some, but not all of these countries surpass the US in PC use per household and or in the share of ICT expenditure. What differs most between Europe and the US in the low level of PC adoption and ICT expenditure in the 'olive belt' ranging from Portugal and Spain on the west to Italy and Greece in the East?

Different authors have analysed the heterogeneity in the sectoral growth patterns within the European countries. Castaldi and Sapio (2008) analyse the value added growth patterns of some sectors for a set of European countries. They follow the idea of potential convergence in the sectoral co-evolution as a result of technological interdependencies in closer geographical areas, known as the *mushroom-like growth process* and developed in Harberger (1998). With data from Eurostat, they describe the value added growth patterns in five-digit NACE sectors for the cases of France, Germany, Italy and the UK for the period 1995–2003. The results show similarities across countries with a lower heterogeneity in the growth patterns of larger sectors. The results also support the idea of the industry life cycle (Gort and Klepper, 1982; Klepper and Graddy, 1990) where large and mature industries converge to higher concentrated industries with reduced firm turnover, in comparison with smaller and younger sectors. Taking a longer time horizon, the properties of sectoral growth show more cross-country disparities, suggesting that structural and country-specific factors are important. European countries display disparities related to their technological sectoral specialization, with more homogenous sectoral growth patterns evident in Germany and UK. Castaldi and Sapio (2008) conclude that the role of the diffusion of technological shocks is the key determinant in the trends of sectoral growth patterns. The results of this analysis are complemented by the results obtained in Inklaar and Timmer (2009). In the case of developed OECD countries since 1970, Inklaar and Timmer (2009) demonstrate different sectoral convergence patterns amongst manufacturing and service sectors, which show a productivity convergence in service sectors that could not be found in manufacturing industries. Cozza *et al.* (2011, 2012) try to shed some more light on understanding the transatlantic productivity gap, not only in terms of productivity but also in terms of R&D investments, considering their important role in explaining the productivity of regions. The study addresses some more conclusions regarding the high degree of heterogeneity in the productivity performance of firms located in different European areas and their comparison with their US counterparts, a subject that had not previously been tacking in the literature. Consistent with previous literature, the authors found a clear dichotomy in the European aggregate: the UK and the Nordic countries appear to exhibit an R&D–productivity pattern similar to the US, whereas the rest of Europe appears to be lagging behind. Overall, Europe is lagging behind the US but within Europe the R&D–productivity link is clearly characterized by increasing returns in R&D-intensive regions. In sum, the specialization patterns of the EU economies and the geographical characteristics of the EU regional locations are some of the main explanations of the gap in productivity and R&D both between Europe and US and also within Europe. The results also show the high returns in labour productivity of internal investments in physical capital, in the case of low-R&D intensive manufacturing sectors.

3. The R&D–ICT Intensity Gap

The consensus about the existence of a positive and significant impact of R&D on productivity remains strong across almost all studies and methods (Hall and Mairesse, 1995; Janz *et al.*, 2004; Klette and Kortum, 2004; Lööf and Heshmati, 2006; Rogers, 2006; Heshmati and Kim, 2011; Ortega-Argilés *et al.*, 2011). However, there is also much evidence which demonstrates that the transatlantic productivity gap is related to the gap and delay between Europe and the US in terms of the application of R&D-driven innovation in general, and in terms of Business R&D in particular (O'Mahony and van Ark, 2003; Blanchard, 2004). Insufficient investment in R&D is often argued to be a key reason why Europe has lagged over the years behind the US in terms of economic growth (Uppenberg, 2009), and many scholars argue that the European delay in terms of private R&D investment is mainly due to a *sectoral composition effect*. This sectoral composition effect arises because the ICT sectors, and the R&D-intensive manufacturing and R&D-intensive service sectors are under-represented in the European economy in comparison with the US (European Commission, 2007a; Mathieu and van Pottelsberghe de la Potterie, 2008; Lindmark *et al.*, 2010; Ortega-Argilés and Brandsma, 2010). As such, this argument implies that any potential productivity gains associated with new technological advancements will proportionately have a lower impact on the EU than the US economy. Moreover, this underperformance will be exacerbates by other issues. In particular, we know that market turbulence, defined in terms of firm entry and exits, is an important driver of productivity growth (Bartelsman and Doms, 2000) as it allows new ideas and technologies to be rapidly introduced into the market place. Most importantly for our purposes, this 'revolving door' entrepreneurial regime appears to be particularly important in high technological industries (Audretsch, 1995; Pilat, 2001), and the lower levels of EU market flexibility may also exacerbate Europe's weaker performance in these sectors. However, as we see more in this chapter, this analysis is somewhat controversial because of the limitations of comparable data and the definition and classification of sectors.

At the same time, other scholars focus their explanations of the transatlantic productivity gap much more on what they regard as a negative *intrinsic effect*, which is explained by lower levels of investments in R&D on the part of EU firms within each sector and a lower translation of inputs into gains in productivity (Erken and van Es, 2007; Erken, 2008; Ortega-Argilés *et al.*, 2010, 2011). The intrinsic effect emphasizes the weaker innovation-transmission mechanisms within the EU economy, rather than the structure of the economy *per se*, as playing a critical and rather adverse role. However, the *sectoral composition effect* and the *intrinsic effect* are not necessarily in conflict with one–another. Both effects may operate simultaneously, and the combination of these two effects may result in the observed productivity transatlantic gap.

In the case of the ICT industries, Lindmark *et al.* (2010) analyse the R&D gap in ICT business sectors between the US and the EU. As with the findings of O'Sullivan (2007) and European Commission (2007b), they found that the ICT business sectors in the EU do not undertake as much R&D as their counterparts in the US. Moreover, the results of the aggregate BERD data (business expenditure on R&D) show that the contribution of the ICT sector is smaller in the EU than in the US for two reasons. First, the ICT sector is smaller in the EU economy than in the US, but this only accounts for one third of the R&D gap. Second, the R&D intensity (BERD/VA) of the ICT sector is smaller in the EU economy and this accounts for the remaining gap. Their results of Lindmark *et al.* (2010) using microdata show that the R&D levels are actually very similar inside and outside the EU when it comes to similar businesses. However, large EU companies within the ICT sectors are more likely to operate in the telecom services subsector, which has a low R&D intensity. In other words, the ICT transatlantic R&D gap reflects, more than anything, the lack of a sufficient presence of EU companies in the higher R&D-intensive components of the ICT sector.

Uppenberg (2009) decomposes aggregate BERD along several dimensions. The sectoral decomposition in his study shows that the business R&D gap between the EU and the US is not the result of different sectoral allocations. Indeed, in his study, he argues that Europe is actually more specialized in relatively R&D-intensive manufacturing sectors than the US, and a shift towards services would actually widen the transatlantic productivity gap. Instead, Uppenberg argues that Europe's lower overall level of R&D intensity appears to be the result of lower levels of R&D intensity in specific individual sectors, and particularly in the case of ICT equipment and other nontransportation equipment industries, as well as in service sectors. Indeed, the low levels of R&D intensity in Europe's services are a major drag on the EU economy, because of their share of overall activity.

In terms of corporate R&D differences between Europe and US, various authors (Castaldi, 2009; Moncada-Paterno-Castello, 2010; Moncada-Paterno-Castello et al., 2010) have documented the relatively higher R&D levels of US firms. The impacts of these differences on productivity growth rates have been examined amongst others by, McMorrow et al. (2010). Their findings suggest that individual industries with higher R&D expenditures and higher adoption rates for ICT-intensive technologies exhibit higher TFP growth rates, although an across the board increase in R&D and ICT does not necessarily significantly affect TFP growth. However, these impacts are not necessarily related to large firms. Using data from the EU R&D Scoreboard, Ortega-Argilés and Brandsma (2010) run a micro-econometric analysis the characteristics of the R&D intensity of firms. Their findings suggest that the higher level of R&D intensity in the US with respect to the EU is mainly due to the greater role that high-R&D intensive small and medium enterprises (SMEs) play in explaining the R&D intensity in US in comparison with the EU. Ortega-Argilés et al. (2011) analyse the returns of R&D and physical capital stocks to labour productivity for a sample of US and EU firms during the period 1990–2008. The analysis tries to shed some line in the comparison between the returns obtained by US and EU firms operating in similar sets of sectors. Consistent with previous literature, the authors found robust evidence of a significant positive relationship of research and development stocks on firm labour productivity across sectors. Amongst the sectors, the R&D returns increase monotonically (both in significance and in magnitude) from the low- to the high-tech sectors, and from the EU to the US. Ortega-Argilés et al. (2011) conclude that US companies seem to be more efficient in translating their R&D investments into productivity gains in comparison with similar firms operating in EU.

In terms of our understanding of the relationship between ICTs, R&D and productivity growth, the work of Sadun and van Reenen (2005) and Stiroh (2002b, 2005) uncovers three important and more general observations. First, on average ICTs do appear to be statistically and significantly associated with higher firm level productivity, and this observation stands in contrast with some of the earlier industry and macro-level studies that struggled to find any effect of ICTs on productivity. The reason why the earlier industry level studies struggled to find much of an impact may be because the industry averages disguise large differences between firms within industries. Second, the magnitude of the association between ICT and company productivity is substantial. Stiroh (2005) reported a 'meta-analysis' looking at the results of 20 different studies of the association of productivity with IT. He investigated the elasticity of productivity with respect to ICT investments or ICT usage, and as a whole he found this elasticity was about 5%, which is much larger than one would expect if ICT was just another form of capital such as buildings. If ICTs were simply a normal form of capital earning the usual market return we would expect that a doubling of the IT capital stock would increase output by approximately the share of IT in total revenues. Because the relevant share was about 1–2%, these elasticities suggest that there are some special features of ICTs compared to other forms of capital. Third, between different studies, there is a huge variation around the average impact of ICTs on firm productivity. Indeed, Stiroh (2005) reports estimates ranging from an upper end of over 25% to –5%. Some of these differences are due to methodological choices such as alternative specifications of the statistical model, but it is more likely that a large amount of this variation is due to genuine differences in the impact of IT across firms and this is reflected in the different results from different datasets.

4. Industry Comparisons and the Diffusion of ICTs

As we have seen earlier, it has been well documented that the growth gap between the EU and the US has been driven by differences in TFP, and the differences have not been homogenous across countries or regions. Moreover, the role of ICTs in this phenomenon appears to be critical although as we have already seen earlier, the nature of the role played by ICTs may be different in different sectors, both inside and outside of the ICT-producing industries. Indeed, research suggests that these issues are also very much evident at the level of many different sectors and many other issues may also influence these relationships.

Analyses that focus on the evidence on the sectoral distribution of growth determinants such as value added, employment or labour productivity across countries with different sorts of data can be found in European Commission (2007a, 2008; and subsequently with the R&D European Scoreboard Data), Castaldi (2009) and Timmer *et al.* (2010) with the EUKLEMS data; Inklaar and Timmer (2009), Uppenberg (2009, 2011) or Nicoletti and Scarpetta (2003, 2005) with the OECD-STAN database, shedding light on the nature of the growth gap between the EU and the US, as well as that between individual EU Member States.

As an example, the work by McMorrow *et al.* (2010) provides a breakdown of the TFP gap between the US and the EU at the industry level[1] over the period 1996–2004 and their work shows that only a small number of industries drove the bulk of the aggregate TFP growth rate in favour of the US during this period. Amongst these industries we can find only one manufacturing industry, namely 'electrical and optical equipment' – which includes telecom, semiconductors and computers – and a number of private service industries including the retail trade, the renting of manufacturing and equipment and other business activities. From their analysis, we can deduce that the industrial composition of the economies is an important part of the explanation of the transatlantic productivity gap.

Pilat (2001) presents a decomposition of labour productivity growth in the business sector in three dimensions (the intrasectoral effect, the net-shift effect and the interaction effect) using the industry decomposition available in the former ISDB-STAN database (2-digit ISIC for services and 3–4 digit ISIC for manufacturing). The intrasectoral effect is the most important contributor to productivity growth in the nonfarm business sector. The net-shift effect also makes and important contribution, but this contribution is different taking into consideration the period under analysis. In the period 1990–1997, for the European countries, the intrasectoral effect appears to be the most important. Similarly, using industry data, Nordhaus (2001) found evidence of productivity spillovers outside durable manufacturing into traditional productivity growth sectors, such as trade and finance.

Adopting a slightly different approach, Castaldi (2009) uses an innovation-based taxonomy of both manufacturing and services industries to decompose the aggregate labour productivity growth of EU, US and Japan in the period 1990–2004. Castaldi argues that structural change relies on an uneven distribution of productivity increases across sectors, in line with the 'mushroom' view of growth of Hagerber (1998). Employment seems to have shifted from manufacturing to services and services account for an important share of labour productivity growth. Information networks, relevant for information diffusion and knowledge sharing, show the highest contribution to aggregate productivity growth. In contrast, although knowledge-intensive services still show some productivity benefits in the US economy, they no longer continue to contribute to the EU economy. As with the findings of other chapters, they appear to demonstrate a relatively slow level of maturity in the European economy mainly by showing an uneven specialization in ICT within Europe and a relatively low contribution by the supplier dominated services in comparison with the US or Japan. Finally, regarding the contribution of manufacturing sectors, the chapter shows that scale-intensive and science-based industries clearly account for an important share of the productivity across all countries.

The Uppenberg (2011) chapter illustrates the composition of GDP growth in the US, the EU and its member countries for the periods 1980–1995, 1995–2001 and 2001–2008 based on the OECD-STAN data, and presents a breakdown of average GDP growth rates into both the contributions of employment and also labour productivity. Productivity growth appeared to be higher in manufacturing than growth in output, and was thus accompanied by a secular decline in the sector's share in total employment. By contrast, market services have seen their share in employment increase over time. In the decade preceding the crisis, output growth in market services showed a healthy combination of productivity and employment increases in the US and also in few EU economies. In the major part of the EU, however, growth in services was heavily dependent on employment and came with disappointingly low productivity advances. In the 2000s, market services accounted for two-thirds in the EU–US productivity growth gap, with manufacturing accounting for the remaining third. Given the growing relative size of the sector, market services' poor productivity performance has increasingly become a drag on overall growth performance of the EU economy.

McMorrow et al. (2010) analyse the industrial determinants of the EU–US TFP growth using EUKLEMS database that allows for the examination of nine EU countries (Inklaar et al., 2008a, b). The analysis is conducted adopting a neo-Schumpeterian growth approach (Aghion and Howitt, 2006) to analyse different TFP determinants such as the rate of innovation and the rate at which state-of-the-art technologies are adopted or diffused throughout the wider economy. The empirical implementation is similar to Nicoletti and Scarpetta (2003), Griffith et al. (2004) or Inklaar et al. (2008a, b). Other control variables such as human capital, R&D, the adoption of ICT technology and market regulations were tested. The human capital effect appears to be significant for explaining the differences in TFP across countries, and as also found in previous analyses, TFP growth appears to be driven by a catching-up phenomena associated with the gradual adoption of new technologies. TFP growth is also significantly driven by developments at the technological frontier in industries with higher R&D expenditures and higher adoption of ICTs, especially since the mid-1990s.

4.1 *The New Economy Effect*

'The European productivity slowdown can be attributable to the slower emergence of the knowledge economy in Europe compared to the United States' (van Ark *et al.*, 2008)

Although, during the 1980s and the first half of the 1990s, most studies found little or no evidence of a significant contribution of ICTs on productivity growth (e.g. Jorgenson *et al.*, 1987; Siegel and Griliches, 1992; Oliner and Sichel, 1994; Berndt and Morrison, 1995), a major consensus in the literature explaining the productivity differential between EU and US since the mid-1990s is that the EU was relatively slower in capturing the impact of the *New Economy* or the *Knowledge Economy* in comparison with the US. The impact of the use of new ICTs as the most important contemporary GPT (general purpose technology) has diffused across all sectors at a slower rate in Europe relative to the US, and these differences themselves differ in different sectors and in different time periods. The so-called Solow paradox argued that although enormous technological progress and investments in ICT production had been realized, hardly any effect on economic growth could be observed (Solow, 1987). Many studies on ICT diffusion and productivity growth using the growth-accounting methodology (Jorgenson and Stiroh, 2000; Oliner and Sichel, 2000; Jorgenson, 2001; Daveri, 2002; Whelan, 2002; van Ark *et al.*, 2008; Timmer *et al.*, 2010) find that productivity growth has accelerated after 1995, particularly in the US, and that this acceleration was linked to rapid technological change in ICT goods production. Jorgenson *et al.* (2008) argued that the US productivity growth after 1995 and up to 2000 was driven by productivity growth in ICT-producing sectors and ICT-capital-deepening effects. Similarly, Timmer and van Ark (2005), Draca *et al.* (2007) and van Ark *et al.* (2008) all find that the differences in ICT-capital deepening and the differences in the contribution of TFP growth in ICT-goods production, explain the major gap in growth rates between Europe and the US after 1995. In contrast, after 2000, productivity growth was driven primarily by TFP growth in ICT-using industries.

Many other studies trying to link the differentials in productivity amongst different economies also argue that growth disparities can be largely explained by the differences in this ICT–GPT-productivity effect in the economies. For example, Jorgenson and Stiroh (1999) and Oliner and Sichel (2000) found evidence that the growth contribution of ICTs in the US economy was small in 1974–1995, and markedly higher in 1996–2000. The Oliner and Sichel (2000) chapter found that the growth rate in labour productivity increased by 1.04 percentage points from 1991–1995 to 1996–1999 for the US. Of this increase, 43% can be attributed to the accumulation of ICT capital in all industries, whereas 36% can be attributed to TFP growth in ICT-producing sectors.

In a similar vein, Stiroh (2002a, 2005) found that IT producing and using sectors essentially account for all of the acceleration in US productivity. The econometric evidence shows that productivity growth was significant in the ICT-using sectors, even after controlling for macro-economic shocks. The analysis was performed for the US industries for the periods 1987–1995 and 1995–2000. The main findings were that the acceleration in productivity is a broad phenomenon across the US industries (not only in ICT-producing sectors) but that growth rates increased the most in ICT-intensive industries. In detail, productivity growth accelerated by 3.5 percentage points per annum (p.a.) in the ICT-using sectors (from 1.2% p.a. pre-1995 to 4.7% p.a. post-1995). It accelerated by 2% in ICT-intensive industries, presenting a small deceleration in the other sectors of the economy. In other words, the US industries have been successful in transforming the new technology into higher productivity.

The question, therefore, is whether the disappointing European growth performance can be attributed to ineffective use of ICT or to the lower levels of technology-intensive firms. O'Mahony and van Ark (2003) performed a comparative study between the US and a small number of European countries (EU-4). The analysis found that European ICT-producing sectors had similar productivity acceleration as in the US. European ICT-*using* sectors (e.g. retail, wholesale and securities trading industries) failed to achieve a similar development showing stagnant productivity growth. Moreover, the authors found that productivity growth in the EU is relatively stable across time in intensively ICT-using sectors, in contrast to a very large acceleration in the US. According to the authors, this is a clear indication that the US is ahead of Europe in terms of productive application of ICT outside the ICT-producing sector itself. In ICT-producing industries, there was acceleration after 1995 of 1.9% per year in the US and a similar 1.6% per year in Europe, but the US started from a higher base. In contrast, the ICT-using industries appear to be the source of the difference.

Beyond ICT-producing sectors, some other sectors also appear to be very important for explaining the productivity gaps. van Ark *et al.* (2003) show that all of the productivity growth differential of the US over Europe in the late 1990s came from these three industries, with retail contributing about 55% of the differential, wholesale 24%, and securities trade 20%. The remaining industries had small positive or negative differentials, netting out to zero. The findings of Oliner and Sichel (2002) seem to predict that at least for the 1990s, all of the productivity revival in retailing was achieved by purchasing new computers, software and communications equipment. US retailers, irrespective of whether they were new establishments of the 1990s or older establishments from the 1980s or before, rapidly adopted new ICT technologies to increase competitiveness. Bar-code readers rapidly became almost universal in both new and old stores. It is likely that the productivity revival in retailing associated with newly built megastores allows for productivity gains beyond just the use of computers, including economies of scale and scope, efficient logistics operations and bulk purchase pricing advantages and greater competition.

On these points, Daveri (2002) argues that although the precise size of the growth effects of ICT in Europe is still subject to large measurement error, the broad picture seems to be clear. In the second half of the 1990s, the growth contributions from ICT capital rose in only six EU countries (UK, Denmark, Finland, Sweden, Ireland and Greece). However, unlike the US, this has not generally been associated with higher labour or TFP growth rates, the only exceptions being Ireland and Greece. Particularly worrying here, is the fact that the large countries in Continental Europe (Germany, France, Italy and Spain) showed stagnating or even mildly declining growth contributions from ICT capital, together with definite declines in TFP growth, compared to the first half of the 1990s. In terms of why this should be the case, van Ark *et al.* (2008) evaluated the effect of structural changes on productivity growth and found that the reallocation of labour between industries has contributed negatively to labour productivity growth after 1995 in Europe. This however, cannot explain the low European growth rates, because the negative reallocation effect is numerically larger for the US.

Inklaar *et al.* (2003) presented a new industry-level database, EUKLEMS data, to analyse sources of growth in Europe. The database contains information of manufacturing and services industries in: France, Germany, Netherlands and United Kingdom, and permits comparisons with the US for the period 1979–2000. The results show that the acceleration in ICT-capital deepening was caused by a relatively small set of service industries in both regions. The differences experienced in growth are mainly due to their relatively lower contribution by these sectors to growth in the EU countries in comparison with the US. The authors also point to the deceleration in non-ICT-capital deepening in the EU-4 linked to the labour restructuring, as two of the causes of the European productivity slowdown in the 1990s.

Similar results can be found in Strauss and Samkharadze (2011) who use the same database, and analyse the decomposition of average annual labour productivity in the EU-15 and the US for the periods 1980–1995, 1995–2001 and 2001–2007. Their analysis shows that for the case of EU-15, ICT capital contributed half a percentage point to annual productivity growth during the period 1995–2001. This temporary acceleration effect in ICT capital did not compensate the decline of TFP growth experienced in the late 1990s. In the US, ICT contributed to accelerating labour productivity growth in the whole period. Finally, with regards to the ICT comparison, their analysis suggests that within the European countries there were disparities. Their analysis shows that ICT growth patterns were similar in the UK and in the US in contrast with Germany, Italy or Spain.

Although as we see there is now a widespread consensus as to the nature of the productivity gap, there are also some slightly differing views. The work of Dahl *et al.* (2011) based on a multicountry sectoral panel dataset, provides econometric evidence of positive and significant productivity effects of ICT in Europe, mainly due to advances in TFP. The impact of ICT in Europe has happened against a negative macro-economic shock, which is not related to ICT. Their main results challenge the consensus in the growth-accounting literature that there has been no acceleration of productivity growth in Europe due primarily to a poor performance of ICT-using sectors. The empirical findings of Dahl *et al.* (2011) suggest that the decline in labour productivity growth after 1995 is a general phenomenon across European industries, in which sectoral productivity growth rates decreased the most in non-ICT-intensive industries. More specifically, the average decline in sectoral growth rates was around 1 percentage point for labour productivity growth after 1995, although this was partly counteracted by a positive effect of around 0.8 percentage points in industries that were ICT-intensive pre-1995. The results weaken when ICT-producers are excluded, although an economically significant differential effect of 0.5 percentage points remains for ICT-users versus remaining sectors.

What we see from these various studies is that the sectoral explanations for the transatlantic productivity gap can be related to a revealed technological disadvantage of the EU in ICT-producing sectors but also, and at least as importantly, is a lower rate of adoption of these GPTs in other ITC-using activities. This ultimately constrains the demand for human capital, ICT diffusion, innovative organizational and management practices associated with the adoption of these new technologies and the diffusion of innovations through embodied technology in new capital formation. However, there are specific sectors in which such weaknesses in ICT-adoption appear to have been particularly problematic, and these are services and retailing.

4.2 *Service Sectors*

The literature that analyses the effects of structural change on aggregate economic growth has also driven the debate on the impact of structural shifts to services on the rate of growth. According to the pessimistic vision expressed by Baumol (1967), the so-called cost-disease argument, the increasing demand for final services will drive productivity down by shifting employment to lower productivity activities with little or no potential for productivity gains. This argument follows the observation (Griliches, 1992, 1994) that services were crucial to the post-1973 slowdown, because productivity in services industries grew much more slowly than productivity in goods-producing industries after the late 1960s. Services, therefore, acted as a brake on US productivity growth, a conclusion that was particularly unsettling because services represented a rapidly increasing share of both US and EU economic activity. In contrast, proponents of a more optimistic view stress instead the role of services as intermediate goods and indirect contributors to productivity growth (Oulton, 2001; Pugno, 2006).

On face value, part of the transatlantic productivity gap explanations may therefore relate to the different composition of the economies. Yet, in Europe, service sectors account for a lower share of overall economic activity than they do in the US, and therefore if the cost disease argument were correct, it ought to favour Europe and minimize the productivity gap (Uppenberg and Strauss, 2010). However, across the Atlantic, 19 percentage points of gross value-added growth from 1995 to 2005 were accounted for by local services, business services and professional and financial services, whereas in the EU-15, these added only 10 percentage points. Clues as to why this is the case come from studies by Bosworth and Triplett (2003, 2004) and Jorgenson et al. (2002, 2005, 2008), which show that some of the biggest contributors to aggregate ICT-capital deepening are a limited number of service industries, in particular trade, finance and business services. Along with TFP growth in ICT-goods manufacturing, TFP acceleration in the ICT-using service industries also appears to be important as well.

Conversely, as Mischke et al. (2010) and Erken (2008) find, the widening productivity gap between Europe and the US was mainly due to the underperforming service sectors in Europe. Local services such as retailing alone account for two-thirds of the productivity shortfall. Yet, within Europe the picture is rather varied. Many chapters have analysed the impacts of service inputs on aggregate productivity growth in a set of different EU countries (Pilat and Lee, 2001; Crespi et al., 2007) and the conclusion that can be extracted from these chapters is that in general that there are positive spillover effects from the computer and ICTs sectors to other service sectors in some countries but not in others. Heterogeneity exists within Europe in terms of these technology transfer mechanisms, and evidence also suggests that these mechanisms have been different across time periods. Bosworth and Triplett (2006, 2003) and Triplett and Bosworth (2004) found that there are important differences in the ICT-related productivity effects between the early 1990s and the early 2000s. Accelerating productivity in services industries played a crucial part in post-1995 US productivity growth, and much of this was related to the adoption of ICTs, which now make a substantial contribution of labour productivity growth in services. This was a major change from the early 1990s, a period in which lagging productivity in services had appeared to be a stifling problem for economic growth.

Finally, following the same reasoning, Strauss and Samkharadze (2011) present a combined argument of the widening of the transatlantic productivity gap in the periods 1995–2001 and 2001–2007. They show that the wider gap was the consequence of a successful combined swift ICT-capital deepening and TFP growth in US market services, in comparison with a limited and lagged ICT adoption and stagnant TFP growth in the EU-15 market services. Their analysis shows that in ICT-using sectors, past ICT investments in services in the US contribute greatly to the actual TFP growth, whereas in the relatively slower ICT adoption by European service firms contributed to lower TFP growth rates in service sectors.

4.3 *The Case of Retailing*

The growth in retailing productivity performance did not occur evenly across the board in retailing but rather was concentrated in 'large stores offering a wide array of goods accompanied by low prices and relatively high use of self-service systems' (Sieling *et al.*, 2001). A complementary finding by Foster *et al.* (2002) based on a study of a large set of individual retail establishments shows that all of retail productivity growth (not just the revival but the entire measured amount of productivity growth over the decade of the 1990s) can be attributed to more productive establishments entering the industry which displaced much less productive existing establishments. In contrast, the typical average existing establishment, which continued in business, displayed zero productivity growth during the 1990s, and this was despite the massive investment of the retail industry in ICT equipment. These observations were supported by van Ark *et al.* (2002) and Foster *et al.* (2006) whose results identify the retail sector as a major factor explaining Europe's poor productivity performance in the late 1990s. Such effects may also be related to differing transatlantic responses to business cycle McMorrow *et al.* (2010). However, just as the US retailing sector has achieved efficiency gains for reasons not directly related to computers, so it appears that Europe has fallen back because European firms are much less free to develop retail innovation associated with new types of stores. Indeed, Baily (1993) suggests that regulation of retail trade plays a major role in explaining the productivity shortfall in retailing for Europe relatively to the US. The reasons why the US–EU productivity performance of retailing appears to have been so different has been argued to be related to specific European growth impediments, which include land use zoning regulations (Baily, 1993) that prevent the carving out of new greenfield sites for megastores in suburban and exurban locations, shop-closing regulations that restrict the revenue potential of new investments, congestion in central-city locations that are near the nodes of Europe's extensive urban public transit systems and restrictive labour rules that limit flexibility in organizing the workplace and make it expensive to hire and fire workers with the near-total freedom to which US firms are accustomed.

5. Other Issues: Market Rigidities, Firm Organization and Entrepreneurship

Other regulatory or institutional issues may also provide some of the explanations of the transatlantic productivity gap (Roeger, 2010), given that both EU product markets and labour markets are generally more regulated than in the US (Hoj *et al.*, 2007). This may be particularly important in service sectors such as distribution, financial services, transport and telecommunications (Goenenc *et al.*, 2001; Pilat, 2001). In addition, firms' organization issues may also influence the ability of non ICT-producing sectors to adopt and adapt ICTs in their operations.

5.1 *Product Markets*

Nicoletti and Scarpetta (2003) analyse industry TFP growth in a panel of OECD countries and find some support for the view that entry liberalization and privatization have a positive impact on TFP. Moreover, this impact appears to be stronger the further away are countries from the technology frontier. However, they also find that restrictive product market regulations have reduced employment rates in some OECD countries, and particularly in those countries where labour market institutions provide strong bargaining power to insiders. In a similar context but using a different theoretical and empirical approach, Griffith *et al.* (2007) investigate the impact of increased product market competition on employment using data across OECD countries during the 1980s and 1990s. Their main conclusion is that conditions in the product market are important determinants of unemployment and interactions between product and labour markets. Using time-varying policy reforms as a source of exogenous variation in product market, conditions have been quantitatively important in explaining movements in unemployment in OECD countries over the past 20 years; the size of these effects varies with labour market institutions. Following these lines of argument McMorrow *et al.* (2010) explore the determinants of the EU–US TFP growth gap using EU KLEMS data, while taking into account these framework conditions such as market regulations. Their findings show that network utilities and network sectors such as retail and logistics are strongly affected by improvements related with flexible product markets.

5.2 *Labour Markets*

The growth accounting literature has mainly decomposed the influences on labour productivity in various ways. Labour productivity can be increased: by improving the quality of labour used in the production process, by increasing the use of capital and improving its quality, by attaining greater overall efficiency in how these factors of production are used together or by generating growth in multifactor productivity (MFP). As such, MFP reflects many types of efficiency improvements, such as improved managerial practices, organizational changes and innovative ways of producing goods and services. van Ark (2002) explained the differences in income growth rates between US and the EU in the second half of the 1990s as being mainly due to the decline in working hours per person in Europe, because of the labour time shortening schemes in countries such as France or Germany and the creation of part-time jobs in countries such as The Netherlands. Blanchard (2004) stresses as well how the differences in the preferences between the leisure and work time between EU and US had a negative consequence in the labour productivity growth in EU, whereas Prescott (2004) argues that the differences in labour participation rates between countries' accounts are due to differences in the income taxes. Inklaar *et al.* (2008a) suggest that the contribution to human capital improvements to TFP growth is mostly related to unmeasured improvements in the quality of labour inputs, and that this effect manifests itself across countries. Finally, Strauss and Samkharadze (2011) introduced another important aspect into the debate, namely a consideration of the impact of demographic ageing. Their analysis shows that transatlantic productivity disparities were in part a result of labour composition effects, and specifically of a labour upskilling effect. The authors therefore suggest that European policies aimed at increasing the competitiveness and growth should devote more importance to the impacts of ageing of on the EU. In particular, growth policies should be focused on increasing productivity per worker, given the potential reduction in the numbers of the working population over the coming decades.

Bourlès and Cette (2007) attribute 0.5 percentage points to the total of 2.5 average annual productivity growth of the US over the period 2000–2004 to a drop in the employment rate (average annual impact of 0.3 percentage points) and a decrease in hours worked (average annual impact of 0.2 percentage points). Indeed, hourly labour productivity levels in a number of European countries are thought to be very close to, or possibly even higher than, the levels 'observed' in the US (see Cette, 2005; Bourlès and Cette, 2006, for a survey). These very high levels of observed productivity in some European countries compared with the US in recent years is generally attributable to lower hours worked and employment rates. Gordon and Dew-Becker (2005) also note that productivity growth is also quite diverse within the EU members. They classify the countries with regard to their productivity performance evolution. Fast-growing European countries including Ireland and Finland have shown a marked acceleration in productivity after 1995, whereas France and Italy have experienced a sharp deceleration. Two-thirds of the growing productivity differentials between the fast-growing EU countries and the slow-growing EU countries have their source in 'old economy' industries, such as non-ICT manufacturing and construction.

These findings above, however, suggest that these may be more than just sectoral effects. Allowing for the different mechanisms operating on labour productivity, Pilat (2001) decomposes the GDP gap in what he calls *demographic effect* that measures the part of the gap that is due demographic factors (based on the working age population to the total population), the *effect of labour utilization* that measures the part of the gap in GDP per capita that is due to differences in labour utilization (by employment rates and average per hours worked) and the *effect of labour productivity* that measures the part of the gap in GDP per capita that is due to difference in GDP per hour worked (Pilat, 2001). The US, together with other countries such as Ireland, Norway, Portugal, Spain and Netherlands, improved its labour productivity and labour utilization at the same time, whereby more workers worked more productively in the period 1990–1999. In contrast, some European countries had strong productivity growth but low employment growth, particularly in the first half of the 1990s. Guisan and Aguayo (2005, 2007) try to explain the uneven growth of European countries relative to the US over 2 decades, while taking into account labour market incentives and human capital expenditure. They argue that although some European countries and regions have reached a very high position in terms of human capital, the EU average is still rather low due to the scale of tax burdens and a lack of investment and over-regulation in education and research in several European countries.

Many chapters (Nicoletti and Scarpetta, 2003; Vanderbussche *et al.*, 2006; Inklaar *et al.*, 2008a, b; McMorrow *et al.*, 2010) show that high skilled workers have a positive effect on TFP growth. However, when comparing the US with EU the overall evidence seems to point to a negative influence of structural rigidities in labour markets on slower EU productivity growth. Although some empirical evidence finds a trade-off between productivity and the employment rate (Belorgey *et al.*, 2006; Bourlès and Cette, 2007), in contrast in the long-term, McGuckin and van Ark (2006) did not find a significant evidence of the effect of hours per worker and participation on labour productivity. But more labour market rigidities do appear to be a major explanation as to why many non ICT-producing EU sectors have been unable to adapt to new ICTs at the same rate as their US counterparts.

5.3 *Organizational and Managerial Issues*

The efficiency and effectiveness of labour and product market responses to the opportunities afforded by technological change may also depend on managerial and organizational issues. Breshanan *et al.* (2002) examined the impact of IT on productivity in over 300 large US companies. Doubling the IT stock was associated with an increase in productivity of 3.6%, but this value increased to 5.8% if a firm became more decentralized. Bloom *et al.* (2005b) demonstrated that for a sample of 7500 establishments located in the UK, in terms of value added per worker, US multinationals appeared to be 23% more productive than the

UK industry average. Non-US multinationals are 16% more productive than the industry average and domestic plants are about 11% less productive. In terms of output per worker, the US advantage over domestic firms is 21.5% and non-US advantage is 17.5%.

These findings are consistent with the widespread evidence that the plants of US multinational firms are more productive than those for most other countries, irrespective of whether the plants are based in the US or in another country. In part, this US productivity advantage is not only linked to greater use of inputs, in that US establishments use about 10% more material and 4% more non-IT capital than non-US multinationals, but also to the fact that US firms use some 40% more IT capital per worker on average than domestic firms, whereas non-US multinationals use only some 20% more. The conclusion of Bloom *et al.* (2005a) is that one reason for the slower growth of productivity in ICT-using sectors in Europe is that US firms have better internal firm organizational systems which allow them to gain more from their ICTs' use.

5.4 *The Entrepreneurial Environment and Culture*

The literature shows that product market regulations act as barriers to entrepreneurship, so following our reasoning in the previous sections, we can assume that the active entrepreneurial culture in the US was also in part due to the beneficial effect of a major flexibility in the product and labour market regulations. Indeed, a 2009 survey by the Global Entrepreneurship Monitor ranked the US ahead of other countries in opportunities for entrepreneurship because it has a favourable business culture, the most mature venture capital industry, close relations between universities and industry and an open immigration policy. Very little research from the field of entrepreneurship has so far examined the impacts of entrepreneurial culture on aggregate productivity growth or on the transatlantic productivity gap, although this would appear to be an area of promise.

6. Measurement Issues

Some commentators have questioned whether the transatlantic productivity gap and the role played by ICTs in this gap is a statistical artefact (Daveri, 2002; Duchêne *et. al.*, 2009) due to measurement errors, and the majority of the chapters examining this issue focus their attention on the disparities in the use of different data, different variables, different calculation for different industries and different methods (Castaldi, 2009; Inklaar and Timmer, 2009; Marattin and Salotti, 2011) in the calculation of ICT.

In the case of ICT sector, problems with the quantification of ICT sector have also been raised by many authors (Dûchene *et al.*, 2009; Lindmark *et al.*, 2010). Current thinking suggests that the definition of ICT should start with the definition at *Frascati Manual* (OECD, 2002). In the case of R&D, the majority of the chapters use BERD data, but the literature shows that BERD data contains some methodological differences between countries in the way sectoral R&D data is classified amongst industries. BERD is sectorally classified either according to the 'principal activity', that is, according to the sector corresponding to the main activity of the company, or according to the 'product field', that is, according to the sector for which the R&D has been conducted. However, the practices differ between countries as to how this is done. For example, in the EU, according to Dûchene *et al.* (2009), a large number of the national statistical offices use product field information to reallocate part of the R&D expenditure to the manufacturing sector for which it has been conducted.

Conversely, in the US, sectoral classification is based on the principal activity criterion. This bias affects the allocation of BERD across the services sector in particular (NSF, 2005).

In the case of aggregate productivity, we know that productivity estimates will be biased if nominal outputs, prices, inputs or cost shares are not measured correctly (Scarpetta *et al.*, 2000; Schreyer, 2001; Rodríguez and Expósito, 2004; Diewert, 2008). As examples, the accounting of changes in prices of goods purchased for resale should be carefully taken account of, as they can lead to a bias in the productivity growth of the trade sector. Another potential problem appears when the definition of outputs present great difficulties in some sectors (Sørensen, 2001; Triplett and Bosworth, 2004, 2008; Crespi *et al.*, 2006; Sørensen and Schjerning, 2008), and the measurement problems in the service sector appear to be particularly severe in the retail, finance and business services. More specific evidence in the subject can be found in the works by Inklaar and Timmer (2008) for the retail sector or by Basu *et al.* (2008), Colangelo and Inklaar (2008) and Inklaar and Wang (2007) for the banking industry. Inklaar *et al.* (2008a) conclude that more theoretical work is needed to provide a firm foundation for applied research.

On these points, Inklaar and Timmer (2008) argue that the standard approach for measuring output and productivity in the trade sector has become obsolete, and the key problem for them is that changes in prices of goods purchased for resale are not accounted for. They outline a consistent accounting framework for measuring trade productivity and provide new estimates, taking into consideration purchase prices of goods sold in a double deflation procedure. The results show stronger productivity improvements in the UK and US as compared to France, Germany and The Netherlands since the mid-1990s, and this finding is robust for various productivity measurement models.

In the case of labour productivity, following the re-basing of European countries' national accounts (from base year 1995 to 2000), the OECD updated its assessments of hourly labour productivity for all of its members. This updating has resulted in some cases in sizeable modifications in relative levels of productivity. These changes have led us to re-estimate, using this new database, the relation explaining hourly productivity variations previously estimated in Bourlès and Cette (2006). Bourlès and Cette (2007) comment that two-thirds of the slowdown of observed productivity at the time of the first oil shock is attributable to an increase in employment rates and to a smaller decrease in working time. Between the first and the second half of the 1970s, annual productivity growth decreased by about one point for the observed indicator and one-third of a point for the structural indicator. The maintenance of strong growth decreases in employment rates and to a smaller decrease in working time. For the 2000–2004 time period, structural productivity slowed down and its growth of about 2% a year was between that of the second half of the 1990s (2.6%) and that of the 1980–1995 time period (1.6%). However, there is no such slowdown for observed productivity, because it is offset by the effects of decreases in the employment rate and average working time. Therefore, since 2000, US productivity gains seem to have been structurally less significant than those of the second half of the 1990s.

As a result of these recalculations, hourly labour productivity levels in a number of European countries are thought to be very close to, or possibly even higher than, the levels observed in the US (Cette, 2005; Bourlès and Cette, 2006, for a survey). These very high levels of observed productivity in some European countries in recent years compared with the US, are generally attributable to lower hours worked and higher unemployment rates (also, in van Ark, 2002). They also find that ICT-intensive industries went through a far less dramatic reduction in productivity growth after 1995 than industries which did not use ICT intensively in production. Although the decline in labour productivity growth after 1995 is a general phenomenon across European industries, the sectoral productivity growth rates decreased the most in non-ICT-intensive industries (Dahl *et al.*, 2011). In effect, the overall slow-down in productivity growth that happened in Europe after 1995 would have been even more dramatic in the absence of the positive impact in ICT-intensive industries.

7. Conclusions

Identifying the differences in the sources of the level of economic development are of interest because they enable the identification of future policy challenges related to participation or productivity, and the possible policy trade-offs within economic policy. However, it is clear that there are no simple or general patterns evident. Amongst the explanations examined in this chapter that are evident in the literature explaining the transatlantic productivity gap which emerged between the US and Europe during the recent decades, we can find: the European lower quality of human capital (Gu *et al.*, 2002; Inklaar *et al.*, 2003), the rigidity of the European labour markets (Gordon and Dew-Becker, 2005; Gomez-Salvador *et al.*, 2006), the relative delay in the diffusion and implementation of ICTs or General Purpose Technologies in the EU (Caselli and Wilson, 2004; Wilson, 2009; Jorgenson, 2011), the higher importance of new managerial practices and organizational investments in US companies (Gu and Wang, 2004; Bloom *et al.*, 2005a; Crespi *et al.*, 2007) and the disparities of the contribution of service sectors to both economies (Inklaar *et al.*, 2003), amongst many others. Moreover, as Bernard and Jones (1996) and Inklaar and Timmer (2009) demonstrate, for advanced OECD countries the patterns of convergence across sectors have differed since 1970. Whereas productivity in market services appeared to converge, this convergence was not found in manufacturing industries. As such, there is no common trend or pattern, which provides a clear-cut explanation of productivity growth, because it depends on the capital intensity, the scale and scope of operations, the technological and innovation capacity and the degree of deregulation. However, although much of the observed productivity gap is very robust to measurement issues, it is also clear that adjusting labour productivity measures for hours worked does close a very large portion of the gap.

It is also clear, however, that the breakdowns by industry demonstrate that ICT-producers and ICT-users such as market services and retail were the industries that most accounted for the differences between the US and EU in terms of productivity gains from the mid-1990s onwards. During the 1980s and early 1990s, the ICT-producing sectors were in the vanguard of the transatlantic productivity gap. However, later on after 1995 it was the differences in performance of the ICT-using sectors, the so-called *New Economy* effect, that accounted for most of the transatlantic productivity gap (Timmer *et al.*, 2010). Although the ICT-intensive industries in Europe performed better than Europe's non-ICT industries, their performance as a whole was below that of the US counterparts.

These weaknesses in ICT-using industries and the lower rate at which the new GPTs general purpose technologies of ICTs were diffused, adopted and adapted in other industries poses a major challenge for EU policy makers. Meister and Verspagen (2004) argue that at the dawn of the 21st century Europe still faced the major productivity gap relative to the US, after many years of catching up. In the second half of the 1990s, Europe developed a process of integration as a way of achieving political stability and peace. The authors argue that the pick in the integration process appear with the European single market, where the potential to explode the economies of scale and the mass production contribute greatly to the European progress. As a result of this and other factors related to the diffusion of technology and the free mobility of goods, services and labour, Europe was able to catch-up to the US over the long postwar period (Pavitt and Soete, 1982; Nelson and Wright, 1992; Tsoukalis, 1997, van Ark *et al.*, 2002) and to significantly close much of the productivity gap that had emerged in the first half of the 20th century.

The extent to which Europe fell behind the US from the mid-1990s suggests that more restructuring is required in the EU economy (Guisan and Aguayo, 2005). Indeed Europe has made significant strides in reforming the labour market, cutting employment and fuelling growth in per capita GDP. However, given high debt and deficit levels, little scope remains to spur growth through short-term stimulus spending. Europe must therefore embrace structural reform and following the findings discussed here the boosting of the performance of service industries would appear to be a critical part of this effort. Increasing R&D investment was the rationale behind the *Lisbon Agenda 2000* which was aimed at making Europe the most dynamic economy in the world by 2010, and which was followed by the setting of the *3% Barcelona target* for the EU R&D/GDP ratio, of which two-thirds was to be accounted for by BERD (European Commission, 2002; European Council, 2002; European Policy Committee, 2002). The emphasis of research and development is behind the concern of the underperformance of European industries intensive on knowledge over the last decade. Although the industries seemed to contribute to the employment, their overall productivity and innovation-related developments were far beyond the ones obtained in the US or Japan. European economic policy aimed at promoting investments in business R&D, being seen as the engine of competitiveness and economic growth to prevent long-term economic decline; and the 2011 *Innovation Union* component of the *Europe 2020 Strategy*, the successor to the Lisbon Strategy adopted in 2010, is based on similar lines of argument (European Commission, 2010).

Note

1. EU9 contains data from Denmark, Germany, Spain, France, Italy, the Netherlands, Austria, Finland and the UK at the NACE A31 industry level using the EUKLEMS database. The name KLEMS refers to capital (K), labour (L), energy (E), materials (M) and services (S).

References

Aghion, P. and Howitt, P. (2006) Appropriate growth policies: a unifying framework. *Journal of the European Economic Association* 4(2–3): 269–314.

van Ark, B. (2002) Measuring the new economy: and international comparative perspective. *Review of Income and Wealth* 48(1): 1–14.

van Ark, B., Inklaar R. and McGuckin, R.H. (2002) *Changing Gear: Productivity, ICT, and Services in Europe and the United States, Mimeograph*. Groningen and New York: University of Groningen and The Conference Board.

van Ark, B., Inklaar R. and McGuckin, R.H. (2003) ICT and productivity in Europe and the United States. Where do the differences come from? *CESifo GroupCESifo Economic Studies* 49(3): 295–318, doi:10.1093/cesifo/49.3.295.

van Ark, B., O'Mahony M. and Timmer, M.P. (2008) The productivity gap between Europe and the United States: trends and causes. *Journal of Economic Perspectives* 22: 25–44.

Audretsch, D.B. (1995) Innovation, growth and survival. *International Journal of Industrial Organisation* 13(4): 441–457.

Baily, M.N. (1993) Competition, regulation and efficiency in service industries. *Brookings Papers on Economic Activity, Microeconomics* 2 (December): 71–159.

Bartelsman, E.J and Doms, M. (2000) Understanding productivity: lessons from longitudinal microdata. *Journal of Economic Literature* 38(3): 569–594.

Basu, S., Inklaar, R. and Wang, J.C. (2008) The value of risk: measuring the services of US commercial banks. Mimeo, 2006 NBER Summer Institute.

Baumol, W.J. (1967) Macroeconomics of unbalanced growth: the anatomy of urban crisis. *American Economic Review* 57(3): 415–426.

Belorgey, N., Lecat, R. and Maury, T.P. (2006) Determinants of productivity per employee: an empirical estimation using panel data. *Economics Letters* 91(2): 153–157.

Bernard, A.B. and Jones, C.I. (1996) Comparing apples to oranges: productivity convergence and measurement across industries and countries. *American Economic Review* 86(5): 1216–1238.

Blanchard, O. (2004) The economic future of Europe, *Journal of Economic Perspectives* 8: 3–26.

Bloom, N., Sadun, R. and van Reenen, J. (2005a) It ain't what you do, it's the way that you do I.T. Testing explanations of productivity growth using US affiliates. Mimeo, Centre for Economic Performance, London School of Economics.

Bloom, N., Dorgan, S., Dowdy, J., van Reenen, J. and Rippin, T. (2005b) Management practices across firms and nations. Mimeo, Centre for Economic Performance, London School of Economics.

Bloom, N., Sadun, R. and van Reenen, J. (2007) Nobody does IT better. *CEPR Policy Insight* 7(June).

Bosworth, B.P. and Triplett, J.E. (2003) Services productivity in the United States: Griliches' Services Volume revisited. Available at http://www.brookings.edu/views/papers/bosworth/20030919.htm (last accessed 24 April 2012).

Bosworth, B.P and Triplett, J.E. (2004) *Productivity in the US Services Sector. New Sources of Economic Growth.* Washington: Brookings Institution Press.

Bosworth, B.P. and Triplett, J.E. (2006) "Baumol's disease" has been cured: IT and multi-factor productivity in U.S. services industries. In D.W. Jansen (ed.), *The New Economy and Beyond: Past, Present and Future* (Chap. 3, pp. 34–60). The Bush School series in the economics of public policy, 5. Cheltenham, PA: Edward Elgar Publisher Ltd.

Bourlès, R. and Cette, G. (2006) A comparison of structural productivity levels in the major industrialised countries. *OECD Economic Studies* 2005(2): 96–138.

Bourlès, R. and Cette, G. (2007) Trends in "structural" productivity levels in the major industrialized countries. *Economic Letters* 95: 151–156.

Berndt, E. and Morrison, C. 1995. High-tech capital formation and economic performance in U.S. manufacturing industries: an exploratory analysis. *Journal of Econometrics* 65: 9–43.

Breshanan, T., Brynjolfsson, E. and Hitt, L. (2002) Information technology, workplace organization and the demand of skill labour. *Quarterly Journal of Economics* 117(1): 339–376.

Caselli, F. and Wilson, D.J. (2004) Importing technology. *Journal of Monetary Economics* 51(1): 1–32.

Castaldi, C. (2009) The relatively weight of manufacturing and services in Europe: an innovation perspective. *Technological Forecasting & Social Change* 76: 709–722.

Castaldi, C. and Sapio, S. (2008) Growing like mushrooms? Sectoral evidence from four large European economies. *Journal of Evolutionary Economics* 18: 509–527.

Cette, G. (2005) Are productivity levels higher in some European countries than in the United States? *International Productivity Monitor* 10(Spring): 59–68.

Colangelo, A. and Inklaar, R. (2008) Risky business: measuring bank output in the Euro Area. Mimeo, University of Groningen and European Central Bank.

Cozza, C., Ortega-Argilés, R. and Piva, M.C. (2011) Can the European heterogeneity tell us more about the transatlantic productivity gap? Mimeo, communication to the ERSA 2011, Barcelona, Spain.

Cozza, C., Ortega-Argilés, R., Piva, M.C. and Baptista, R. (2012) Productivity gaps among European regions. In Z. Acs and D.B. Audretsch (eds.), *Technology Transfer in a Global Economy* (forthcoming). New York: Springer Science + Business Media, Inc.

Crespi, G., Criscuolo, C., Haskel, J. and Hawkes, D. (2006) Measuring and understanding productivity in UK market services. *Oxford Review of Economic Policy* 22(2): 186–202.

Crespi, G., Haskel, J.E. and Haskel, J. (2007) Information technology, organizational change and productivity. CEPR Discussion Paper 6105.

Dahl, C.M., Kongsted, H.C. and Sørensen, A. (2011) ICT and productivity growth in the 1990s: panel data evidence on Europe. *Empirical Economics* 40: 141–164.

Daveri, F. (2002) The new economy in Europe, 1992–2001. *Oxford Review of Economic Policy* 18(3): 345–362.

Dew-Becker I. and Gordon, R.J. 2008. The role of labor market changes in the slowdown of European productivity growth, NBER Working Papers, 13840, National Bureau of Economic Research, Inc.

Diewert, E. (2008) What is to be done for better productivity measurement. *International Productivity Monitor* 16(Spring): 40–52.

Draca, M., Sadun, R. and van Reenen, J. Productivity and ICTs: a review of the evidence. In R. Mansell, C. Avgerou, D. Quah and R. Silverstone (eds), *The Oxford Handbook of Information and Communication Technologies.* (pp. 100–147) Oxford: Oxford University Press.

Duchêne, V., Lykogianni, E. and Verbeek, A. (2009) EU R&D in services industries and the EU-US R&D investment gap. European Commission, Joint Research Centre, Institute for Prospective Technological Studies and Directorate General Research, IRMA Working Paper Series 03/2009-JRC50911.

Economic Policy Committee (22 January 2002) Report on Research and Development. EPC/ECFIN/10/777-EN Final. Brussels.

Erken, H. (2004) An international comparison of productivity performance: the case of Netherlands. In G.M.M. Gelauff, S.E.P. Klomp and T.J.A. Roelandt, (eds), *Fostering Productivity, Patterns, Determinants and Policy Implications* (pp. 9–28). Amsterdam: Elsevier.

Erken H. and van Es, F. (2007) Disentangling the R&D shortfall of the EU vis-à-vis the US. Jena Economic Research Papers 2007107.

European Commission (2002) European Competitiveness Report 200. Commission Staff Working Paper, SEC(2002) 528. Office for Official Publications of the European Communities, Luxembourg.

Erken, H.P.G. (2008) *Productivity, R&D and Entrepreneurship.* ERIM Ph.D. Series Research in Management. Rotterdam: Erasmus University Rotterdam.

European Commission (2007a) Data on business R&D: comparing BERD and the scoreboard. Joint Research Centre, Institute for Prospective Technological Studies and DG RTD Scientific and Technical Research Series, EU23364 EN, ISSN 1018–5593, Office for Official Publications of the European Communities, Luxembourg.

European Commission (2007b) *Key Figures 2007 on Science, Technology and Innovation. Towards a European Knowledge Area.* Luxembourg: Office for Official Publications of the European Communities.

European Commission (2008) The 2008 EU industrial R&D investment scoreboard. Joint Research Centre, Institute for Prospective Technological Studies and DG RTD Scientific and Technical Research Series, EU23530 EN, ISSN, 1018–5593.

European Commission (2010) Communication from the Commission to the European Parliament, the Council, the European Economic and Social Committee and the Committee of the Regions. Europe 2020 Flagship Initiative Innovation Union, SEC(2010) 1161.

European Council (2002) Presidency conclusion. Brussels: Barcelona European Council.

Foster, L., Haltiwanger, J.C. and Krizan, C.J (2002) The link between aggregate and micro productivity growth: evidence from retail trade. NBER Working Papers 9120.

Foster, L., Haltiwanger, J.C. and Krizan, C.J. (2006) Market selection, reallocation and restructuring in the US retail trade sector in the 1990s. *Review of Economics and Statistics* 88(4): 748–758.

Goenenc, R., Maher, M. and Nicoletti, G. (2001) The implementation and the effects of regulatory reform: past experience and current issues. *OECD Economic Studies* 32: 11–98.

Gomez-Salvador, R., Musso, A., Stocker, M. and Turunen, J. (2006) Labour productivity developments in the Euro Area. European Central Bank Occasional Paper 53.

Gordon, R.J. (2004) Five puzzles in the behavior of productivity, investment and innovation. NBER Working Paper 10660.

Gordon, R.J. and Dew-Becker, I. (2005) Why did Europe's productivity catch-up sputter out? A tale of tigers and tortoises. Federal Research Bank of San Francisco. *Journal Proceedings.*

Available at http://www.frbsf.org/economics/conferences/0511/1_ProductivityCatchup.pdf (last accessed 24 April 2012).

Gort, M. and Klepper, S. (1982) Time paths in the diffusion of product innovations. *Economic Journal* 92(367): 630–653.

Griffith, R., Redding, S.J. and van Reenen, J. (2004) Mapping the two faces of R&D: productivity growth in a panel of OECD industries. *Review of Economics and Statistics* 86: 883–895.

Griffith, R., Harrison, R. and Macartney, G. (2007) Product market reforms, labour market institutions and unemployment. *Economic Journal* 117(519): C142–C166.

Griliches, Z. (ed.) (1992) *Output Measurement in the Service Sectors: Studies in Income and Wealth* (Vol. 56). Cambridge, MA: National Bureau of Economic Research.

Griliches, Z. (1994) Productivity, R&D, and the data constraint. *American Economic Review* 84(1): 1–23.

Gu, W. and Wang, W. (2004) Information technology and productivity growth: evidence from Canadian industries. In D. Jorgenson (ed.), *Economic Growth in Canada and the United States in the Information Age.* (pp. 57–81). Ottawa: Industry Canada.

Gu, W., Kaci, M., Maynard, J.P. and Sillamaa, M.A. (2002) The changing composition of the Canadian workforce and its impact on productivity growth. In J.R. Baldwin, T.M. Harchaoui, (eds), *Productivity Growth in Canada* (pp. 69–75). Ottawa: Statistics Canada.

Guisan, M.C. and Aguayo, E. (2005) Employment, development and research expenditure in the European Union: analysis of causality and comparison with the United States 1993–2003. *International Journal of Applied Econometrics and Quantitative Studies* 2(2): 21–30.

Guisan, M.C. and Aguayo, E. (2007) Wages, productivity and human capital in the European Union: econometric models and comparison with the USA 1985–2005. *Applied Econometrics and International Development* 7(1): 43–56.

Hall, B.H. and Mairesse, J. (1995) Exploring the relationship between R&D and productivity in French manufacturing firms. *Journal of Econometrics* 65: 263–293.

Harberger, A.C. (1998) A vision of the growth process. *American Economic Review* 92: 220–239.

Heshmati, A. and Kim, H. (2011) The R&D and productivity relationship of Korean listed firms. *Journal of Productivity Analysis* 36: 125–142.

Hoj, J., Jimenez, M., Maher, M., Nicoletti, G. and Wise, M. (2007) Product market competition in OECD countries: taking stock and moving forward. OECD Economics Department Working Paper No. 575, September 2007.

Inklaar, R. and Timmer, M.P. (2008) Accounting for growth in retail trade: an international productivity comparison. *Journal of Productivity Analysis* 29: 23–31.

Inklaar, R. and Timmer, M.P. (2009) *Productivity Convergence Across Industries and Countries: The Importance of Theory-Based Measurement.* Groningen, The Netherlands: Groningen Growth and Development Centre Research Memorandum GD-109.

Inklaar, R., O'Mahony, M. and Timmer, M. (2003) *ICT and Europe's Productivity Performance Industry-Level Growth Account Comparisons with the United States.* Groningen, The Netherlands: Groningen Growth and Development Centre Research Memorandum GD-68.

Inklaar, R., Timmer, M.P. and van Ark, B. (2008a) Data for productivity measurement in market services: an international comparison. *International Productivity Monitor* 16(Spring): 71–81.

Inklaar, R., Timmer, M.P. and van Ark, B. (2008b) Market services productivity across Europe and the US. *Economic Policy* 23: 139–194.

Inklaar, R and Wang, J.C. 2007. Not Your Grandfather's Bank Any More? Consistent Measurement of Non-Traditional Bank Output. Mimeo.

Janz, N., Lööf, H. and Peters, B. (2004) Firm level innovation and productivity – is there a common story across countries? *Problems and Perspectives in Management* 2: 1–22.

Jorgenson, D.W. (2001) Information technology and the US economy. *American Economic Review* 90(1): 1–32.

Jorgenson, D.W. (2011) Innovation and productivity growth. *American Journal of Agricultural Economics* 93(2): 276–296.

Jorgenson, D.W. and Stiroh, K.J. (1999) Information technology and growth. *American Economic Review Essays and Proceedings* 89(2): 109–115.

Jorgenson, D.W. and Stiroh, K.J. (2000) Raising the speed limit: US economic growth in the information age. *Brookings Papers on Economic Activity* 1: 125–211.

Jorgenson, D.W., Gollop, F.M. and Fraumeni, B. (1987) *Productivity and US Economic Growth.* Cambridge: Harvard University Press.

Jorgenson, D.W., Ho, M.S. and Stiroh, K.J. (2002) Information technology, education, and the sources of economic growth across US industries. US: Federal Reserve System.

Jorgenson, D.W., Ho, M.S. and Stiroh, K.J. (2005) *Information Technology and the American Growth Resurgence.* Cambridge: MIT Press.

Jorgenson, D.W., Ho, M.S. and Stiroh, K.J. (2008) A retrospective look at the U.S. productivity growth resurgence. *Journal of Economic Perspectives* 22(1): 3–24.

Klepper, S. and Graddy, E. (1990) The evolution of new industries and the determinants of market structure. *Rand Journal of Economics* 21(1): 27–44.

Klette, J. and Kortum, S. (2004) Innovating firms and aggregate innovation. *Journal of Political Economy* 112: 986–1018.

Lindmark, S., Turlea, G. and Ulbrich, M. (2010) Business R&D in the ICT sector: examining the European ICT R&D deficit. *Science and Public Policy* 37(6): 413–428.

Lööf, H. and Heshmati, A. (2006) On the relation between innovation and performance: a sensitivity analysis. *Economics of Innovation and New Technology* 15: 317–344.

Maddison, A. (2001) *The World Economy: A Millennial Perspective.* Paris: OECD.

Marattin, L. and Salotti, S. (2011) Productivity and per capita GDP growth: the role of the forgotten factors. *Economic Modelling* 28(3): 1219–1225.

Mathieu, A. and van Pottelsberghe de la Potterie, B. (2008) A note on the drivers of R&D intensity. CEPR Discussion Paper 6684.

Maudos, J., Pastor, J.M. and Serrano, L. (2008) Explaining the US-EU productivity growth gap: structural change vs. intra-sectoral effect. *Economic Letters* 100(2): 311–313.

Mc Morrow, K., Roeger, W. and Turrini, A. (2010) Determinants of TFP growth: a close look at industries driving the EU-US TFP gap. *Structural Change and Economic Dynamics* 21: 165–180.

McGuckin, R.H. and van Ark, B. (2004) *Performance 2003, Productivity, Employment and Income in the World's Economies.* New York: The Conference Board.

McGuckin, R.H. and van Ark, B. (2006) *Productivity and Participation: An International Comparison.* Groningen: Groningen Growth Development Centre, Research Memorandum GD-78.

Meister, C. and Verspagen, B. (2004) European Productivity Gaps: Is R&D the Solution? *Current Issues of Economic Growth, Workshops-Proceeding of OeNB Workshops.* Vienna, Austria: Oesterreichische National Bank.

Mischke, J., Regout, B. and Roxburgh, C. (2010) Why Europe lags behind the United States in productivity. Regulation and market barriers continue to hold back the continent's service sectors. McKinsey Quarterly October 2010.

Moncada-Paterno-Castello, P. (2010) New insights on EU-US comparison of corporate R&D. IPTS Working Papers Series on Corporate R&D and Innovation, January 2010.

Moncada-Paterno-Castello, P., Ciupagea, C., Smith, K., Tuebke, A. and Tubbs, M. (2010) Does Europe perform too little corporate R&D? A comparison of EU and non-EU corporate R&D performance. *Research Policy* 39: 523–535.

Nelson, R.R. and Wright, G. (1992) The rise and fall of American technological leadership: the Postwar era in an historical perspective. *Journal of Economic Literature* 30: 1931–1964.

Nicoletti, G. and Scarpetta, S. (2003) Regulation, productivity and growth: OECD evidence. *Economic Policy* 36(April): 9–72.

Nicoletti, G. and Scarpetta, S. (2005) Product market reforms and employment in OECD countries. OECD Economics Department Working Paper 472.

Nordhaus, W.D. (2001) Productivity growth and the new economy. NBER Working Paper 8096, January.

NSF (National Science Foundation) (2005) *National Patterns of Research and Development Resources: 2003.* Arlington, VA: NSF 05–308, National Science Foundation.

O'Mahony, M. and van Ark, B. (eds) (2003) EU productivity and competitiveness: an industry perspective. Can Europe resume the catching-up process? Luxembourg: European Commission.

O'Sullivan, M. (2007) What policies are needed to overcome the EU's R&D deficit?. European Commission DG-RTD, Knowledge for Growth Advisory Group, Policy Debate number 1.

Available at http://ec.europa.eu/invest-in-research/pdf/download_en/policy_debate.pdf. (last accessed 24 April 2012).

Oliner, S. and Sichel, D. (1994) Computers and output growth revisited: how big is the puzzle?. *Brookings Papers on Economic Activity* 2: 273–317.

Oliner, S. and Sichel, D. (2000) The resurgence of growth in the late 1990s: is information technology the story? *Journal of Economic Perspectives* 14: 3–22.

Oliner, S. and Sichel, D. (2002) Information technology and productivity: where are we now and where are we going? US: Federal Reserve System.

Ortega-Argilés, R. and Brandsma, A. (2010) EU-US differences in the size of R&D intensive firms: do they explain the overall R&D intensity gap?. *Science and Public Policy* 37(6): 429–441.

Ortega-Argilés R., Piva, M., Potters, L. and Vivarelli, M. (2010) Is corporate R&D investment in high-tech sectors more effective?. *Contemporary Economic Policy* 28: 353–365.

Ortega-Argilés, R., Potters, L. and Vivarelli, M. (2011) R&D and productivity: testing sectoral peculiarities using micro data. *Empirical Economics* 41(3): 817–839.

Oulton, N. 2001. Must the growth rate decline? Baumol's unbalanced growth revisited. *Oxford Economic Papers* 53: 605–627.

Pavitt, K. and Soete, L. (1982) International differences in economic growth and the international location of innovation. In H. Giersch (ed.), *Emerging Technologies: The Consequences for Economic Growth, Structural Change and Employment*. Tübingen, Germany: Mohr.

Pilat, D. (2001) Productivity growth in the OECD area: some recent findings. *International Productivity Monitor* 3(Fall): 32–43.

Pilat, D. and Lee, F.C. (2001) Productivity growth in ICT-producing and ICT-using industries: a source of growth differentials in the OECD?, OECD, DSTI/DOC(2001)4, June, Paris. Organization for Economic Cooperation and Development.

Prescott, E.C. (2004) Why do Americans work so much more than Europeans?. *Federal Reserve Bank of Minneapolis Quarterly Review* 28: 2–13.

Pugno, M. (2006) The service paradox and endogenous economic growth. *Structural Change and Economic Dynamics* 17: 99–115.

Rodríguez, X.A. and Expósito, P. (2004) Models of productivity in European Union, the USA and Japan. *Applied Econometrics and International Development* 4(4): 27–42.

Roeger, W. (2010) Assessing alternative strategies to promote growth in the EU. *EC Economic Papers, European Commission/DG ECFIN*, December 2010.

Rogers, M. (2006) R&D and productivity in the UK: evidence from firm-level data in the 1990s. University of Oxford, Economics Series Working Papers 255.

Rogerson, R. (2008) Structural transformation and the deterioration of European labor market outcomes. *Journal of Political Economy* 116(2): 235–259.

Sadun, R. and van Reenen, J. (2005) Information technology and productivity: it ain't what you do it's the way that you do I.T. EDS Innovation Research Programme Discussion Paper Series. Intellectual Property, Technology and Productivity, No. 002.

Scarpetta, S., Bassanini, A., Pilat, D. and Schreyer, P. (2000) Economic growth in the OECD area: recent trends at the aggregate and sectoral level. Economics Department Working Papers, 248, June.

Schreyer, P. (2001) *Measuring Productivity – OECD Manual: Measurement of Aggregate and Industry-Level Productivity Growth*. Paris: OECD.

Siegel, D. and Griliches, Z. 1992. Purchased services, outsourcing, computers, and productivity in manufacturing, NBER chapters, In *Output Measurement in the Service Sectors* (pp. 429–460), National Bureau of Economic Research, Inc.

Sieling, M., Friedman, B. and Dumas, M. (2001) Labor productivity in the retail trade industry, 1987–99. *Monthly Labor Review* 124(12): 3–14.

Solow, R.M. (1987) We'd better watch out. *New York Times*, book review, July 12.

Sørensen, A. (2001) Comparing apples to oranges: productivity convergence and measurement across industries and countries: comment, *American Economic Review* 91(4): 1160–1167.

Sørensen, A. and Schjerning, B. (2008) Productivity measurement in manufacturing and the expenditure approach. *Review of International Economics* 16(2): 327–340.

Stiroh, K.J. (2002a) Information technology and the US productivity revival: what do the industry data say? *American Economic Review* 92: 1559–1576.

Stiroh, K.J. (2002b) *Reassessing the Role of IT in the Production Function: A Meta-Analysis*. New York: Federal Reserve Bank of New York.

Stiroh, K.J. (2002c) Are ICT spillovers driving the "New Economy"?. *Review of Income and Wealth* 48(1): 33–58.

Stiroh, K.J. (2005) Reassessing the impact of IT in the production function: a meta-analysis and sensitivity tests, *Annals of Economics and Statistics/Annales d'Économie et de Statistique*. Contributions in memory of Zvi Griliches (79/80): 529–561.

Strauss, H. and Samkharadze, B. (2011) ICT capital and productivity growth. *EIB Papers* 16(2): 8–28.

Timmer, M.P. and van Ark, B. (2005) Does information and communication technology drive EU-US productivity grwoth differentials? *Oxford Economic Papers* 57: 693–716.

Timmer, M.P., Inklaar, R., O'Mahony, M. and van Ark, B. (2010) *Economic Growth in Europe. A Comparative Industry Perspective*. Cambridge, UK: Cambridge University Press Ed.

Triplett, J.E. and Bosworth, B.P. (2004) *Services Productivity in the United States: New Sources of Economic Growth*. Washington, DC: Brookings Institution Press.

Triplett, J.E. and Bosworth, B.P. (2008) The state of data for services productivity measurement in the United States. *International Productivity Monitor* 16: 53–70.

Tsoukalis, L. (1997) *The New European Economy Revisited*, 3rd ed. Oxford, UK: Oxford University Press.

Uppenberg, K. (2009) Innovation and economic growth. EIB Papers 1/2009, European Investment Bank, Economic and Financial Studies.

Uppenberg, K. (2011) Economic growth in the US and the EU: a sectoral decomposition. In productivity and growth in Europe. long-term trends, current challenges and the role of economic dynamism. *EIB Papers* 16(1): 18–52.

Uppenberg, K. and Strauss, H. (2010) Innovation and productivity growth in the EU service sector. EIB Working Papers, July 2010.

Vanderbussche, J., Aghion, P. and Meghir, C. (2006) Growth, distance to frontier and composition of human capital. *Journal of Economic Growth* 11(2): 97–127.

Whelan, K. (2002) Computers, obsolescence and productivity. *Review of Economics and Statistics* 84(3): 445–461.

Wilson, D.J. (2009) IT and beyond: the contribution of heterogeneous capital to productivity. *Journal of Business and Economic Statistics* 27(1): 52–70.

4

A SURVEY OF THE INNOVATION SURVEYS

Shangqin Hong, Les Oxley and Philip McCann

1. Introduction to Innovation

At the micro level, the importance of innovation has been stressed by numerous commentators. In general, we know that firms engage in innovative activities because they are hoping to develop a new product or process that will allow them to increase profits and maintain or improve their market position over time. In some highly successful innovation cases, significant innovations can afford a firm a dominant market position and long-term monopoly rents, but more typical innovation outcomes tend to relate to more modest, but nonetheless important, market gains. As a general principle, Baumol (2002) regards innovation as a 'life-and-death matter for a firm', in which the constant need of fighting for survival and the threat of competition encourage firms to innovate. As such, innovation is a fundamental part of competition, and consequently also the overall growth outcomes realized due to the competition. But what exactly innovation is, and what exactly is the role played by innovation processes in growth, is actually rather less obvious that at first appears. In practice, different firms conduct innovation differently: some conduct research and development (R&D) in house and actively pursue patenting; others co-operate with outside partners or acquire technology externally via licensing; other engage in less-formalized means of promoting innovation such as supporting good practices in design, marketing research and staff training, all of which have becoming increasingly popular. Yet, given the high costs and uncertainty often associated with innovation, the pay-off of an innovation investment is difficult to forecast. Certainly, the benefits of engaging in innovative activities have been advocated by many authors, including Crepon *et al.* (1998) who suggested that firm productivity is positively correlated with innovation outputs, Banbury and Mitchell (1995) who identified a positive relationship between long-term survival and the rate at which firms are able to develop new products and processes, and Jin *et al.* (2004) who conclude that innovative firms outperform non-innovative ones. Yet, still difficulties remain as to what exactly we understand as innovation, what exactly is the growth role played by innovation, and how are we to capture empirically innovation and its role in economic growth.

At the most basic level, all innovations or innovation processes contain three underlying elements, namely, newness, improvement and the overcoming of uncertainty (Gordon and

Innovation, Entrepreneurship, Geography and Growth, First Edition.
Edited by Philip McCann and Les Oxley. Chapters © 2013 The Authors.
Book compilation © 2013 Blackwell Publishing Ltd. Published 2013 by Blackwell Publishing Ltd.

McCann, 2005). Newness, or novelty, is an essential part of innovation, although such newness could be understood as something novel to the firm or to the industry as a whole. Improvement implies that what is novel or new is also in some way superior to what currently exists, but such superiority can only be determined by the market, and demonstrated in terms of sales revenues. Finally, all innovations are undertaken by firms in order to try to improve their price-making monopoly or monopolistic positions, or at least not too reduce such positions, and this is so as to reduce the long-run uncertainty faced by the firm which results from being primarily a price-taker. Beyond these general features, however, our theoretical and conceptual understanding of innovation has developed significantly since the early 1980s. More noticeable, however, are the major changes that have been experienced in empirically oriented innovation research as a result of the introduction of firm-level innovation surveys. Nowadays collecting innovation-related data via firm-based surveys have become a common practice for many countries such as Canada, United States, Malaysia, Taiwan, Australia as well as in almost all EU countries. These survey-lead approaches have transformed our understanding of the nature and determinants of innovation and also increased our understanding of the role played by innovation in growth. At the same time, the surveys themselves have also been adapted as our conceptual understanding of innovation has increased. As such, the balance of innovation-related research has shifted from a theoretical to a primarily empiricist-lead agenda, and increasingly combined both quantitative and qualitative approaches.

The objective of this chapter is examine how our understanding of innovation has evolved over the last few decades, to identify the major theoretical and empirical influences on our understanding, and to assess the role which innovation surveys have played in this evolution. The rest of this chapter is organized as follows. Section 2 discusses the major theoretical and conceptual trends influencing our understanding of innovation over the last three or four decades and the role played by innovation surveys. Section 3 discusses the origination of innovation surveys by looking at various measures of innovation employed, and Section 4 outlines different innovation surveys by type and region/nation. Section 5 provides an overview of the survey variables used in econometrics studies and their significance. Section 6 provides some brief final remarks.

2. Evolutions in Our Understanding of Innovation

Our understanding of the roles which innovation, technology and new firm formation play in economic growth has been slowly developing over many decades. Classical authors including Marx, Marshall and Schumpeter all speculated on the role which technology and knowledge played in transforming the economy, by focusing on the distributional, clustering and restructuring aspects of technological change, respectively. However, it is Schumpeter (1934, 1939) who is most notably associated with the phenomenon of innovation, which he described in terms of processes of 'creative destruction', and the sense in which creative destruction processes operate is twofold. Firstly, competitive processes in a context of technological change serve to sweep away older technology vintages and modes of production in favour of new ideas and methods. At the same time, competition itself serves to drive technological change. Schumpeter (1942, p. 84) contended that 'it is not that kind of competition (price) which counts, but the competition from the new commodity, the technology and the new source of supply'. As such, competition drives technological change, which itself transforms the nature of competition, and the dynamics of growth always contain both elements of transformation. Importantly, both aspects of these dynamics are also subject to both risk and uncertainty, the former being quantifiable and the latter not (Knight, 1921). Risk aspects of technological change tend to dominate in periods during which technologies are only changing slowly and incrementally. In contrast, the uncertainty elements tend to dominate in periods when technologies are changing fundamentally. As such, the fact that certain aspects of technological change are not only risky but also unquantifiable provides precisely the opportunities that certain entrepreneurs need in order to overcome their inherited positioning in the production system and to reconfigure the system as a whole. Indeed, the history of industrial economics (Piore and Sabel, 1984; Best, 1990) demonstrates that the processes by which these transformations take place sometimes entail upheavals on a scale which are far more profound than simply the churning of varieties of existing types of firms. At intermittent intervals, the old order of production (of both goods and services) is reconfigured on a fundamental level, and this is often due to the widespread emergence of a new general-purpose technology (GPT) (George et al., 2004; Lipsey et al., 2005). Such GPTs are typically understood as being of a scientific-technological nature, such as the introduction of the steam engine, railways, electricity, the Internet and the miniaturization of microprocessors. However, in terms of the links between innovation and economic transformation, it is also possible to consider organizational, institutional changes and infrastructural changes as being of equal importance. For example, the widespread organizational changes evident at various points in manufacturing related to the advent of the interchangeability of parts (Best, 1990), the mass production system and the introduction just-in-time (JIT) production systems have also been mirrored in fundamental organizational changes in many transport services and logistics-related sectors at different points in time (Levinson, 2006). Importantly, in each of these cases, technical innovations in one sector have been translated into organizational and behavioural innovations in other sectors. Similarly, technical and organizational innovations often imply the need for institutional and governance innovations, as has been witnessed during the last two decades of modern globalization (McCann and Acs, 2011). The fall of the Berlin Wall and the opening up of the BRIICS countries Brazil, Russia, India, Indonesia, China and South Africa (McCann, 2009) are fundamentally institutional innovations based on national domestic political and governance choices. However, these national governance innovations themselves drive fundamental organizational and technical choices on the part of individual firms, relating to issues such as the outsourcing and off-shoring of production and the use of advanced information and communications technologies (ICTs) to realize such production ambitions. As such, the sources of innovation are multi-dimensional, and the impacts and outcomes of innovation are also multi-faceted.

The first modern analytical insights into these aspects of innovation derive from the work of Pavitt (1984). Pavitt's seminal analysis demonstrated that the sources of innovation can be variously internal or external to an industry, and the nature of the sources also has critical implications for the organization of the industry structure and also the competitive behaviour of the industry participants. For some industries, innovations are driven primarily by upstream segments of the sector, whereby the downstream elements of the sector embody these innovations in their products or services. Meanwhile, in others, downstream segments play a more important role, whereby upstream productivity gains depend on the performance of the final producers. At the same time, in some industries, the productivity gains are driven primarily by embodying and adapting to new technologies that emanate from outside of the industry, as is the case, for example, in the modern global financial services sector, which has transformed itself by capitalizing on the opportunities afforded by new ICTs, the advances of which were largely external to the financial services sector.

The timing of these Pavitt-type insights is significant because the 1980s was precisely the period during which modern thinking regarding the role and importance of innovation in growth processes first began to emerge in earnest. Of major significance here were the competitiveness arguments of Porter (1980, 1985) who for the first time communicated to a wide-ranging business and academic audience the important relationships between firm competition and decision-making and broader themes of technology and innovation. Central to Porter's early arguments were the role that innovation plays in driving competition, but his approach was rather different to that of Schumpeter. Porter's perspective was from the point of view of the firm-specific decision maker, and primarily from the point of view of the firm-level strategy maker operating in a medium- or large-sized firm (Porter, 1985, 1986), rather than an individual entrepreneur. Moreover, during the 1980s, Porter's arguments were not primarily concerned with the impacts on creative destruction on the industries and markets, but rather more on the impacts on the firm itself. However, this thinking changed in 1990, in which Porter (1990) turned his attention and that of his numerous academic and business readers, to the roles which institutional structures play in driving competition, productivity and performance. In particular, Porter (1990) examined the role which geography, and the formal and informal institutional context which underpins geographical clusters, plays in enhancing innovation processes in general. The arguments extend the discussions of innovation beyond technical science issues, and also move the discussions beyond the impacts on the firm. For many observers, Porter's (1990) work was one of the very first times that innovation as a phenomenon was simultaneously linked to firm-specific competition, as well as the systems relationships between all actors including institutions, in an explicitly geographical setting. However, more recent analysis has also adopted and pushed forwards this systems-type thinking, variously stressing the role played by national (Lundvall, 1985; Nelson, 1993; Freeman, 1995), technological (Carlsson and Stankiewicz, 1991), sectoral (Breschi and Malerba, 1997, see also Malerba and Orsenigo, 1993, 1995) and regional systems of innovation (Morgan, 1997). Indeed, the original Pavitt's (1984) classification scheme, which was initially built on manufacturing sectors, has subsequently been updated to include service industries (Archibugi, 2001) and also different types of clusters and geographical network systems (Iammarino and McCann, 2006). What is common in all of these innovation systems lines of enquiry is the assumption that innovation is not simply due to technical or science-related advances, but is just as much an organizational, institutional and social phenomenon as it is a technical-science-related phenomenon. Innovation is seen to be multi-dimensional, and technology is the result of such innovation processes and systems. Technology is therefore the result of social interactions, just as much as scientific interactions.

These assumptions which emerged primarily during the 1980s and early 1990s were very different from those underpinning the traditional neo-classical growth accounting models (Swan 1956; Solow, 1957) in which technology was assumed to be exogenous, disembodied and more or less freely available to all competitive market participants. Neo-classical thinking about knowledge–technology interactions itself shifted somewhat its emphasis in the light of product variety and knowledge spillovers (Romer, 1990) and human capital models (Lucas, 1988) of endogenous growth. Yet, even here, there is little room for innovation per se, except perhaps as a partially disembodied technological feature, with the major focus being on the nature of the interactions between the factors. It is only with Aghion and Howitt (1992) that innovation begins to be more formally incorporated into growth models in a more systematic way, whereby new firms, products and varieties drive quality improvements that supersede existing vintages and thereby drive growth in a Schumpeterian framework. Since then, numerous chapters have discussed different aspects of the role of innovation, but beyond the original Aghion and Howitt (1992, 1998), there have been surprisingly little formal theoretical progress on the role played by innovation. A few specific lines of enquiry (Scotchmer, 2004; Lipsey *et al.*, 2005; Andersson and Beckmann, 2009) have derived important insights relating with the role of incentives, creativity and discovery and different waves and types of technological change in growth. Yet, apart from these few research agendas, almost all subsequent theoretical work regarding the role played by innovation in growth has been of a largely qualitative and descriptive nature (Foray, 2004, 2009; Swann, 2009) in which the role of knowledge generation, knowledge spillovers, knowledge diffusion and knowledge transactions in fostering innovation is discussed from a perspective which is largely akin to that of the various innovation systems approaches alluded to above.

In marked contrast, over the last two decades, the vast majority of the subsequent breakthroughs in our understanding of the nature and role of innovation in growth processes have been in terms of the empirical modelling and measurement of the determinants of innovation. The major modern approaches to measuring the features and impacts of innovation first emerged in the late 1980s following the patent citation work of Jaffe and co-authors (1989, 1993) and the analyses by Acs and Audretsch (1988, 1990) of the small business administration data. Both approaches suggested that new knowledge was a key feature of economic performance, but the relationships between knowledge, innovation and firm types were for the first time examined empirically. These empirical approaches represented a major potential breakthrough because while, on the one hand, theoretical arguments from the international business literature suggested that large firms were systematically more likely to be more innovative than other firm types, on the other hand, some Schumpeterian arguments tended to point to the advantages afforded to small firms (Ortega-Argilés *et al.*, 2009; Ortega-Argilés and Brandsma, 2010). Yet, without comprehensive data and testing, the debate could not be satisfactorily resolved either way.

During the 1990s and following Porter's (1990) seminal contributions, a range of new directions in empirical research opened up regarding the role of geography in innovations systems. Krugman (1991) had argued that knowledge leaves no trace geographically, but very quickly a range of evidence started to emerge using patent data (Jaffe 1989; Jaffe *et al.*, 1993), micro-survey data from the U.S. Small Business Administration (Acs and Audretsch, 1988a,b; Feldman, 1994; Audretsch and Feldman, 1996) and bespoke industry or sectoral surveys (Audretsch and Stephan, 1996; Anselin *et al.*, 1997; Arita and McCann, 2000), which demonstrated that knowledge does indeed leave geographical traces. Increasingly, innovation came to be seen as also related to geography, clustering, networks and agglomeration, as Porter (1990) had highlighted, and this was reflected in a shift during the 1990s from national, technological and sectoral ways of thinking to an increasing regional innovations systems approach. More recently, and initially building primarily on Italian observations (Putnam, 1993; Becattini *et al.*, 2009), additional institutional elements have been added to the debates that allow for the role played by good governance, trust and social capital in facilitating innovation processes.

As can be seen, our understanding of the nature and role which innovation plays in growth has evolved over time. Today, innovation is regarded as a multi-dimensional issue, and one which may differ in different contexts, allowing for different drivers of innovation to dominate in different contexts. On this point, one of the key issues which will emerge in the following sections is that our understanding of which of the drivers of innovation are dominant in which particular contexts, also depends in part on the available data. As has already been mentioned, most of the breakthroughs in our understanding of innovation issues over the last two decades have emerged from investigations of new data sources. At the same time, however, as we will also see shortly, the availability of data for innovation analyses in part also depends on how society perceives innovation issues. These perceptions do differ over time and also between different countries, and these differences both reflect, and are reflected by, the different histories associated with efforts at innovation survey data collection.

3. Measures of Innovation

A fundamental and immediate challenge for any innovation-related research is how to measure the variable of interest, namely, innovation. Currently, there are two types of measures; *indirect* and *direct*, measures of innovation. Conventionally, innovation is measured by proxies including R&D and patent-based indicators. R&D expenditure is an *indirect* measure as it only measures inputs devoted to innovative activities and patent-based indicators focus solely on the successful generation of commercial applications. There is, however, a long history of using these measures. The practice of using R&D can be traced back to the 1930s (Holland and Spraragen, 1933), and the use of patents was popularized by Schmookler (1950, 1953, 1954). For a number of reasons, including ease of measurement and perhaps for ease of international comparisons, most national statistical agencies continue to report some form of R&D and patent statistics.

The problem with these indirect measures is that they are relatively narrow due to their potentially weak linkages with innovation and the induced large firm bias. For econometric analyses, a preferred option is to use direct measures of innovation, which can either be objective or subjective. Measuring innovation as an output, such as the number of innovations or an 'innovation count', is an objective measure that collects information from new product/process announcements, specialized journals, databases, etc. As a result of its collection method, this measure tends to be biased towards radical/product innovation as opposed to incremental/process innovation where unsuccessful innovations are automatically excluded. Carter and Williams (1957, 1958) were the first to use the output approach, on behalf of the *Science and Industry Committee* (UK), where they conducted a survey of the sources of innovation by examining 201 significant innovations from 116 firms and their characteristics. The same approach was used by the U.S. *National Science Foundation* (NSF) (Little, 1963; Mansfield, 1968; Myers and Marquis, 1969) and the *Organization for Economic Co-Operation and Development* (OECD, 1968; Pavitt and Wald, 1971).

Since the late 1970s, the use of subjective measures of innovation has become increasingly popular. Instead of focusing on output, the subjective measures consider innovation as an activity and a range of innovation-related data are collected via firm-based surveys. This approach generally provides discrete measures of innovation, measures which may be subject to human error/bias, and with potentially low response rates as there may be limited representativeness. Germany adopted the activity approach as early as 1979 (Meyer-Krahmer, 1984), and Italy followed in the mid-1980s (Archibugi *et al.*, 1987). Aiming to harmonize national methodologies and collect standardized information on firms' innovation activities, the first edition of the *Oslo Manual* was published in 1992 under the joint effort of the OECD and EU's statistical service *Eurostat*, and this made what is known as the 'activity approach' the official, preferred method for measuring innovation.

3.1 *Innovation Surveys Around the World*

First of all, before going into details of individual surveys, it is important to distinguish the differences between a complementary innovation survey and a 'true' innovation survey. A 'true' innovation survey is a survey that is custom-designed to collect a full set of innovation data, while there are two types of complementary surveys, whereby type I surveys only focus on a specific aspect of innovation, while type II surveys not only contain questions encountered in the innovation surveys but also information on many other variables.

A typical example of a type I complementary survey is a R&D survey. The NSF and the U.S. Census Bureau (Census) have been collecting a broad range of firm-level R&D data annually between 1953 and 2008 using the *Survey of Industrial Research and Development* (SIRD). Similarly, the Agency for Science, Technology and Research (A*STAR) and the Department of Statistics (DOS) in Singapore introduced their annual *National Survey of R&D* in 2002, also since 2004, Statistics New Zealand (SNZ) has been conducting an R&D survey every second year. Other examples of type I surveys include 2007 *Survey of Commercialization of Innovation* by Statistics Canada, and the 1997 *Survey on Organizational Changes and Computerization* by France's National Institute for Statistics and Economic Studies. Compared to type I complementary surveys, type II surveys have a wider focus and are often used as substitutes by researchers if no 'true' innovation surveys are readily available at the time. A few prominent examples are the World Bank administered *Investment Climate Survey*, the Chinese National Bureau of Statistics' annual survey on large and medium size enterprises, and the *Spanish Survey of Entrepreneurial Strategies* (ESEE).

Nonetheless, collecting innovation data via 'true' innovation surveys are the most preferable approach. In Europe, the *Community Innovation Survey* (CIS) is the main statistical instrument of the European Union which is the main source of data for the *European Innovation Scoreboard* and is based on the *Oslo Manual* approach. The first survey was conducted in 1993 covering a three-year time span, and following a legislative change in 2007, the survey frequency was increased from every four to every two years. Latin American countries have also been very active in terms of conducting innovation surveys. In response to the publication of the *Oslo Manual*, the *Bogota Manual* was drafted during 1999–2000. Intended to complement the *Oslo Manual*, additional guidelines were added to suit the differences between regions. Three rounds of survey have been conducted since 1995 with a total of 12 countries participating. However, only Argentina and Chile completed all three rounds. In addition to the collective effort, many countries also had their own official innovation surveys, including those listed below.

Malaysia's National Survey of Innovation (NSI) is conducted by Malaysian Science and Technology Information Centre (MASTIC). Adopting the OECD guideline, four NSIs have been carried out since 1995 and the latest survey was conducted in 2005 covering periods from 2002 to 2004. The main focus of the survey is on product and process innovation in manufacturing sector.

In South Korea, the Korean Innovation Survey (KIS) is carried out every three years by the Science and Technology Policy Institute (STEPI). The available datasets are:

- Technology Innovation Survey 2000 (1996–1999)
- KIS 2002: Manufacturing Sector (2000–2001)
- KIS 2003: Service Sector (2001–2002)
- KIS 2005: Manufacturing Sector (2002–2004)
- KIS 2008: Manufacturing sector (2005–2007)

Based on the *Oslo Manual*, both technological and non-technological innovations are included in 2005 and 2008 survey.

The Taiwanese Technological Innovation Survey (TTIS) is jointly conducted by the National Science Council (NSC) and the Ministry of Economic Affairs (MOEA) in 2002 and 2005, respectively. The sampling frame was generated by a stratified random sampling process based on firm size and industry, and it is representative of the population of traditional Taiwanese manufacturing firms.

Canada has an ongoing program to measure the product and process innovation. A series of surveys of innovation and technologies has been conducted every three to four years since the early 1990s. The Survey questionnaire was designed by the *Science, Innovation and Electronic Information Division* of *Statistics Canada* in collaboration with *Industry Canada, Natural Resource Canada*, and various government departments.

In the United States, innovation surveys are a relatively new phenomenon. In order to broaden the relevance and usefulness of the R&D statistics, NSF replaced SIRD by the *Business R&D and Innovation Survey* (BRDIS), the pilot questionnaire of which was mailed out in January 2009 to collect data for calendar year 2008.

The collection of innovation statistics in Australia began in the 1990s. The first two surveys in 1994 and 1997 primarily focused on the manufacturing and mining industries, whereas services and non-technological innovations were excluded. The practice has continued in the 2000s, and two more surveys were conducted in 2004 and 2006. Since 2007, an integrated *Business Characteristics Survey* (BCS) has been introduced, and a longitudinal dataset has been created and updated annually. Such a change allows for more comprehensive data integration and gives greater flexibility in terms of the measurement of a range of business characteristics. The characteristics of innovation outputs are released biennially.

Finally, in New Zealand, the main survey instrument for the collection of innovation data is the *Business Operations Survey (BOS)*, which is a modular survey developed by SNZ. The survey has been operating annually since 2005 and uses an integrated collection approach with the innovation module running every second year. The innovation module is intended to replace the *Innovation Survey*, which was last run in 2003. In 2006, a two-year feasibility project 'Improved Business Understanding via Longitudinal Database Development' (IBULDD) was implemented by SNZ aiming to link business-related data from both administrative databases and sample survey datasets, and a prototype Longitudinal Business Database (LBD) was created as a result.

In addition to the efforts made by national governments, various research institutes around the world have also undertaken their own innovation surveys. For example, *InnovationLab (Ireland) Ltd.*, an academic spin-off from the *Northern Ireland Economic Research Centre* created the *Irish Innovation Panel* (IIP) by linking five postal surveys on product and process innovation. The Fraunhofer Institute for Systems and Innovation Research (ISI) has conducted the *German Manufacturing Survey* every two to three years since 1993. The survey was internationalized in 2001 to meet the demands for internationally comparative data and the *European Manufacturing Survey* (EMS) was established as a result.

Rather than using secondary data, many authors have also opted for primary source data by constructing independent innovation surveys, which allow them to focus on a specific sector or issues. Moreover, authors also prefer different survey methods in different contexts, and here, we highlight some notable examples.

Panne and Beers (2006) carried out a postal survey during September 2000 and August 2002 on a sample of 398 innovative Dutch firms that were selected using the Literature-

Based Innovation Output (LBIO) method, and two years after product launch, all participating firms were re-contacted for follow-up. Alegre and Chiva (2008) surveyed 82 Italian and 100 Spanish firms in the Ceramic tile industry between June and November 2004, and the questionnaire was addressed to company directors. Weterings and Boschma (2009) gathered cross-sectional data on 265 software firms located in the Netherlands through two consecutive telephone surveys conducted during 2002 and 2003. Zhang *et al.* (2009) employed a web-based interview method and surveyed 104 wholly owned manufacturing subsidiaries of multi-national companies (MNCs) located in three Chinese economic development zones. Finally, using multiple survey methods (i.e. a telephone survey combined with personal interviews and a WWW-survey), Kaufmann *et al.* (2003) surveyed Austrian firms in the manufacturing and service sectors during 2000 and 2003. Supported by the Austrian National Bank, their initiative was a part of a two-year project for Austria (RINET).

3.2 *Survey-Related Researches*

Given the wide range of innovation surveys now available and the impacts that these empirical approaches have had on our overall understanding of innovation, a review of the different survey-related approaches to studying innovation, and also the findings uncovered by such approaches, becomes necessary. In this section, examples of the types of independent explanatory and dependent response variables used in survey-based approaches are discussed, and the relationship between the use of these variables and our more general conceptual understanding of the roles which the factors captured by these variables plays in innovation.

3.2.1 *Dependent Variables*

If we recall our earlier discussion on the different measures of innovation, we saw that both direct and indirect measures of innovation were discussed. Based on our review of such surveys, it becomes clear that the dependent variables typically used by authors in their analyses often comprise certain features. Indirect measures of innovation are often used as dependent variable, and the major types of indirect measures are related to R&D expenditure, patent indicators and direct measures of innovation.

Grabowski (1968) was particularly interested in the determinants of research expenditures in the drugs, chemicals and petroleum refining industries, and in his analysis, research intensity was considered as a more appropriate dependent variable than the actual research expenditures due to the large-scale differences between firms. Similar to many others, his choice of the appropriate size deflator was the total sales of the firm (Levin *et al.*, 1985; Lunn and Martin, 1986). However, alternative size deflators have been used. For example, the total assets and the number of employees were also used as a check for model consistency, and such deflators are preferred by some other authors including Artes (2009) and Crepon *et al.* (1998). Cuervo-Cazurra and Un (2007) analysed the influence of a regional economic integration agreement by focusing on the relative investment in internal R&D as well as the internal and external R&D intensity. Here, total sales were used as the deflator, while Crepon *et al.* (1998) preferred to use a stock measure of research rather than a flow measure and as a consequence they used the actual research capital per employee.

In the absence of a 'completely satisfactory index of inventive output', Scherer (1965) chose patent statistics as the principal-dependent variable for his work, and specifically 'the number of U.S. invention patents received' by the sampled firms in 1959. Krammer (2009) explored the determinants of innovation at a national level in Eastern European transition countries, where the 'new-to-the-world' notion of innovation was approximated by the number of patents that the *U.S. Patent and Trademark Office* (USPTO) issued to European Economic community (EEC) inventors. Scellato (2006) sourced patent portfolio information from the European Patent Office while examining the impact of financial constraints on innovation activities in the Italian manufacturing sector. In addition to registered patent counts, Beneito (2006) also considered 'utility model counts' as measures of innovation output. According to the definition provided by the *World Intellectual Property Organization* (WIPO), both patents and utility models are exclusive rights granted for an invention, and for a limited period of time unless authorized any commercial use of the protected invention is prohibited. The term of protection for a utility model is shorter than for patents, but it is cheaper and easier to obtain and maintain because of its less stringent requirements. Instead of counts, patent propensity is another dependent variable used in innovation research (Schmiedeberg, 2008), which takes the form of a dichotomous variable, which equals one if the patenting activity is observed and zero otherwise.

In contrast to the patent-based research discussed above, the most common approach currently adopted in econometric studies is to use *direct measures* of innovation. In addition to 'patent propensity', Santamaria *et al.* (2009) included two additional dichotomous variables to capture the different innovation outputs (i.e. product and process innovation). Todtling *et al.* (2009) had a sole focus on product innovation, but went a step further by defining 'new to the firm' and 'new to the market' innovations. Weterings and Boschma (2009) included both dichotomous variables for the 'introduction of new products or services' and the 'percentage of turnover due to the sales of those new products or services' in their analysis. Utilizing data from the *Taiwanese Technological Innovation Survey* (TTIS), Tsai (2009), Tsai and Hsieh (2009) and Tsai and Wang (2009)) measured the innovation performance based on 'innovative product sales' and 'innovative sales productivity' (i.e. innovative product sales per employee). Kirner *et al.* (2009) separated product and process innovation and adopted five innovation output indicators, namely, the 'share of turnover with new products', 'share of turnover with new product-related services', 'labour productivity' (turnover input/employee), 'rework/scrap rate' and 'production lead time'. Finally, Mol and Birkinshaw (2009) were keen to discover the source of management innovation. In their approach, to qualify as an innovator, the firm has to make major changes in at least one of the following areas: (a) implementation of advanced management techniques; (b) implementation of new or significantly changed organizational structure; (c) changing significantly firm's marketing concepts/strategies, for example, marketing methods. They create a single scale variable which takes the value 0 if there is no effective management innovation activity within the firm, with 1 added for each type of management innovation the firm engaged in, such that the upper bound is set at 3.

3.2.2 *Independent Variables*

In terms of independent explanatory variables, researchers have typically developed their models differently depending on the specific focus of the study. Assessing a wide range of independent variables sourced from the existing innovation literature, we can assign most variables used to one of three categories: (i) firm characteristics, (ii) firm behaviour or strategy and (iii) the overall competitive environment.

Table 1. Determinants of Innovation – Firm Characteristics.

Category	Subcategory	Variables	Selected References
Acquired	Firm Size	Employment	Brewin *et al.* (2009) and Harris *et al.* (2009)
		Total sales	Artes (2009) and Cuervo-Cazurra and Un (2007)
	Financial capability	Debt to equity ratio	Cuervo-Cazurra and Un (2007) and Munari *et al.* (2010)
	Production capacity		Armbruster *et al.* (2008)
	Business makeup	Ownership	Ortega-Argilés *et al.* (2005), Huergo (2006), Tsai (2009) and Munari *et al.* (2010)
		Export status	Leiponen and Byma (2009) and Falk (2008)
		Part of business/ multiplant group	Frenz and Ietto-Gillies (2009) Frenz and Ietto-Gillies (2009)
		Outsourcing/ subcontracting	Cuervo-Cazurra and Un (2007) and Kirner *et al.* (2009)
	Stock of knowledge	Absorptive capacity	Tsai (2009) and Tsai and Hsieh (2009)
		Capital/assets	Kafouros *et al.* (2008) and Zhang (2009)
		Employment	Hewitt-Dundas and Roper (2008) and Freel (2003)
	Firm age		Saliola and Zanfei (2009) and Weterings and Boschma (2009)
	Product	Diversity	Santamaria *et al.* (2009) and Siegel and Kaemmerer (1978)
		Complexity	Kirner *et al.* (2009)
	Geography/location		Srholec (2010) and Saliola and Zanfei (2009)
Inherent	Sector profile	Industry dummies	Veugelers and Cassiman (1999) and Faems *et al.* (2005)
		Technology level	Raymond *et al.* (2009) and Todtling *et al.* (2009)

In terms of firm characteristics, firm characteristics' variables can either be 'acquired' or 'inherent' properties of the firm. As suggested by the description, acquired characteristics can vary over a period of time due to the intentional or unintentional actions of the firm, whereas the inherent sectoral characteristics are harder to change, and examples of survey-based approaches using these different characteristics to capture innovation are given in Table 1.

A classic example of an acquired firm characteristic is the firm size. Given four principal dimensions of size, such as employees, sales, income generated and assets (Adelman, 1951), the number of people employed and the total sales are typically used to measure firm size. Pavitt *et al.* (1987) highlighted the advantages of firm size in R&D and pointed to a U-shaped relationship between innovation intensity and firm size (Tether, 1998; Tether, *et al.*, 1997). This implies that both large and small firms have innovation intensities above the average where the medium-sized firms have a below average intensity. It is worth stressing, however, that the criteria for 'small' and 'large' firms can differ markedly for different studies. In the Pavitt *et al.*'s (1987) chapter, large firms are classified as having more than 10,000 employees; the employment bracket for medium firms is between 2000 and 9999, and small firms have between 500 and 1000 employees. Nowadays Small and Medium Enterprises (SMEs) are generally understood in USA as being those firms with less than 500 employees, while in EU, it is 250. Therefore, care should be exercised when comparing results across countries, studies and time periods.

Other size-related characteristics are the 'financial capability', the 'production capacity' and 'business make-up' of a firm. In terms of financial capability, larger firms tend to face fewer resource constraints than smaller firms, especially when undertaking innovative activities. 'Debt to equity ratio' is one of the most well-known measures of a company's financial leverage and this is calculated by dividing its total liabilities by stockholders' equity. Himmelberg and Petersen (1994) argued that, given the imperfection of the capital market, internal finance is 'the principal determinant of the rate at which small, high-tech firms acquire technology through R&D'.

'Production capacity' may also impact on a firm's innovation performance. Armbruster *et al.* (2008) identified a positive correlation between the degree of capacity utilization and organizational innovation. However, it is also possible that a limited production capacity may reduce the possibility of product innovation, and production batch sizes could also affect a firm's innovativeness (Love and Roper, 1999).

'Business make-up' can include many other aspects of a firm, including the firm's ownership, export status, organizational structure and outsourcing or subcontracting practices. In terms of these dimensions, the literature suggests that family owners are more risk averse than non-family firms, and as a result, tend to invest less in terms of R&D (Munari *et al.*, 2010), while, on the other hand, publicly owned firms may have fewer incentives to make productivity improvements, and hence may have fewer incentives to innovate (Huergo, 2006). Focusing on MNCs and firms with overseas investments, Lin and Chen (2007) argued that innovation may be required in order for a firm to gain competitive advantages when competing in an international arena. For these types of firms, variables with different levels of detail are used by authors to capture a firm's export status. At one extreme, a dummy variable is used, which takes a value 1 if the firm participates in exporting and 0 otherwise (Huergo, 2006). Others, however, prefer quantitative measures such as 'export intensity as percentage of sales' (Panne and Beers, 2006). Mol and Birkinshaw (2009) viewed exports from a geographic perspective and asked the firm whether its largest market were 'local, regional, national or international'.

Sectoral characteristics are also typically inherent rather than acquired. The most recognizable sector-related variables are a firm's industry classification. Almost all cross-sector studies include some form of industrial dummies to isolate the sector effect on innovation. In particular, given the likelihood of differences in innovative capacity between high-tech and low-tech firms, variables capturing an industry's technology level are included by some authors (Kafouros *et al.*, 2008; Todtling *et al.*, 2009), although the number of studies using such an approach is less than might be expected, largely because many data sources preclude the use of such variables. However, while different branches of an individual industry may innovate differently, it has also been suggested that such variations may also exist within individual firms. Here, the role of 'business structure' (i.e. the internal corporate networks of subsidiaries) is argued to influence innovation because the knowledge transfers between each unit are likely to affect the overall innovation performance of the firm (Frenz and Ietto-Gillies, 2009). In a multi-plant of multi-national context, firms or establishments with access to the business group's resources may be more likely to innovate (Cantwell and Iammarino, 2003; Leiponen, 2006). Similar arguments have also been made for outsourcing and subcontracting practices, in that once the decision has been made to subcontract some of its production, the firm makes a conscious decision to invest in managing external sources of technology and knowledge (Cuervo-Cazurra and Un, 2007), and these decisions will influence innovation patterns. For these various reasons, different measures of organizational structure have been developed in order to enable researchers to identify whether the firm is a single-location company, a subsidiary of some other company, a main office or headquarters, or a branch establishment.

The remaining acquired characteristics that have been considered include the stock of knowledge, the firm age, the product characteristics and the firm's geographic locality. The 'stock of knowledge' variables measure the firm's existing technological knowledge base from various perspectives. Of these, the most important feature is probably the 'absorptive capacity', which is the ability of a firm to recognize, assimilate and apply the valuable, new and external information flows to its own commercial requirements (Cohen and Levinthal, 1990). In general, it is associated with a firm's ongoing in-house R&D activity (Stock *et al.*, 2001). Tsai (2009) recognized that the existing knowledge base is accumulated from periods of previous learning and the intensity of earlier efforts at learning, so he opted for a more nuanced measure by dividing the firm's total expenditures on in-house R&D activities and training programs for technological activities in the past three years by its current number of employees, where the numerator is a stock measure. In addition to absorptive capacity, knowledge can also be embedded within a firm's physical and human capital. Santamaria *et al.* (2009) explored the importance of knowledge diffusion for innovation performance and suggested that the use of machinery and advanced technology such as automatic machines, robots, CAD/CAM, or combinations of these procedures is critical for the innovation success of low-and-medium technology (LMT) firms. To approximate the knowledge embedded in a firm's human capital, education-related variables such as percentage of graduates in the workforce or the share of employees with higher education are used as the most common measures employed (Leiponen, 2006; Hewitt-Dundas and Roper, 2008).

'Firm age' is generally measured in years, although based upon existing empirical evidence, there are somewhat divergent views on its relationship with innovation. Hurley and Hult (1998) proposed the idea that younger firms are more innovative and that firms become less receptive to innovation opportunities as they age because of bureaucracy, which limits the infusion of new lifeblood into the organization and also new ideas. Other evidence, however, showed that older firms are able to accumulate innovative knowledge and experience and generate more innovations as a result (Sorensen and Stuart, 2000).

The product or service that they produce is the core of all businesses, and firms with more diversified product lines may be able to utilize innovative opportunities better, raising the expected pay-offs to R&D investment. Santamaria *et al.* (2009) found that it is easier for diversified firms to develop and adapt new technologies to improve their activities and processes. In their schema, to be diversified means that their main product has to represent less than 50% of sales at the three-digit industry level. Other product characteristics that may impact a firm's innovation performance are the complexity of the product. 'Complex products tend to stand at the end of the supply chain and thus naturally incorporate various innovation steps along this chain. Innovations developed and introduced by different suppliers become part of the final product' (Kirner *et al.*, 2009). On the one hand, the more innovations that are embodied within the product, the greater are the opportunities for capturing market shares, at least in times when technology is not dramatically changing. On the other hand, in times of radically technological change, such as during period when new GPTs are appearing, the greater complexity of a product may actually hamper the ability to adjust to the new innovation opportunities.

In innovation studies, location is a variable that is often used to control for inter-regional or inter-country difference in the innovative environment (Alegre and Chiva, 2008; Falk, 2008). In recent years, the literature on the geographical determinants of innovation has increased dramatically (Audretsch, 2003; Herrera *et al.*, 2010), and in particular, the role of agglomeration as the key catalyst of innovation has been explored by many researchers. Sedgley and Elmslie (2004) found that agglomeration has positive effects on innovative outputs, even after controlling for differences in human capital, high-tech industry structure and R&D university infrastructure. In contrast, Simonen and McCann (2008, 2010) found that by carefully decomposing the elements of a firm's co-operation relations as well as its inherited characteristics, the population density and local labour acquisition features associated with agglomeration tended to reduce innovation outputs. The implication here is that agglomeration as a variable is something of a catch-all variable incorporating many different innovation mechanisms, which, when decomposed into its transactional elements, reveals the residual congestion costs effects. Of course, the geographical context can also be acquired rather than inherited by firm relocation behaviour, and the relationships between locational choices and innovation behaviour also depend on the innovation objectives of the firm, the importance of accessibility and face-to-face interactions for knowledge flows, and the travel and opportunity costs of accessing such knowledge (McCann, 2007b). As such, geography is neither entirely exogenous nor endogenous to the innovation-optimization problem.

3.2.3 *Firm Behaviour and Strategy*

Firm behaviour and strategy regarding innovation relate to the specific activities and choices that could help to make a firm a successful innovator. It has been suggested that innovative firms are less risk adverse (Khan and Manopichetwattana, 1989a) and more optimistic about business (Souitaris, 2002), and as such, are more willing to adapt and change in response to market opportunities and innovation challenges than non-innovators. The focus of this chapter is on innovating firms, and for the purpose of this survey, behaviour and strategy variables are split into 'general practice' and 'innovation-related' practices and examples of these different approaches in survey-based innovation analyses are given in Table 2.

The first 'general practice' variable discussed is a firm's investment behaviour. In endogenous growth theories, the interactions between capital and labour are regarded as being critical for a firm's innovation performance. Compared to capital investment, investment in labour, that is, human capital, is intangible and arises from, for example, vocational training and further education. However, such training involves choices on the part of the firm as to whether to invest in new equipment or alternatively in the upgrading or acquiring of

Table 2. Determinants of Innovation – Firm Behaviour and Strategy.

Category	Subcategory	Variables	Selected references
General practice	Investment	Capital	Cohen and Levinthal (1989) and Leiponen (2005)
		Labour	Swan and Newell (1995) and Baumol (2005)
	Input	Source	Cuervo-Cazurra and Un (2007) and Saliola and Zanfei (2009)
	External communication		Weterings and Boschma (2009) and Jong and Hippel (2009)
	Strategy/ management		Schmiedeberg (2008) and Pekovic and Galia (2009)
Innovation practice	R&D	Dummy	Hewitt-Dundas and Roper (2008)
		Expenditure	Herrera et al. (2010) and Leiponen and Byma (2009)
		Intensity	Kafouros et al. (2008) and Panne and Beers (2006)
		Employment	Weterings and Boschma (2009)
	Co-operation	Partners	Huergo (2006) and Tsai and Wang (2009)
		Activities	Mol and Birkinshaw (2009) and Leiponen (2006)
	Technological management		Herrera and Nieto (2008) and Jong and Hippel (2009)
	Informal practice	Design	Santamaria et al. (2009) and Kirner et al. (2009)
		Marketing	Marsili and Salter (2006)
		Quality control	Beneito (2006)

new labour skills. Such human capital enhancing behaviour has also become increasingly popular among businesses, and represents an increasing awareness of the role of human capital as well as physical capital. Yet, the issue is not straightforward. A certain amount of technical training is indispensable for any innovator (Baumol, 2005), and Swan and Newell (1995) emphasized the positive influence of on-the-job training, in particular, on innovation. Obviously, education supports technical progress by allowing mastery of existing scientific knowledge and methods and increases the technical competence in general. On the other hand, it may also hinder innovation by impeding unorthodox thinking and imagination. This argument also applies to general recruitment processes, in which the search for educational attainment and entrepreneurial talent is qualitatively quite different. However, it is also clear that a well-educated and experienced workforce enhances innovative activity, in that in the long run, the continuous investment in human capital will become the firm's inherited knowledge base or stock of knowledge discussed above.

Another general practice strategic choice faced by firms which influences innovation relates to internal production versus outsourcing and contracting. Inputs that are transferred into the firm would have knowledge and technology embodied within (Caelile, 2002).

Cuervo-Cazurra and Un (2007) and the external advanced technologies obtained from high-quality input suppliers may reduce the need for internal R&D on the part of the firm itself. Saliola and Zanfei (2009) looked at the amount of inputs bought locally by multi-national subsidiaries as an approximation of the degree of local embeddedness of the market relationship between multi-nationals and local firms. Their findings suggested that an increase in the share of locally purchased inputs leads to significant performance advantages in innovation on the part of the outsourcing firm. Presumably, such a mechanism would operate by fostering local knowledge exchanges, as argued by the Porter (1990) and Feldman (1994) amongst others.

Rather than open-market contracting, perhaps, a more efficient general practice way to acquire and embody market or technological information is to communicate directly with suppliers of raw materials, machinery and equipment (Rothwell, 1992) and likewise also with customers. The highest level of communication is carried out in terms of co-operation between a firm and other firms, customers or institutions, as discussed shortly. A firm can also obtain new or external information by networking internally or with others (Souitaris, 2002), but importantly, networking often involves the need to redesign organizational structures and processes so as to best fit the firm's competitive environment (Souitaris, 2002, p. 883). The communication with customers, in particular, can take the form of personal visits (Rochford and Rudelius, 1992), feedback via phone or post (Chiesa *et al.*, 1996) or quantitative market research (Khan and Manopichetwattana, 1989b).

With regard to 'innovation-related' practices, the importance of R&D to innovation has been emphasized for many years. However, and similar to human capital investment, R&D investment is a type of intangible investment which, along with other drivers, contributes to innovation behaviour, processes and outcomes. Since the widespread adoption of direct measures of innovation resulting from the use of *Oslo Manual*-type innovation surveys, the previous tendency of using R&D as the left-hand side regressor in economic models has declined and instead R&D is nowadays almost always used as a right-hand side variable. Here, total R&D expenditure and R&D expenditure as the percentage of total sales have remained the most popular measures of R&D effort, followed by an R&D dummy and R&D employment.

But R&D itself is neither homogenous nor necessarily inherited, and for this reason, many authors have also separated internal and external R&D in their research, based on the belief that each contributes differently to the innovation process (Beneito, 2006; Frenz and Ietto-Gillies, 2009). The argument here is that as a result of globalization, external R&D often takes the form of outsourcing, partnerships and alliances that are frequently chosen by firms as a means of technology acquisition. A very common practice here is for the firm to co-operate with universities or research institutions (Bonaccorsi and Piccaluga, 1994; Lopez-Martinez *et al.*, 1994), government institutions, or public and private consultants (Bessant and Rush, 1995), but R&D co-operation may also include joint ventures with other customer, supplier or competitor firms (Rothwell, 1992; Swan and Newell, 1995). As such, at one end of the spectrum, financial institutions and government might participate in innovation co-operation relationship as funding providers (Souitaris, 2002). At the other end of the spectrum, firms can purchase technological know-how from external providers via licensing, which can be seen as an alternative form of intangible investment directly boosting the input of knowledge and ideas. There are also a range of other co-operation relationships with varying degrees of knowledge-exchange intensity (Arita and McCann, 2000), and in regression analyses, authors have often focused on co-operation with partners and joint-venture-type activities as independent variables driving innovation.

Other innovation-related practices also include the use of a 'technological strategy', which is defined as a set of integrated actions involving various departments throughout the company and requires multiple steps in order to upgrade the overall general technological level of the firm. The existence of a technological strategy demonstrates the intention of a firm to innovate and an overall encompassing technological strategy can help provide continuity and consistency, and the economies of scale and scope require for innovative activities. The establishment of an R&D department may also have a similar effect. The rationale for these types of approaches is that from survey data, it becomes clear that firms tend to have higher innovation rates if there is a well-defined and well-communicated business strategy, with a long-term horizon, including plans for new technology investment (Koc and Ceylan, 2007). Moreover, the decision to use different types of intellectual property protections may also enhance innovation outcomes (Jong and Hippel, 2009), both via a stronger legal grounding and also by associated governance learning effects.

In these discussions so far, the innovation-related practices considered are mainly formal practices with a strong innovation focus. However, some informal practices should not be ignored, as they are also potentially beneficial to the overall innovation process. Design is an integral part of product development, and Laestadius *et al.* (2005) claim that the creative process can be rational, innovative or artistic. Marsili and Salter (2006) were interested in the relationship between design and innovation performance and defined design activities as 'the stages of detailed development that are necessary to translate the first prototype into successful production'. It is worth noting that there is obviously considerable overlap between the concepts of design and R&D, and this causes some difficulties in terms of interpretation of the roles played by these activities (Glaeser, 2005; McCann, 2007a). Indeed, while setting the rules for collection on R&D statistics, the *Frascati Manual* (OECD, 2003) identified the difficulty of drawing the line between experimental development[1] and design with the variability depending on industrial situation. Quoting from the *Oslo Manual*, 'Some elements of industrial design should be included as R&D if they are required for R&D' (OECD, 2005, p. 94). However, notwithstanding these difficulties, there are still good arguments that suggest that it is still important to distinguish between design and creative activities from other R&D activities. Kirner *et al.* (2009) pointed out that firms which develop the customised design of their products according to a customer's specifications perform better in terms of product innovation than firms which do not employ such design approaches. In a similar vein, marketing and quality control are the other two informal innovation practices that have been investigated by innovation researchers. The key results show that R&D marketing integration enables the firm to develop a product that meets the customer's needs (Kahn, 2001), while quality control helps with the identification of, and the avoidance of further, existing problems on the production floor.

3.2.4 *The Overall Environment of the Firm*

The final set of explanatory variables used in innovation regressions relate to the overall environment variables, and examples of the use of these types of variables in innovation research are given in Table 3.

There are many aspects of the competitive context of a firm which fall under the heading of the firm's 'environment', such as the market structure of the firm's industry, the firm's market share within that industry, the number of competitors in the industry, the regulatory context, the level of price competition and also the regional economic context. In general, Herfindahl-type indices are the most popular measures of market structure. The Herfindahl

Table 3. Determinants of Innovation – Overall Environment.

Category	Subcategory	Variables	Selected references
Market	Structure	Market share	Santamaria *et al.* (2009) and Tingvall and Poldahl (2006)
		Price competition	Okada (2004) and Cuervo-Cazurra and Un (2007)
		Competitor	Huergo (2006) and Kraft (1989)
	Demand		Becker and Egger (2009) and Santamaria *et al.* (2009)
Regional	Environment		Panne and Beers (2006) and Srholec (2010)
Institutional	Technological related		Harris *et al.* (2009) and Hewitt-Dundas and Roper (2008)
	Non-technological related		Mahagaonkar *et al.* (2009)

index is the sum of the squared market shares of the firms in the industry and is used by the U.S. competition authorities as a guideline for making decisions on approving mergers and acquisitions (Clyde and Reitzes, 1995). Some authors have taken a simpler option to reflect the market condition, opting for the firm's 'number of competitors' (Huergo, 2006), while others focused on price variables such as price-cost margins and intensity of price competition (Aghion *et al.*, 2005; Cuervo-Cazurra and Un, 2007). In some cases, the concentrations of clients and suppliers are also used to gain a further understanding of the market environment in which the firm operates in Cuervo-Cazurra and Un (2007). More mixed and pragmatic approaches can also be employed. For example, when examining the role of market structure on influencing short-term and long-term R&D decisions, Artes (2009) included both a concentration ratio and a market share dummy in his analysis. Here, the concentration ratio was the sum of market shares of the main four industries in the product markets where the company operates, weighted by the share of the sales in these markets on total sales of the company, while the market share dummy indicates whether the firm had a non-significant market share. Yet, even despite strong monopoly power, changes in market demand can affect both innovation efforts and outcomes substantially. Flaig and Stadler (1994) included demand volatility as a determinant of product and process innovations; Sadowski and Sadowski-Rasters (2006) captured the influence of market growth by looking at sales growth between years and the impacts on innovation; Huergo (2006) employed two dummy variables (i.e. expanding and contracting demand) to control for fluctuations in the innovation environment.

The final broad group of issues to consider here are the variables that are used to capture the regional and institutional environment. Given that no region is the same, the work of many authors (Porter, 1990; Feldman, 1994; Audretsch and Feldman, 1996) suggests that the unique properties of the region can directly or indirectly influence the firm's innovative behaviour. On this point, Brouwer *et al.* (1999) find that Dutch firms in urban agglomerations devote a higher percentage of their R&D to product development than rural firms, and firms in central regions have higher probabilities of announcing new products in journals. However, the model of McCann (2007b) suggests that when we discuss innovation, the environment cannot be treated as being either entirely exogenous. Firms are able to move and relocate, and as such, the influence of the environment on innovation is in part endogenous to the innovation-optimization choices available to the firm, which themselves depend on the geography–time settings and the optimized frequency of interaction between people (McCann *et al.*, 2010). Moreover, this argument can be extended by going beyond traditional regional–geographical understanding of boundaries to include institutional variables that capture wider policy settings. Many countries, including some developing countries, use national or regional technology and innovation policies to achieve particular economic goals. Although regional technology and innovation policies are typically set within an individual jurisdiction, they often induce some unintended spatial and firm-related effects outside the region. A good example here is the innovation policies of the European Union. Sternberg's international comparison (1996) suggested that the unintended spatial impacts of technology policies are often far greater than the intended impacts. This broader line of thinking has given rise to the publication of series of new survey-based analyses of innovation, the most important of which are the EU surveys and the recent OECD analyses.

In Europe, the European Commission conducts a survey on R&D business investment trends[2] and this is used primarily for monitoring purposes. Similarly, the EU Industrial R&D Investment Scoreboard (European Commission, 2005, 2011)[3] is used for monitoring EU innovation strategies and collects data from the latest audited company reports and accounts as well as from Eurostat. The scoreboard is based on companies whose registered offices are located within the EU and the same number with registered offices outside the EU. Nowadays there are the 2004–2011 editions of the scoreboard with information from 2000 in some of the companies. The scoreboard is mainly used for comparisons and benchmarking purposes, rather than econometric analyses, and there is now also a EU Regional Innovation Scoreboard[4] which uses fewer indicators than the national innovation scoreboard.

Whereas these EU scoreboards are primarily used for monitoring purposes, the 2009 NESTA report (Anyadike-Danes *et al.*, 2009) on economic and social outcomes in UK cities and regions was intended to provide an analytical base for policy-making. The report suggests that a very small percentage of firms, and in particular fast-growing firm, account for a very large percentage of employment growth. Moreover, this growth tends to be particularly marked in certain places. Entrepreneurship and innovation appear to be spatially concentrated and the report provides normative arguments regarding why SMEs should be prioritized by policy, and more controversially, in particular high-growth places. This argument is slightly different to that which is offered by the OECD (2011) report *Regions and Innovation Policy*, which classified all OECD regions into particular types of places according to their combinations of innovation features. The OECD report is based on the OECD regional database plus numerous case studies conducted under the auspices of the OECD territorial and urban policy reviews, and the argument of the report is that all regions differ significantly and there can be no one-size-fits-all policy. As such, innovation policies must be tailored to the context, but essential elements of all policies are that they ensure that all relevant stakeholders have the incentives to maximize their engagement. The importance of this multi-level governance agenda has been highlighted for many years by the OECD, and implies that the policy design issues relating to governance and institutional coordination are critical, and must be appropriate for the context. What might be appropriate an innovation policy in a large decentralized and centrally located economy such as Germany is unlikely to be appropriate in a small and geographically isolated economy such as New Zealand. These governance and more contextually nuanced arguments also reflect a more general and fundamental shift in the thinking about innovation away from a hard science and R&D-centred discussion based on capital expenditure and technical infrastructure to something which also includes softer governance and institutional issues.

4. Final Remarks

Given all data collection and research efforts undertaken, it is clear that our empirical awareness of innovation has been pushed forward significantly over the least two decades. Yet, overall, it is still quite surprising how little we know about the subject of innovation, even though there is almost universal agreement regarding its crucial role in economic growth and development. What is clear is that empirical work on innovation has now far outstripped theoretical work on innovation, much of which is still struggling with variants of neo-classical growth-accounting framework. Yet, while the widespread growth in surveys has allowed researchers to increase our understanding of innovation, there are still major problems around data quality. Innovation researchers often have problems accessing the data, because the micro innovation data administrated by the state is often considered to be highly confidential, and the independent surveys and data produced by research institutes are often generally very expensive. As such, it is often the case that only a small number of people are able to fully access the data. At best, national statistical agencies report only summary statistics on their national surveys. If we really want to understand innovation, its role in economic growth and the underlying drivers, which foster innovation, it is essential that access is maximized to the detailed data that are available.

Notes

1. Three main categories of R&D activities: basic research, applied research and experimental development.
2. http://iri.jrc.es/research/survey_2010.htm
3. http://www.proinno-europe.eu/page/european-innovation-scoreboard-2009;
   http://www.proinno-europe.eu/inno-metrics/page/innovation-union-scoreboard-2010.
4. http://www.proinno-europe.eu/page/regional-innovation-scoreboard.

References

Acs, Z.J. and Audretsch, D.B. (1990) Innovation in large and small firms: an empirical analysis. *American Economic Review* 78(4): 678–690.

Acs, Z.J. and Audretsch, D.B. (1988b) *Innovation and Small Firms.* Cambridge, MA: MIT Press.

Adelman, M.A. (1951) The measurement of industrial concentration. *The Review of Economics and Statistics* 33(4): 269–296.

Aghion, P., Bloom, N., Blundell, R., Griffith, R. and Howitt, P. (2005) Competition and innovation: an inverted U-relationship. *Quarterly Journal of Economics* 120: 701–728.

Aghion, P. and Howitt, P. (1992) A model of growth through creative destruction. *Econometrica* 60(2): 322–352.

Aghion, P. and Howitt, P. (1998) On the macroeconomic effects of major technological change. *Annales d'Economie et de Statistique* 3: 49–50.

Alegre, J. and Chiva, R. (2008) Assessing the impact of organizational learning capability on product innovation performance: an empirical test. *Technovation* 28: 315–326.

Andersson, A.E. and Beckmann, M.J. (2009) *Economics of Knowledge: Theory, Models and Measurements*. Cheltenham: Edward Elgar.

Anselin, L., Varga, A. and Acs, Z. (1997) Local geographic spillovers between university research and high technology innovations. *Journal of Urban Economics* 42(3): 422–448.

Anyadike-Danes, M., Bonner, K., Hart, M. and Mason, C. (2009) *Measuring Business Growth: High-Growth Firms and Their Contribution to Employment in the UK*. London: NESTA.

Archibugi, D. (2001) Pavitt's taxonomy sixteen yearss on: a review article. *Economic of Innovation and New Technology* 10(5): 415–425.

Archibugi, D., Cesaratto, S. and Sirilli, G. (1987) Innovative activity, R&D and patenting: the evidence of the survey on innovation diffusion in Italy. *Science Technology Industry Review* 2: 135–190.

Arita, T. and McCann, P. (2000) Industrial alliances and firm location behaviour: some evidence from the US semiconductor industry. *Applied Economics* 32(11): 1391–1403.

Armbruster, H., Bikfalvi, A., Kinkel, S. and Lay, G. (2008) Organizational innovation: the challenge of measuring non-technical innovation in large-scale surveys. *Technovation* 28: 644–657.

Artes, J. (2009) Long-run versus short-run decisions: R&D and market structure. *Research Policy* 38: 120–132.

Audretsch, D.B. (2003) Innovation and spatial externalities. *International Regional Science Review* 26(2): 167–174.

Audretsch, D.B. and Feldman, M.P. (1996) R&D spillovers and the geography of innovation and production. *American Economic Review* 86(3): 630–640.

Audretsch, D.B. and Stephan, P. (1996) Company-scientist locational links: the case of biotechnology. *American Economic Review* 86(3): 641–652.

Banbury, C.M. and Mitchell, W. (1995) The effect of introducing important incremental innovations on market share and business survival. *Strategic Management Journal* 16: 161–182.

Baumol, W.J. (2002) *The Free-Market Innovation Machine: Analyzing the Growth Miracle of Capitalism*. New York: Princeton University Press.

Baumol, W.J. (2005) Education for innovation: entrepreneurial breakthroughs versus corporate incremental improvements. *Innovation and the Economy* 5: 33–56.

Becattini, G., Bellandi, M. and De Propis, L. (eds) (2009) *A Handbook of Industrial Districts*. Cheltenham, UK: Edward Elgar Publishers Ltd.

Becker, S.O. and Egger, P.H. (2009) Endogenous product versus process innovation and a firm's propensity to export. *Empirical Economics, First Online*. DOI: 10.1007/s00181–009–0322–6.

Best, M.H. (1990) *The New Competition: Institutions of Industrial Restructuring*. Cambridge, MA: Harvard University Press.

Beneito, P. (2006) The innovative performance of in-house and contracted R&D in terms of patents and utility models. *Research Policy* 35: 502–517.

Bessant, J. and Rush, H. (1995). Building bridges for innovation: the role of consultants in technology transfer. *Research Policy* 24(1): 97–114.

Bonaccorsi, A. and Piccaluga, A. (1994) A theoretical framework for the evaluation of university-industry relationship. *R&D Management* 24(4): 229–247.

Breschi, S. and Malerba, F. (1997) Sectoral innovation systems: technological regimes, schumpeterian dynamics, and spatial boundaries. In C. Edquist (ed.), *Systems of Innovation: Technologies, Institutions and Organizations*. London and Washington: Pinter.

Brewin, D.G., Monchuk, D.C. and Partridge, M.D. (2009) Examining the adoption of product and process innovations in the Canadian food processing industry. *Canadian Journal of Agricultural Economics* 57: 75–97.

Brouwer, E., Budil-Nadvornikova, H. and Kleinknecht, A. (1999) Are urban agglomerations a better breeding place for product innovation? An analysis of new product announcements. *Regional Studies* 33(6): 541–550.

Caelile, P.R. (2002) A pragmatic view of knowledge and boundaries: boundary objects in new product development. *Organization Science* 13(4): 442–255.

Cantwell, J. and Iammarino, S. (2003) *Multinational Corporations and European Regional Systems of Innovation*. London, UK: Routledge.

Carlsson, B. and Stankiewicz, R. (1991) On the nature, function, and composition of technological systems. *Journal of Evolutionary Economics* 1(2): 93–118.

Carter, C.F. and Williams, B.R. (1957) *Industry and Technical Progress: Factors Governing the Speed of Application of Science*. London: Oxford University Press.

Carter, C.F. and Williams, B.R. (1958) *Investment in Innovation*. London: Oxford University Press.

Chiesa, V., Coughlan, P. and Voss, C.A. (1996) Development of a technical innovation audit. *Journal of Product Innovation Management* 13(2): 105–136.

Clyde, P.S. and Reitzes, J.D. (1995) The effectiveness of collusion under antitrust immunity, the case of liner shipping conferences. Available at http://www.ftc.gov/reports/shipping.pdf. (accessed September 15, 2011).

Cohen, W.M. and Levinthal, D.A. (1989) Innovation and learning: the two face of R&D. *The Economic Journal* 99(397): 569–596.

Cohen, W.M. and Levinthal, D.A. (1990) Absorptive capacity: a new perspective on learning and innovation. *Administrative Science Quarterly* 35(1): 128–152.

Crepon, B., Duguet, E. and Mairesse, J. (1998) Research, innovation and productivity: an econometric analysis at the firm level. NBER Working Paper 6696.

Cuervo-Cazurra, A. and Un, C.A. (2007) Regional economic integration and R&D investment. *Research Policy* 36: 227–246.

European Commission (2005) *2004 EU Industrial R&D Investment Scoreboard*. Luxembourg: European Commission.

European Commission(2011) *2011 EU Industrial R&D Investment Scoreboard*. Luxembourg: European Commission.

Faems, D., Looy, B.V. and Debackere, K. (2005) Interorganisational collaboration and innovation: toward a portfolio approach. *Journal of Product Innovation Management* 22: 238–250.

Falk, M. (2008) Effect of foreign ownership on innovation activities: empirical evidence for twelve European countries. *National Institute Economic Review* 204(1): 85–97.

Feldman, M.P. (1994) *The Geography of Innovation*. Boston: Kluwer Academic Publishers.

Flaig, G. and Stadler, M. (1994) Success breeds success. The dynamics of the innovation process. *Emporical Economics* 19: 55–68.

Foray, D. (2004) *The Economics of Knowledge*. Cambridge, MA: MIT Press.

Foray, D. (eds) (2009) *The New Economics of Technology Policy*. Cheltenham, UK: Edward Elgard.

Freel, M.S. (2003) Sectoral patterns of small firm innovation, networking and proximity. *Research Policy* 32: 751–770.

Freeman, C. (1995) The "National System of Innovation" in historical perspective. *Cambridge Journal of Economics* 19(1): 5–24.

Frenz, M. and Ietto-Gillies, G. (2009) The impact on innovation performance of different sources of Knowledge: evidence from the UK Community Innovation Survey. *Research Policy* 38: 1125–1135.

George, D.A.R., Oxley, L. and Carlaw, K.I. (2004) *Surveys in Economic Growth: Theory and Empirics*. Oxford: Blackwell.

Glaeser, E.L. (2005) Review of Richard Florida's the rise of the creative class. *Regional Science and Urban Economics* 35(5): 593–596.

Gordon, I.R. and McCann, P. (2005) Innovation, agglomeration, and regional development. *Journal of Economic Geography* 5(5): 523–543.

Grabowski, H.G. (1968) The determinants of industrial research and development: a study of the chemical, drug, and petroleum industries. *The Journal of Political Economy* 76(2): 292–306.

Harris, R., Li, Q.C. and Trainor, M. (2009) Is a higher rate of R&D tax credit a panacea for low levels of R&D in disadvantaged regions? *Research Policy* 38: 192–205.

Herrera, L., Munoz-Doyague, M.F. and Nieto, M. (2010) Mobility of public researchers, science knowledge transfer, and the firm's innovation process. *Journal of Business Research* 63(5): 510–518.

Herrera, L. and Nieto, M. (2008) The national innovation policy effect according to firm location. *Technovation* 28(8): 540–550.

Hewitt-Dundas, N. and Roper, S. (2008) Ireland's innovation performance:1991 to 2005. *ESRI Quarterly Economic Commentary* 2008(2): 46–68.

Himmelberg, C.P. and Petersen, B.C. (1994) R & D and internal finance: a panel study of small firms in high-tech industries. *The Review of Economics and Statistics* 76(1): 38–51.

Holland, M. and Spraragen, W. (1933) *Research in Hard Times*. Washington: Division of Engineering and Industrial Research, National Research Council.

Huergo, E. (2006) The role of technological management as a source of innovation: evidence from Spanish manufacturing firms. *Research Policy* 35: 1377–1388.

Hurley, R.F. and Hult, G.T.M. (1998) Innovation, market orientation and organizational learning: a integration and empirical integration and empirical examination. *Journal of Marketing* 62(3): 42–54.

Iammarino, S. and McCann, P. (2006) The structure and evolution of industrial clusters: transactions, technology and knowledge spillovers. *Research Policy* 35(7): 1018–1036.

Jaffe, A.B. (1989). Real effects of academic research. *American Economic Review* 79(5): 957–970.

Jaffe, A.B., Trajtenberg, M. and Henderson, R. (1993) Geographic localization of knowledge spillovers as evidenced by patent citations. *The Quarterly Journal of Economics* 108(3): 577–598.

Jin, Z., Hewitt-Dundas, N. and Thompson, N.J. (2004) Innovativeness and performance: evidence from manufacturing sectors. *Journal of Strategic Marketing* 12(4): 255–266.

Jong, J.P.J.d. and Hippel, E.v. (2009) Transfers of user process innovations to process equipment producers: a study of Dutch high-tech firms. *Research Policy* 38: 1181–1191.

Kafouros, M.I., Buckley, P.J., Sharp, J.A. and Wang, C. (2008) The role of internationalization in explaining innovation performance. *Technovation* 28: 63–74.

Kahn, K.B. (2001) Market orientation, interdeparmental integration, and product development performance. *The Journal of Product Innovation Management* 18: 314–323.

Kaufmann, A., Lenhner, P. and Todtling, F. (2003) Effects of the Internet on the spatial structure of innovation networks. *Information Economics and Policy* 15(3): 402–424.

Khan, A.M. and Manopichetwattana, V. (1989a) Innovative and non innovative small firms: types and characteristics. *Management Science* 35(5): 597–606.

Khan, A.M. and Manopichetwattana, V. (1989b) Models for distinguishing innovative and non-innovative small firms. *Journal of Business Venturing* 4(3): 187–196.

Kirner, E., Kinkel, S. and Jaeger, A. (2009) Innovation paths and the innovation performance of low-technology firms – an empirical analysis of German industry. *Research Policy* 38: 447–458.

Knight, F.H. (1921) *Risk, Uncertainty and Profit* (Hart, Schaffner and Marx Prize Essays, Vol. 31). Boston and New York: Houghton Mifflin.

Koc, T. and Ceylan, C. (2007) Factors impacting the innovative capacity in large-scale companies. *Technovation* 27(3): 105–114.

Kraft, K. (1989) Market structure, firm characteristics and innovative activity. *Journal of Industrial Economics* 37: 329–336.

Krammer, S.M.S. (2009) Drivers of national innovation in transition: evidence from a panel of Eastern European countries. *Research Policy* 38: 845–860.

Krugman, P. (1991) *Geography and Trade*. Cambridge, MA: MIT Press.

Laestadius, S., Pedersen, T. and Sandven, T. (2005) Towards a new understanding of innovativeness and of innovation based indicators. *Journal for Perspectives on Economic Political and Social Integration* 11(1–2): 75–122.

Leiponen, A. (2005) Skills and innovation. *International Journal of Industrial Organisation* 23: 303–323.

Leiponen, A. (2006) Managing knowledge for innovation: the case of business-to-business services. *Journal of Product Innovation Management* 23: 238–258.

Leiponen, A. and Byma, J. (2009) If you cannot block, you better run: small firms, cooperative innovation, and appropriation strategies. *Research Policy* 38(9): 1478–1488.

Levin, R.C., Cohen, W.M. and Mowery, D.C. (1985) R&D appropriability, opportunity and market structure: new evidence of some schumpeterian hypothesis. *American Economic Review* 75: 20–24.

Levinson, M. (2006). *The Box: How the Shipping Container Made the World Smaller and the World Economy Bigger*. Princeton: Princeton University Press.

Lin, C.Y.-Y. and Chen, M.Y.-C. (2007) Does innovation lead to performance? An empirical study of SME in Taiwan. *Management Research News* 30(2): 115–132.

Lipsey, R.G., Carlaw, K.I. and Bekar, C.T. (2005) *Economic Transformations: General Purpose Technologies and Long Term Economic Growth.* Oxford, UK: Oxford University Press.

Little, A.D. (1963) Patterns and problems of technical innovation in American Industry. Report C-65344 submitted to the NSF, Washington.

Lopez-Martinez, R.E., Medekkin, E., Scanlon, A.P. and Solleiro, J.L. (1994) Motivations and obstacles to university and industry co-operation (UIC): a Mexican case. *R&D Management* 24(1): 17–31.

Love, J.H. and Roper, S. (1999) The determinants of innovation: R&D, technology transfer and networking effects. *Review of Industrial Organization* 15(1): 43–64.

Lucas, R.E. (1988). On the mechanics of economic development. *Journal of Monetary Economics* 22: 3–42.

Lunn, J. and Martin, S. (1986) Market structure, firm structure and research and development. *Quarterly Review of Economics and Business* 26: 31–44.

Lundvall, B.Å. (1985) *Product Innovation and User-Producer Interaction, Industrial Development* (Research Series 31). Aalborg: Aalborg University Press.

Mahagaonkar, P., Schweickert, R. and Chavali, A.S. (2009) Sectoral R&D intensity and exchange rate volatility: a panel study for OECD countries: Kiel Working Paper Number 1531.

Malerba, F. and Orsenigo, L. (1993) Technological regimes and firm behavior. *Industrial and Corporate Change* 2(1): 45–71.

Malerba, F. and Orsenigo, L. (1995) Schumpeterian patterns of innovation. *Cambridge Journal of Economics* 19(1): 47–65.

Mansfield, E. (1968) *Industrial Research and Technological Innovation: An Econometric Analysis.* New York: Norton.

Marsili, O. and Salter, A. (2006) The dark matter of innovation: design and innovative performance in Dutch manufacturing. *Technology Analysis & Strategic Management* 18(5): 515–534.

McCann, P. (2007a) Observational equivalence? Regional studies and regional science. *Regional Studies* 41(9): 1209–1222.

McCann, P. (2007b) Sketching out a model of innovation, face-to-face interaction and economic geography. *Spatial Economic Analysis* 2: 117–134.

McCann, P. (2009) Globalisation, multinationals and the BRIICS countries. In R. Lattimore, and R. Safadi (eds.), *Globalisation and Emerging Economies.* Paris: OECD.

McCann, P. and Acs, Z.J. (2010) Globalisation: Countries, cities and multinationals. *Regional Studies* 45(1): 17–32.

McCann, P., Poot, J. and Sanderson, L. (2010) Migration, relationship capital and international travel: theory and evidence. *Journal of Economic Geography* 10(3): 361–387.

Meyer-Krahmer, F. (1984) Recent results in measuring innovation output. *Research Policy* 13: 175–182.

Mol, M.J. and Birkinshaw, J. (2009) The sources of management innovation: when firms introduce new management practices. *Journal of Business Research* 62: 1269–1280.

Morgan, K. (1997) The learning region: institutions, innovation and regional renewal. *Regional Studies* 31(5): 491–503.

Munari, F., Oriani, R. and Sobrero, M. (2010) The effects of owner identity and external governance systems on R&D investments: a study of Western European firms. *Research Policy* 39(8): 1093–1104.

Myers, S. and Marquis, D.G. (1969) *Successful Industrial Innovation: A Study of Factors Underlying Innovation in Selected Firms* (pp. 69–17). Washington: NSF.

Nelson, R.R. (eds) (1993). *National Innovation Systems: A Comparative Analysis.* New York: Oxford University Press.

OECD (1968) Gaps in technology. General Report, Paris.

OECD (2003) *Frascati Manual 2002: Proposed Standard Practice for Surveys on Research and Experimental Development.* Paris: OECD.

OECD (2005) *Oslo Manual: Guidelines for Collecting and Interpreting Innovation Data,* 3rd edn. Paris: OECD.

Okada, Y. (2004) R&D and productivity in Japanese manufacturing industries. NBER Working Paper 11540.

Ortega-Argilés, R. and Brandsma, A. (2010) EU-US differences in the size of R&D intensive firms: do they explain the overall R&D intensity gap? *Science and Public Policy* 37(6): 429–441.

Ortega-Argilés, R., Moreno, R. and Suriñach, J. (2005) Ownership structure and innovation: is there a real link? *Annals of Regional Science* 39(4): 637–662.

Ortega-Argilés, R., Vivarelli, M. and Voigt, P. (2009) R&D in SMEs: a paradox? *Small Business Economics* 33(1): 3–11.

Panne, G. v. d. and Beers, C. v. (2006) On the Marshall-Jacobs controversy: it takes two to tango. *Industrial and Corporate Change* 15(5): 877–890.

Pavitt, K. (1984) Sectoral patterns of technical change: towards a taxonomy and a theory. *Research Policy* 13: 343–373.

Pavitt, K., Robson, M. and Townsend, J. (1987) The size distribution of innovation firms in the UK: 1945–1983. *The Journal of Industrial Economics* 35(3): 297–326.

Pavitt, K. and Wald, S. (1971) *The Conditions for Success in the Technological Innovation.* Paris: OECD.

Pekovic, S. and Galia, F. (2009) From quality to innovation: evidence from two French employer survey. *Technovation* 29(12): 829–842.

Piore, M.J. and Sabel, C.F. (1984) *The Second Industrial Divide.* New York: Basic Books.

Porter, M.E. (1980) *Competitive Strategy.* New York: Free Press.

Porter, M.E. (1985) *Competitive Advantage.* New York: Free Press.

Porter, M.E. (ed.) (1986) *Competition in Global Industries.* Boston: Harvard Business School Press.

Porter, M.E. (1990) *The Competitive Advantage of Nations.* London: Macmillan.

Putnam, R.D. (1993) *Making Democracy Work: Civic Traditions in Modern Italy.* Princeton, NJ: Princeton University Press.

Raymond, W., Mohnen, P., Palm, F. and Loeff, S.S.v.d. (2009) Innovative sales, R&D and total innovation expenditures: panel evidence on their dynamics. Working Papers 2009s-29, CIRANO.

Rochford, L. and Rudelius, W. (1992) How involving more functional areas within a firm affects the new product process. *Journal of Product Innovation Management* 9(4): 287–299.

Romer, P.M. (1990) Endogenous technological change. *Journal of Political Economy* 98(5): 71–102.

Rothwell, R. (1992) Successful industrial innovation: critical factors for the 1990s. *R&D Management* 22(3): 221–239.

Sadowski, B.M. and Sadowski-Rasters, G. (2006) On the innovativeness of foreign affiliates: evidence from companies in The Netherlands. *Research Policy* 35: 447–462.

Saliola, F. and Zanfei, A. (2009) Multinational firms, global value chains and the organization of knowledge transfer. *Research Policy* 38: 369–381.

Santamaria, L., Nieto, M.J. and Barge-Gil, A. (2009) Beyond formal R&D: taking advantage of other sources of innovation in low- and medium-technology industries. *Research Policy* 38: 507–517.

Scellato, G. (2006) Patents, firm size and financial constraints: an empirical analysis for a panel of Italian manufacturing firms. *Cambridge Journal of Economics* 31: 55–76.

Scherer, F.M. (1965) Firm size, market structure, opportunity, and the output of patent inventions. *The American Economic Review* 55(5): 1097–1125.

Schmiedeberg, C. (2008) Complementarities of innovation activities: an empirical analysis of the German manufacturing sector. *Research Policy* 37: 1492–1503.

Schmookler, J. (1950) The interpretation of patent statistics. *Journal of the Patent Office Society* 32(2): 123–146.

Schmookler, J. (1953) Patent application statistics as an index of inventive activity. *Journal of the Patent Office Society* 35(7): 539–550.

Schmookler, J. (1954) The level of inventive activity. *Review of Economics and Statistics,* 36(2): 183–190.

Schumpeter, J.A. (1934) *The Theory of Economic Development.* Cambridge, MA: Harvard University Press.

Schumpeter, J.A. (1939) *Business Cycles* (Vol. 1). New York: McGraw-Hill.

Schumpeter, J.A. (1942) *Capitalism, Socialism and Democracy.* New York: Harper and Row.

Scotchmer, S. (2004) *Innovations and Incentives.* Cambridge, MA: MIT Press.

Sedgley, N. and Elmslie, B. (2004) The geographic concentration of knowledge: scale, agglomeration, and congestion in innovation across U.S. States. *International Regional Science Review* 27: 111–137.

Siegel, S. and Kaemmerer, W. (1978) Measuring the perceived support for innovation in organizations. *Journal of Applied Psychology* 63(5): 553–562.

Simonen, J. and McCann, P. (2008) Firm innovation: The influence of R&D cooperation and the geography of human capital inputs. *Journal of Urban Economics* 64(1): 146–154.

Simonen, J. and McCann, P. (2010) Knowledge transfers and innovation: The role of labour markets and R&D cooperation between agents and institutions. *Papers in Regional Science* 89(2): 295–309.

Solow, R.M. (1957) Technical changes and the aggregate production function. *The Review of Economics and Statistics* 39(3): 312–320.

Sorensen, J.B. and Stuart, T.E. (2000) Aging, obsolescence, and organizational innovation. *Administrative Science Quarterly* 45(1): 81–112.

Souitaris, V. (2002) Technological trajectories as moderators of firm-level determinants of innovation. *Research Policy* 31: 877–898.

Srholec, M. (2010) A multilevel approach to geography of innovation. *Regional Studies* 44, forthcoming.

Sternberg, R. (1996) Government R&D expenditure and space: empirical evidence from five advanced industrial economies. *Research Policy* 25(5): 741–758.

Stock, G.N., Greis, N.P. and Fischer, W.A. (2001) Absorptive capacity and new product development. *Journal of High Technology Management Research* 12: 77–91.

Swan, T.B. (1956) Economic growth and capital accumulation. *Economic Record* 32(63): 334–361.

Swan, J.A. and Newell, S. (1995) The role of professional associations in technology diffusion. *Organisation Studies* 16: 846–873.

Swann, G.M.P. (2009) *The Economics of Innovation: An Introduction.* Chetenham: Edward Elgar

Tether, B.S. (1998) Small and large firms: sources of unequal innovations? *Research Policy* 27(7): 725–745.

Tether, B.S. Smith, I.J. Thwaites, A.T. (1997) Smaller enterprises and innovation in the UK: The SPRU innovations database revisited. *Research Policy* 26: 19–32.

Tingvall, P.G. and Poldahl, A. (2006) Is there really an inverted U-shape relation between competition and innovation? *Economics of Innovation and New Technology* 15(2): 101–118.

Todtling, F., Lehner, P. and Kaufmann, A. (2009) Do different types of innovation rely on specific kinds of knowledge interactions? *Technovation* 29: 59–71.

Tsai, K.-H. (2009) Collaborative networks and product innovation performance: toward a contingency perspective. *Research Policy* 38: 765–778.

Tsai, K.-H. and Hsieh, M.-H. (2009) How different types of partners influence innovative product sales: does technological capacity matter? *Journal of Business Research* 62(12): 1321–1328.

Tsai, K.-H. and Wang, J.-C. (2009) External technology sourcing and innovation performance in LMT sectors: an analysis based on the Taiwanese Technological Innovation Survey. *Research Policy* 38: 518–526.

Veugelers, R. and Cassiman, B. (1999) Make and buy in innovation strategies: evidence from Belgian manufacturing firms. *Research Policy* 28: 63–80.

Weterings, A. and Boschma, R. (2009) Does spatial proximity to customers matter for innovative performance? Evidence from the Dutch software sector. *Research Policy* 38: 746–755.

Zhang, J., Hoenig, S., Benedetto, A.D., Lancioni, R.A. and Phatak, A. (2009) What contributes to the enhanced use of customer, competition and technology knowledge for product innovation performance? A survey of multinational industrial companies' subsidiaries operating in China. *Industrial Marketing Management* 38: 207–218.

5

KNOWLEDGE DYNAMICS, STRUCTURAL CHANGE AND THE GEOGRAPHY OF BUSINESS SERVICES

Tommaso Ciarli, Valentina Meliciani and Maria Savona

1. Introduction

Economic progress has been associated widely with the increasing volume and complexity of knowledge in economies and societies (Machlup, 1980; Aghion and Howitt, 1992; Metcalfe *et al.*, 2006). Some contributions have attempted to unpack the concept and measurement of knowledge, especially with respect to technological progress, distinguishing between scientific and technological knowledge (Metcalfe, 2002), codified and tacit knowledge (Cowan and Foray, 2000; Foray, 2006) and learning processes required to acquire the know-how and know-what (Lundvall and Johnson, 1994; Archibugi and Lundvall, 2001; Jensen *et al.*, 2007) related to invention and innovation. Knowledge has been studied from the perspective of cognitive studies nested in evolutionary economics (Nelson and Nelson, 2002) to articulate the links between individual know-how and learning, and cultural systematized know-how known as 'technology'. We are not concerned here with the epistemological debates around the concept of knowledge, that is beyond the scope of this chapter. Our intention is to re-focus the 'knowledge economy' debate – associated with the emergence of services – in terms of its economic and historical roots, by examining the sectoral and spatial concentration of knowledge activities. The motivation for this task lies in the excitement over building a 'Knowledge-based' Europe which increasingly has come to dominate the policy lexicon. We believe that anchoring this debate through a revision of the theoretical roots of knowledge, its evolution and its influence on the emergence of knowledge-intensive services will be useful input to policy discourse (Godin, 2006).

The aim of this chapter, therefore, is to provide a selected review of the role of knowledge and technological progress as a determinant of the sectoral and spatial concentration of economic activities. To do this, we explore how the role of knowledge has evolved in relation to: (i) the shift in the relative importance of science and technology in the economy;

Corresponding author: SPRU, Science and Technology Policy Research, Freeman Centre, University of Sussex, Falmer, Brighton, BN1 9QE. E-mail: M.Savona@sussex.ac.uk

Innovation, Entrepreneurship, Geography and Growth, First Edition.
Edited by Philip McCann and Les Oxley. Chapters © 2013 The Authors.
Book compilation © 2013 Blackwell Publishing Ltd. Published 2013 by Blackwell Publishing Ltd.

(ii) the resulting change in the composition of sectors and the rise of business services (BS); (iii) the spatial concentration of BS as an outcome of the increasing volume and complexity of knowledge and the need to manage it through spatial proximity.

Recalling the fundamental distinction between *episteme* and *techne* proposed by Mokyr (2002), and in line with the history of technology perspective, we would argue that the contemporary increased complexity and size of bodies of knowledge have brought about a shift in the relative importance between scientific knowledge and technology, accompanied by dramatically increased access to – and standardization of – epistemic knowledge afforded by Information and Communication Technologies (ICTs), and continuously increasing specialization in narrowly based expertise (see also Witt, 2010). Sectoral structural change in history can therefore be interpreted as the growing necessity to deal with an ever-increasing volume of knowledge. Spatial agglomeration of economic activities has resulted from this process of increased partitioning of knowledge in disciplines and specialties, which has required specialized functions and processes to cope with increasingly complex production activities.

We revisit the historical debate around the growth and economic impact of services to show that the counterpositioning of different views – neo-industrialist 'pessimist' versus post-industrialist 'optimist' – is the outcome of the respective concern for whether physical capital accumulation or increasing knowledge-intensive activities should be the driver of growth (see for instance Evangelista, 1999). Following a review and empirical examination of the main determinants of growth in BS, we link them to the spatial concentration of services, by revisiting the Marshallian agglomeration economies argument focusing especially on the presence of Hirschmanian linkages.

Section 2 reviews the theoretical and historical perspectives linking the evolution of knowledge from a technological perspective, to sectoral structural change, reprising some historical accounts from the British Industrial Revolution. Section 3 refers to the 'capital versus knowledge' debate in relation to the growth of services within a historical perspective, and proposes an interpretation of this growth linked to intermediate demand, supported by some empirical evidence. Section 4 presents an argument, in the spirit of Marshallian agglomeration economies, for knowledge dynamics and structural change to be considered from the perspective of spatial concentration of BS. This emphasizes the specific role of backward and forward linkages put forward by Hirschmann (1958) and shows some evidence of the concurrent role of intermediate demand and agglomeration economies in determining the spatial concentration of BS. Section 5 concludes.

2. Knowledge, Technology and Structural Change

Industrial revolutions are characterized by radical changes to knowledge, technology and the economic structure (Kuznets, 1973; von Tunzelmann, 1995; Abramovitz and David, 2001). We can observe far-reaching advances in useful knowledge (Rosenberg, 1974) and fundamental changes in the relationship between knowledge and technologies – i.e. prescriptive and procedural knowledge – (Mokyr, 2009). At the same time, we have witnessed a reorganization of production with the advent of the factory system and the concentration of capital (von Tunzelmann, 1995), changes in industrial relations, wages (Lazonick, 1981) and the distribution of income (Lindert, 1994), all of which have been accompanied by changes in institutions (Berg and Bruland, 1998), the emergence of new social and economic classes (McCloskey, 2009) and the emergence of demand for and supply of new final goods (Berg, 2002).

Some of these structural changes have been integrated in growth theories (Mokyr and Voth, 2010) that focus variously on the relations between economic power, political power and technological change (Acemoglu *et al.,* 2005; Acemoglu and Robinson, 2006), on the institutional determinants of markets and the division of labour (Greif, 2006), on transitions in population growth and human capital (Galor, 2010) and on the relations between the organization of production, distribution of wages and demand patterns (Ciarli *et al.*, 2010; Ciarli and Lorentz, 2010).

Competing theories introduce the broader concept of shifting technological paradigms, 'in some respects metaphors of the interplay between continuity and ruptures in the process of incorporation of knowledge and technology into industrial growth' (Dosi, 1982, p. 161). Shifting paradigms imply changes in a number of dimensions, including technology – a set of pieces of knowledge, accompanied by social struggles and shifts in prices and distribution shares – which define long-term trajectories of technological progress. Freeman and Perez (1988), in their interpretation of long economic waves and business cycles, argue that a shift in a technol-economic paradigm associated with an industrial revolution involves, among other things, new firm organizations, different skills compositions, product mixes, patterns of consumption and changes in the location of investment.[1] Thus, there is an intrinsic link between knowledge advances and their realization in economic activities which shape the industrial structure.

A wealth of contributions in economic history investigate why the industrial revolution occurred in one specific part of the world, despite the technological advances (inventions and new techniques) that had occurred in several other world regions. It has been argued, in particular, that the shift in the technological paradigm accompanying the first industrial revolution in Britain brought about dramatic changes in the way new knowledge emerged, was selected, stored and applied to techniques and production, concentrated in specific regions of the world before later diffusing more widely. There is an intrinsic link between advances in knowledge and the specific locations in which they translate into economic activity (Mokyr, 2007b, 2002; Allen, 2011).

Looking back, we can identify aspects of the interactions between knowledge, technology and structural change. Technology is one form of knowledge (Johnson, 2005), and the relationship between knowledge and techniques is key to understanding the paradigm shifts that accompany industrial revolutions (Mokyr, 2002).[2] Technological change leads to structural changes that include a new organization of production – division of labour, new workforce compositions and new markets and institutions. The channels through which the process takes place are constituted by final and intermediate demand for technological knowledge that require knowledge specialization and storage (Witt and Zellner, 2009; Mokyr, 2010), and ever-increasing specialization in narrowly based expertise (see also Witt, 2010). Intermediate demand for specialized knowledge functions explains other types of structural change, including that which led to the growth of BS, as discussed in this chapter.

2.1 *Knowledge and Technology*

The literature distinguishes between exogenous and endogenous interpretations of technological change (Mokyr, 2010). 'Internalists' refer mainly to endogenous change in which the external environment acts as a selection device. 'Externalists' refer mainly to responses induced by (economic) incentives such as needs or factor prices. The social construction of technology offers a different view, which tends to overlook the endogenous process and focuses on the relations among the actors in the economy who carry and transfer knowledge, culture and specific interests, rather than simply reacting to economic incentives (Law, 1986).

A comprehensive long-run theory of knowledge and technology evolution is proposed by Mokyr (2010), and related works (Mokyr, 2000, 2002, 2007a, 1998). Mokyr (2002, p. 116), in his historical account of the British Industrial Revolution, argues that 'The productivity and growth implications of revolutions in knowledge are at the core of much of the literature in the economics of technological change and productivity measurement. Oddly however, economists have not gotten into the black box of knowledge evolution in the past (with the notable exception of Nelson, Schrerer and Rosenberg). [...] Traditional measures of growth and productivity underestimate the rate of progress considerably as they are unable to measure the impact of the emergence of new goods and services and even needs'. Central to Mokyr's argument is that knowledge dynamics proceeds alongside technical progress. The overall 'useful' knowledge of a system, Ω – propositional knowledge, or *episteme*, is defined as the union of the 'useful' knowledge of all the individuals in society. Hence, an increase in knowledge may be defined as a discovery by one individual in society, of a property of nature, that can be used to improve societal welfare.[3] Useful knowledge maps onto a set of 'feasible techniques', λ – prescriptive knowledge, or *techne*. This defines what society could do, but not necessarily what it is doing because different techniques can be invented within the same Ω.

Knowledge dynamics arise first through the selection of techniques responding to incentives, user needs and production processes. The selection of techniques, in turn, affects shifts in the direction of knowledge. Selection does not imply that the knowledge is lost – although it may mean that the knowledge becomes outdated and is labelled as inaccurate. This reflects the need for devices for storing the base of knowledge, and a language that allows assessment and replication of a specific knowledge–technique relation.[4] Second, according to Mokyr, a selection mechanism operates on the knowledge set, but this is based on scientific and social persuasion.[5]

In referring to the first industrial revolution, Mokyr (2009) explains the dramatic change in the rate of invention and technological change, particularly in Britain, through the relationship between *episteme* and *techne*, that is, the interaction between micro-inventions – due to artisans' practice – and macro-advances in knowledge, which, since the enlightenment, have focused on practical problems (see also Ziman, 1976). Limitations in the set of knowledge would explain, for example, why it took nearly 200 years of wood scarcity to achieve machines that used coal in Britain (Rosenberg, 1974).[6]

A competing explanation for the changes in knowledge and technologies is economic incentives, including demand for intermediate inputs that increase production efficiency and final demand for goods that increase well-being (Schmookler, 1966). Changes in consumer needs and demand provide producers with a market for ideas, and markets emerge for potential new commodities and services. Invention provides the inventor and initial supplier with a monopolistic market until other suppliers manage to imitate and produce the same commodity/service. However, according to Schmookler, the actual change in knowledge is relatively exogenous since the inventions can occur only within an innovation possibility curve (Ahmad, 1966).

Relative factor costs act as an incentive to search for new production techniques. In the attempt to find cheaper ways to produce a good, producers will find techniques that enable savings on costly inputs (Hicks, 1932). This is how Allen (2009) explains the long-term emergence of technological innovations. In the context of the first industrial revolution, it paid to invent new technologies (and to advance knowledge) because of the relative high costs of labour, coal and capital, and the living standards high in Britain compared to competing countries. Higher wages with respect to the rest of the world, due to the internalization and sectoral specialization, required the overall costs of production to be lowered by saving on labour.[7] High wages with respect to the minimum living standard wage, coupled with only marginal differences in the price of goods with the rest of Europe, increased the market for new 'luxury' goods. Also, the high wage/energy ratio, due mainly to the low price of energy in Britain, suggested that energy-intensive technologies were more profitable than labour-intensive technologies. Finally, the high relative cost of labour with respect to the cost of renting capital due mainly to the high nominal wages induced the search for capital-intensive production processes.[8] Allen uses similar arguments to explain why technologies that were already invented – and for which the cost of invention had been internalized – were adopted only after some decades in Europe: given the factor costs in other European countries, the price of the new capital-intensive technologies was too high to be profitable. However, incremental innovations, via learning by using the new machines, made their later use profitable in other countries.

The source of technological change, then, is demand for an invention rather than a change in scientific research or a closer link between the scientist and the craftsman, induced by lower cost of access to knowledge. Demand is driven first by the usefulness of the invention, then through some sort of 'serendipity' the invention required to reduce the cost of production paves the way to a scientific and technological revolution.

Since scientific knowledge and invention run in parallel, similar reasoning can be applied to the growth in scientific knowledge. According to Allen, although some innovations were not initially linked directly to science, they became linked at a later stage or generated spinoffs that induced the innovation at the basis of the industrial revolution.[9]

2.2 *Technology and Structural Change*

Changes in knowledge and technology play an important role in the economic structure. The accumulation of knowledge in producers and buyers continuously changes the environment, the transactions and the possible forms of organizing production, requiring new institutions (Metcalfe, 2002).

The technology-induced structural changes that have accompanied the industrial revolutions fall into three groups of related dimensions, organization of production, sectoral composition and income classes, each of which is associated with a certain evolution of knowledge – that is, knowledge accumulation and complexification, knowledge standardization, knowledge specialization and fragmentation.

For instance, the transition to modern growth, which was characterized also by the closer interaction between scientific knowledge and techniques, is marked by transport technologies including the high pressure steam engine, mechanization and mass production and the application of thermodynamics to electricity and communication (Mokyr, 2010). Mechanization was crucial for standardizing production and substituting for skilled labour. It had the effect of reinforcing a selected set of knowledge and techniques and strengthening specific knowledge paradigms. It reduced the need for craft techniques, knowledge and practices, which were substituted by a standardized knowledge set. Both knowledge and techniques become more standardized, and labour practices subject to tighter controls.[10]

Knowledge also became more specialized, with individuals forced to focus on specific aspects of the knowledge set. The specialization of knowledge and the mechanization of production gave way to increased division of labour and transactions among intermediate sectors, which altered the sectoral composition of the economy. Finally, the factory system induced concentration in the ownership of capital, which, together with the sectoral and skill division of labour, led to the emergence of different income classes, and demand for different goods and services.

During the second industrial revolution technical progress 'rested as much on industry-based science than on science-based industry' (Mokyr, 2002), whereas the third industrial revolution saw the establishment of directed, systematized and organized efforts to create new knowledge in *ad hoc* research and development (R&D) departments. The revolution in the cross-fertilizing dynamics of propositional and prescriptive knowledge was driven by ICTs – and earlier by the printing press, which granted unprecedented access to the epistemic knowledge base at dramatically lower cost (Cowan and Foray, 2000; Foray, 2006). The cost of accessing knowledge was reduced further by its codification. This led to an increase in the volume of knowledge that were required to be managed for its economic use (von Tunzelmann, 1995; Witt, 2009) and the consequences for the division of labour, specialization and structural changes in the sectoral composition of economies. This is discussed in more length in the next section.

3. Structural Change and the Raise of (Knowledge-Intensive) BS

The argument proposed earlier – of the changing nature and size of knowledge over time and the consequent evolution of the sectoral division of labour – underpins our analysis of one of the most relevant cases of structural change: the growth of services and especially BS. Awareness of a possible link between knowledge dynamics and the growth of services has emerged slowly, and is rarely considered within the framework of the history of technology (see for instance Lee, 1994). The literature on services has developed in parallel with the evolving theory of value and is characterized by shifting concerns. Pre-occupation about the intangibility of services and the erosion of capital accumulation following tertiarization has translated into over-optimism about their knowledge content. The lack of any reference to services in the history of technology has brought about these radical shifts in the way services are regarded, from being a 'threat' leading to de-industrialization (Kaldor, 1966) to becoming a mean of leveraging knowledge provision and diffusion. The latter view emerged from the rhetoric surrounding the 'New Economy' (for a review see Beyers, 2002) and, more specifically, the 'Knowledge Economy' (Marrano *et al.*, 2009).[11] These categories are often associated with Knowledge Intensive Business Services (KIBS) and the widespread diffusion of ICTs.

We briefly review the historical debate around the growth of services and then try to unpack the foundations of overused categories, such as the 'Knowledge Economy', and identify two main, interrelated views on growth in BS. The first view relates to the increasing importance of intermediate demand for service functions as an outcome of the knowledge-related division of labour across sectors described earlier (see also Witt, 2009). The second is related to the role of technology – particularly ICTs – in the processes of knowledge complexification on the one hand, and knowledge standardization on the other, which have favoured demand for specialized functions.

3.1 *'Much Ado About Services': From the Classical Tradition of Unproductive Hands to the Cost Disease*

The somewhat controversial debate around the determinants and impact of the growth in services dates back certainly to the 1930s, although historians, basing their claims on historical data, assert that its roots are much older (see for instance Lee, 1994). The controversy around services over time has pitted optimistic advocates of the *post-industrial era* (Fourastié, 1949; Bell, 1976) against sceptical *neo-industrialists* (Baumol, 1967; Fuchs, 1968; Gershuny, 1978; Cohen and Zysman, 1987). The debate has lost some of its spark in recent years, but has not reached any sort of agreement despite the availability of better longitudinal data on services. In addition, the role of technical change and knowledge evolution has entered the debate, potentially providing support for both sides. On the one hand, service sectors are excluded from the race for technical progress and – at best – are passive adopters of technology from elsewhere. On the other hand, services represent the main engine of the new knowledge-based economy. The historical roots of this debate can be found in the classical tradition of the theory of value and its interesting developments, which are briefly sketched later.[12]

Before the concept of knowledge began diffusing through the academic and policy lexicon, the main concern around the growth of services was the intangibility of output and the quasi-absence of capital intensity, which were seen as responsible for the productivity gap between manufacturing and services and which sparked a literature pre-occupied with the threat of 'deindustrialisation' (Kaldor, 1966). This stream of 'neo-industrialist' literature (Delaunay and Gadrey, 1992) is rooted in the earliest speculation about the role of services, the *classical tradition*, and reached maturity with Baumol's and Fuchs's attempts to interpret the causes of the productivity slowdown that occurred in the advanced countries, relative to the early post-World War II period (Baumol and Bowen 1966; Baumol, 1967; Fuchs, 1977, 1968; Baumol, *et al.,* 1989).

Adam Smith – and later the classical theory of value – viewed the spread of (public) services as a 'threat' to the accumulation of capital, industry and the wealth of nations, which was in contrast to the mercantilist view.[13]

'Unproductive labour adds to the value of nothing. It does not fix or realize itself in any particular subject or vendible commodity. His services generally perish in the very instant of their performance, and seldom leave any trace of value behind them, for which an equal quantity of services could afterwards be procured' (Smith, 1776, Book II, opening paragraph of Ch. III). Productive labour, such as wage–labour, on the other hand, is substantiated in a physical output and generates profit on the capital investments to which it is applied, therefore contributing to capital accumulation. A crucial distinction within the classical theory of value is whether this immaterial labour belongs to the commercial or the industrial sphere.[14]

Prophecies of erosion of capital accumulation due to the increasing presence of *unproductive hands* – which Smith identifies as the *men of speculation* despite some, such as protection, security and defence, being *honourable, useful and necessary* – are the forerunners of the neo-industrialist view. Smithian *unproductive hands* found an echo in Baumol's (Baumol and Bowen, 1966) *cost disease of a string-quartet performance*. The concept of *cost disease* has remained implacably associated with the productivity performance of service industries, since the second generation debate on the nature of services growth and its consequences on productivity slowdown in the 1960s sparked by Baumol (Baumol and Bowen,

1966).[15] The concept was extended by Baumol first in a very influential chapter (Baumol, 1967), and then in further contributions (Baumol *et al.,* 1985, 1989; Baumol, 2001).

Over time, the conceptual categories characterizing services have become blurred, and seen as a single (black!) box of misfortune: immateriality of output implies lack of capital intensity, which was considered synonymous with technology stagnancy. This has been seen by some as limiting technical progress which translates into low productivity, although measurement issues are contentious.[16] This quickly led scholars to regard tertiarization as responsible for the slowdown in aggregate productivity and the systematic increase in costs and prices in the advanced economies.

The reversal of this process of demonization in the current literature is sometimes difficult to understand. How have services been rescued from representations as the technology and productivity laggard? Which segments of services have benefited from this upturn? The Baumol–Fuchs idea of a *structural burden* of services slowing aggregate labour productivity growth is being challenged empirically (Peneder *et al.,* 2003; Cainelli *et al.,* 2006; Savona and Lorentz, 2006). In what follows we try to understand how this radical shift has been justified conceptually and highlight the important role of knowledge for a particular branch of services.

3.2 *Knowledge Dynamics, Intermediate Demand and KIBS Growth*

As referred to earlier, the rhetoric of the 'Knowledge economy' has reversed the concerns of the classical tradition and the neo–industrialists, and reprised the enthusiasms of the pioneers of the 'post-industrial' society (Clark, 1940; Fisher, 1945; Fourastié, 1949; Bell, 1976). KIBS are perceived as being at the core of the Knowledge economy (Miles *et al.,* 1995; Muller and Zenker, 2001; Muller and Doloreux, 2009), although few contributions go beyond mere definition of KIBS to disentangle – from a conceptual and an empirical perspective – how the alleged contribution of KIBS to the knowledge economy functions from the perspective of the history of technology as described earlier.

There is little consensus on the exact boundaries of KIBS, although they have been defined as *a set of service activities whose use as intermediary inputs affects the quality and efficiency of production activities by complementing or substituting for in-house service functions* (Kox and Rubalcaba, 2007, p. 4). Recent work focuses on what is special about KIBS (Miles *et al.,* 1995; Muller and Zenker, 2001; Muller and Doloreux, 2009). Muller and Doloreux (2009) consider the numerous definitions of KIBS in the literature and identify three fundamental characteristics:

- KIBS rely on professional knowledge, usually measured in terms of labour qualifications and the quality of human capital involved in the transaction between client and provider;
- KIBS either represent primary sources of knowledge or use knowledge to provide intermediate inputs to clients;
- KIBS clients typically are businesses or public organizations rather than final users.

These characteristics support the argument in this work that the growing complexity and volume of knowledge – facilitated in great part by the diffusion of ICTs in the economy – has led to an increasing need for knowledge-specialized functions, especially at the level of private and public organizations. Therefore, the determinants of KIBS growth lie in the interrelated role of intermediate demand and the diffusion of ICTs. Knowledge dynamics in its aspects of structural change, as hinted at in Section 2, has resulted in greater complexity of the organization of manufacturing production and distribution and significant increase in coordination problems, which has increased the services content of many manufactured goods, well beyond the simple 'outsourcing' or 'contracting out' of services (Francois and Woerz, 2007). These processes, since the early 1970s, have increased demand for (KIB) services as intermediate inputs (Francois, 1990; Rowthorn and Ramaswamy, 1999; Guerrieri and Meliciani, 2005; Savona and Lorentz, 2006; Montresor and Vittucci Marzetti, 2011). The use of general and abstract knowledge in innovation opens up the possibility for a division of labour in inventive activity – division of innovative labour, leading to the emergence of a *market for knowledge* and making it possible to disentangle the tacit from the codified components of technological knowledge, with the former being produced by specialized knowledge suppliers and traded through the market (Arora and Gambardella, 1994). In this perspective KIBS can be seen as a dynamic interface between codified and quasi-generic knowledge (produced and stored in universities and R&D laboratories) and tacit knowledge embedded within firms.

ICTs play an important role in enabling the division of innovative labour, thereby favouring the growth of KIBS and associated structural change. On the one hand, KIBS are major players in the ICT sector (as providers of computer and software consultancies); on the other hand, ICTs have increased the stockability and transportability of information, releasing it from some time-spatial indivisibilities and constraints characterizing the production, storage and transmission of information and codified knowledge. This process has favoured the emergence of new firms, markets and sectors and is changing the organization/size of existing ones. The increased codification and commoditization of knowledge inputs and outputs promoted a shift from the neo–industrialist to the post-industrialist view. BS now are perceived mainly as providers and diffusers of knowledge, contributing positively to aggregate labour productivity and economic growth (Kox and Rubalcaba, 2007). Therefore, the diffusion of ICTs and the growth of KIBS can be understood as interdependent processes reshaping the structure of knowledge flows and the technological interdependences in the economy with *knowledge-intensive business services (...) replacing the manufacturing sector (...) as the providers of strategic inputs to the rest of the system* (Antonelli, 1998, p. 192).

We can examine this paradigmatic change based on Input–Output (I/O) data, as in Guerrieri and Meliciani (2005),[17] and extending the analysis to cover a longer period in order to compare the long-term role of intermediate and final demand in the rise of manufacturing and in two groups of service sectors: Financial, Communication and Business services (FCB), and other services.[18]

Table 1 presents the stylized facts in the literature: (i) services have gained share at the expense of the manufacturing sector; (ii) growth in FCB services has been much more marked than growth in other services; (iii) shares of FCB services in intermediate demand have especially increased; (iv) in 2005 the share of FCB services in total intermediate demand equals that in all manufacturing sectors (about 30%). These trends are confirmed for both periods (although they are more marked in earlier time span) and in all the countries considered.[19]

If intermediate demand following the new, knowledge-related division of labour is the main driver of this structural change, then it is likely that it has played a major role in the location of these sectors. We next investigate the factors behind the spatial concentration of BS and examine the extent to which this depends on the location of client industries and the implications in relation to knowledge concentration/diffusion.

Table 1. Share of FCB Services of Intermediate, Final Demand and Gross Output.

Shares	OECD I/O Tables		Eurostat I/O tables	
	Share mid-70s	Share 1990	Share 1995	Share 2005
Man ID	0.56	0.49	0.37	0.32
Man FD	0.42	0.41	0.33	0.33
Man GO	0.41	0.37	0.34	0.33
FCB ID	0.14	0.23	0.27	0.32
FCB FD	0.10	0.12	0.13	0.15
FCB GO	0.13	0.19	0.19	0.22
Other ser ID	0.13	0.14	0.17	0.18
Other ser FD	0.22	0.22	0.29	0.30
Other ser GO	0.21	0.22	0.24	0.25

Notes: Man = manufacturing; ser = services; ID = Intermediate Demand; FD = Final Demand; GO = Gross Output

4. Knowledge Dynamics and Spatial Agglomeration of BS

Despite the emergence of ICTs, which has favoured information, standardization and eased the access to and transferability of knowledge, we argue and show empirically that proximity between BS and its clients still matters. We extend the analysis of knowledge dynamics and structural change to the spatial concentration of BS. Few contributions address knowledge concentration in relation to service specialization (Muller and Zenker, 2001; Raspe and Van Oort, 2006; Doloreux and Shearmur, 2011), and no studies include the specific role of intermediate demand as an explicit explanatory factor. We reprise the argument put forward by Meliciani and Savona (2011), isolating the specific aspects of agglomeration economies that explain the location patterns of BS. Beyond classical localization and urbanization externalities, and in line with the arguments proposed earlier, we suggest that BS localize on the basis of existing regional sectoral specialization, and the existence of backward and forward linkages, *à la* Hirschmann (1958).

4.1 *Urbanisation Externalities and Knowledge Density*

Marshall (1920) in his seminal contribution identified the main determinants of spatial concentration of economic activities (for a historical review see McCann and van Oort, 2009). These are imputable first and foremost to the well-known *industrial atmosphere*, that is, an environment conducive to knowledge spillovers among the actors. Also, a labour market able to provide a reservoir of specialist skills is a necessary condition for localization decisions. Finally, and interestingly, economic activities tend to be concentrated in locations where substantial presence of local consumers and supplier markets is ensured.

   In the case of services, there are two factors in the spirit of Marshallian agglomeration sources, which would seem to apply to localization patterns. The first is related to *urbanization externalities*, which are independent of the sectoral structure, refer to the urban and population density and facilitate knowledge spillovers (Glaeser *et al.*, 1992; Henderson *et al.*, 1995; Glaeser, 1999). The second is the presence of clients and supplier markets, described by Hirschmann (1958) as the existence of sectoral backward and forward linkages.

Oort *et al.* (2009) make the case for analysis of the geographic, dynamic and sectoral context-dependency aspects in order to understand knowledge dynamics. Leaning towards more sectoral-specific analyses, Coombes (2000) and Van Oort (2007) find that localization externalities are positively related to services employment growth and more than to employment growth in other sectors, arguing that service sectors benefit more from concentration than other economic activities do.

Large urban areas have been found to be attractors of BS (Jacobs, 1969; Duranton and Puga, 2005). Duranton and Puga (2005) find that functional specialization in BS is driven by multinational firms, which choose to locate their headquarters functions in large urban regions. Such a location makes it possible for the headquarters to buy inputs locally from specialized business service firms in areas such as R&D, marketing, financing, law, exporting, logistics, etc. Also, the location of the headquarters favours the co-location of specialized intermediate BS firms from which the headquarters can buy locally when choosing to outsource various services. This is in line with the argument put forward in the previous sections that knowledge dynamics are shaped by the need to manage a stock of knowledge growing in complexity and size, which requires an increasing specialization in activities dealing with particular parts of this knowledge. Knowledge seems to flow more easily if spatial and sectoral contiguity are relatively high.

A further inducement for knowledge-intensive services to locate in regions with large urban areas is their need for skilled labour and human capital, both of which tend to be concentrated in cities (Glaeser, 1999; Faggian and McCann, 2009). Urbanization externalities are linked also to the more intensive access to ICTs in urban areas and the availability of technology specialist skills (Acs *et al.*, 2002; Raspe and Van Oort, 2006; Doloreux and Shearmur, 2011).

The concentration of BS in large urban areas is a well-established, empirical stylized fact: Table 2 presents a list of the European regions specialized in the group of BS identified in Meliciani and Savona (2011), including R&D, computer and related services, and other business sectors, in 2005.[20]

In line with the urbanization literature, many of the regions with the highest values are regions where capital cities are located (Glaeser *et al.*, 1992; Glaeser, 1999). This applies to high-income countries and also to Spain, Portugal, Greece and some new entrant eastern European countries. If we exclude regions with capital cities, there appear to be important *country effects* in the spatial map of specialization in BS. In fact all the Dutch regions and the majority of United Kingdom and German regions appear to be highly specialized in these branches. However, none of the regions in new entrant countries, and (with the exception of the regions already mentioned that are home to capital cities) Portugal, Greece, Norway shows a comparative advantage in BS. Regions in Spain, France and Italy show a more variable pattern although on average they are not specialized in BS. The geography of BS that emerges from Table 2 confirms the findings in Wood (2006) that KIBS tend to be more clustered in the countries of southern Europe (and mainly in cities) and more dispersed in northern countries where they are present in cities but also in regions where there are manufacturing and service user sectors. This applies especially to Germany where there is a virtuous co-location of high-tech manufacturing and BS. This supports the conjecture that – in the case of BS – an important dimension of agglomeration economies responsible for their location is linked to the structure of intermediate demand and, in particular, to region-specific Hirschmann linkages, which are addressed in the next section.

Table 2.   EU Regional Comparative Advantage in BS.

Region	CA	Region	CA
Inner London	5.81	Flevoland	1.42
Région de Bruxelles-Capitale	3.54	East Anglia	1.38
Comunidad de Madrid	3.14	Dorset and Somerset	1.37
Ile de France	2.98	Oberbayern	1.36
Berkshire, Bucks and Oxfordshire	2.68	East Wales	1.35
Utrecht	2.48	Kent	1.35
Lisboa	2.41	South Yorkshire	1.33
Noord-Holland	2.21	Derbyshire and Nottinghamshire	1.32
Bedfordshire, Hertfordshire	2.19	Limburg (NL)	1.32
Hamburg	2.11	Hannover	1.32
Surrey, East and West Sussex	2.05	Prov. Antwerpen	1.29
Darmstadt	2.03	Mittelfranken	1.27
Rhone-Alpes	1.98	Kassel	1.26
Oslo og Akershus	1.95	Merseyside	1.26
Kozép-Magyarorszàg	1.95	Provence-Alpes-Cote d'Azur	1.26
Hampshire and Isle of Wight	1.95	Liguria	1.25
Wien	1.94	Essex	1.25
Cheshire	1.91	Piemonte	1.24
Zuid-Holland	1.89	Eastern Scotland	1.20
Bremen	1.88	Lancashire	1.20
Bucuresti (SRE 2002)	1.84	Prov. Brabant Wallon	1.20
Greater Manchester	1.79	Pais Vasco	1.19
Lombardia	1.78	Emilia-Romagna	1.18
Gloucestershire, Wiltshire and Bristol/Bath area	1.71	Saarland	1.16
Outer London	1.70	Provincia Autonoma Trento	1.15
Koln	1.69	Valle d'Aosta	1.15
West Midlands	1.67	Friesland (NL)	1.14
Lazio	1.65	North Yorkshire	1.11
Noord-Brabant	1.64	Toscana	1.10
Herefordshire, Worcestershire and Warks	1.64	Friuli-Venezia Giulia	1.09
Karlsruhe	1.62	Devon	1.09
Dusseldorf	1.62	Attiki	1.08
Berlin	1.59	Leipzig	1.07
Prov. Vlaams Brabant	1.59	Tees Valley and Durham	1.06
Bratislavsky kraj	1.59	Mazowieckie	1.06
Leicestershire, Rutland and Northants	1.55	Etela Suomi	1.05
Stuttgart	1.55	Shropshire and Staffordshire	1.05
Gelderland	1.49	Zeeland	1.04
South Western Scotland	1.49	Oberosterreich	1.04
Catalana	1.48	Veneto	1.02
Overijssel	1.48	Detmold	1.02
Northumberland, Tyne and Wear	1.48	Umbria	1.01
West Yorkshire	1.44	Region Autonoma da Madeira (PT)	1.00

Notes: CA = comparative advantage

Table 3. Share of BS on Total Input and Output of Selected Industries, 2005, Av. EU-27.

Sectors	Share on inputs	Share on output
Agriculture and fishing	0.04	0.02
Mining and quarrying	0.09	0.05
Electricity, gas, water, constr.	0.10	0.05
High-tech manufacturing	0.11	0.07
Medium-high-tech manufacturing	0.07	0.05
Medium-low-tech manufacturing	0.05	0.04
Low-tech manufacturing	0.06	0.04
High-tech KIBS	0.27	0.12
KIBS	0.15	0.07
Less KIBS	0.17	0.08
Financial intermediation	0.27	0.12
Non-market services	0.19	0.08

4.2 Backward and Forward Linkages

Hirschmann (1958), in a seminal contribution, reprises Marshall's explicit acknowledgement of consumer and supplier markets as important dimensions of agglomeration economies, and identifies different types of externalities, depending on whether activities are related through backward or forward linkages. Forward linkages imply that certain sectors are concentrated where clients are located; backward linkages relate to the migration of sectors to locations where new or growing sectors that provide them with inputs are located.[21]

We argue that the spatial equivalent of the role of intermediate demand for the growth of BS is given by the presence of forward linkages in the regions where they tend to be concentrated. Location patterns of BS follow and are shaped by prior specialization in sectors which are intensive users of those functions provided by BS that serve the purpose of managing highly complex knowledge. The location of customer industries is particularly relevant since these services typically are supplied to firms through strong supplier user interactions (Muller and Zenker, 2001) and are heavily reliant on geographical proximity. Doloreux and Shearmur (2011) indirectly support this view by arguing that KIBS are a core actor in innovative regions, enhancing the network of collaborations for innovation, which would suggest that KIBS do not only provide a one-directional transfer of specialized information, but are co-producers of knowledge in a process that involves their clients intimately (see also Muller and Doloreux, 2009). The presence of a high density of forward linkages, à la Hirschmann, strengthens the effects of urbanization externalities on regional BS specialization.

But what are the intermediate sectors that make the most use of BS? Are there regularities in the patterns of inter-industry linkages between BS and other manufacturing and service industries? Before examining in depth the spatial evidence supporting our conjectures, we investigate the input–output linkages between BS and other industries by distinguishing user industries according to their knowledge intensity. Table 3 reports the shares of the group of BS.[22]

This evidence shows that: (i) the set of knowledge-intensive services considered here is mostly used by other services sectors; (ii) among these sectors financial intermediation and high tech KIBS (because we exclude within sector use the only remaining high tech KIBS is R&D) are particularly high users of KIBS themselves; (iii) there are no important differences across other services sectors – distinguishing either between knowledge-intensive services and less knowledge-intensive services, or between market and non-market services; (iv) among manufacturing sectors, our group of services is used mostly by high-tech industries; (v) results are similar for both input and output shares with the only exception that the difference in the size of the use between services and manufacturing is more marked when computed in terms of input shares.

Overall, it seems that knowledge-intensive industries tend to feed into each other, which implies that regional specialization of BS might tend to reinforce the processes of knowledge-related polarization and that regions specialized in knowledge-intensive man-ufacturing will tend to be favoured by the localization of KIBS, in a self-reinforcing virtuous circle. The reverse would apply in peripheral regions.

Meliciani and Savona (2011) conducted a spatial econometric analysis of the determinants of specialization in BS taking account of the whole set of intermediate demand, technology, urbanization economies – the determinants of BS specialization mentioned earlier – proxying Hirschmann linkages by intermediate demand from manufacturing and services industries. Later, we extend some of the empirical evidence in Meliciani and Savona (2011) on the spatial correlation of BS specialization and its determinants.

Figures 1– 3 show Moran's scatterplots and report the associated global Moran coeffi-cients respectively for specialization in BS, in manufacturing sectors that are high users of BS and in service sectors that are high users of BS.[23]

All variables are spatially correlated (with a Moran value of, respectively, 0.344, 0.424 and 0.277 – all significant at 1%). In the case of specialization in BS, as shown by the

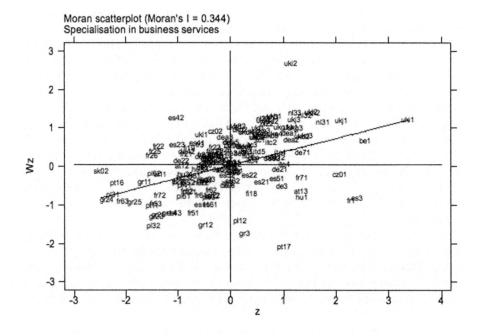

Figure 1. Moran's Scatterplot of Specialization in Business Services.

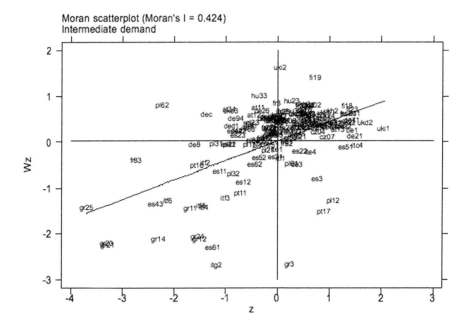

Figure 2. Moran's Scatterplot of Specialization in High-Manufacturing Users of BS.

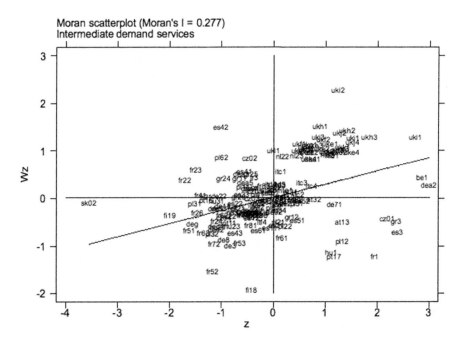

Figure 3. Moran's Scatterplot of Specialization in High Service Users of BS.

Table 4. Correlation Coefficients Between BS, Intermediate Demand and Proxies for Agglomeration Economies and Knowledge at the Regional Level.

Variables	BS	ID	ID MANU	ID SERV	PD	ICT	S&T	R&D	CD
Business services (BS)	1								
Intermediate demand (ID)	0.809	1							
Intermediate demand manufacturing (ID MANU)	0.568	0.547	1						
Intermediate demand services (ID SERV)	0.76	0.98	0.37	1					
Population density (PD)	0.69	0.644	0.470	0.605	1				
ICT	0.512	0.366	0.555	0.276	0.409	1			
Human resources in S&T (S&T)	0.55	0.393	0.374	0.342	0.393	0.531	1		
Public R&D	0.36	0.24	0.216	0.222	0.262	0.320	0.381	1	
Capital dummies (CD)	0.432	0.462	0.275	0.438	0.509	0.15	0.306	0.33	1

local Moran statistics, we find many capital regions with negative local Moran coefficients; we also find a cluster of highly specialized regions including Dutch, Belgian and German regions and another cluster of UK regions; clusters with low values include Polish regions and a group of Portuguese and Spanish regions (Norte and Centro Portugal and the Spanish region of Extremadura). With respect to intermediate manufacturing demand, clusters of high intermediate demand regions include the UK South Eastern (but not central) regions; three Hungarian regions including the region of the capital and the two Western regions of Transdanubia; clusters of low manufacturing intermediate demand include the cluster of Portuguese and Spanish regions (again Norte and Centro Portugal and Extremadura and also Andalucia in Spain); the cluster of Greek regions and also a cluster of Southern Italian regions. Finally, BS service user sectors tend to follow a location pattern that is similar to that for BS with highly specialized capital regions surrounded by de-specialized regions and clusters of specialized regions especially in the United Kingdom and Northern-Central Europe. Specialization in BS service user sectors appears to be slightly less spatially correlated than specialization in BS. Overall the figures show that BS and high BS users sectors are spatially correlated and that there are some similarities in their location patterns.

Table 4 presents the correlation coefficients for BS specialization, specialization in BS user sectors and other variables proxying, respectively, for agglomeration economies (population density and dummies for capital cities) and the regional knowledge base (patents in ICT, public R&D, resources in Science and Technologies in universities).

BS are very strongly correlated with total potential intermediate demand (from both services and manufacturing) showing the relevance of the co-location of BS and user sectors and supporting the role of forward linkages in the location of BS. This appears to be more important in the case of services compared to manufacturing. BS are also highly correlated with population density, confirming the importance of agglomeration economies. For the variables capturing the *knowledge environment*, correlation coefficients are high (although lower than those of demand and population density) especially for ICT and human resources in Science and Technology (S&T) in universities, while the correlation coefficient of public R&D, although significant, is much lower. This might reflect the fact that public R&D is less concentrated than other innovation variables.

Overall, despite the increased standardization of knowledge that has been taking place over time and which has favoured the process of production fragmentation and the rise of BS, and despite the increase in knowledge transferability due to the development of ICTs, we observe that BS tend to cluster in space and to localize close to their client industries. This is supported by empirical evidence on the intensity and 'identity' of BS users and their spatial localization.

5. Concluding Remarks

This chapter revisited the debate on the 'knowledge economy' as synonymous with the emergence of services in terms of its economic and historical roots, and examined the sectoral and spatial concentration of knowledge-intensive BS. We have provided a historical account of the emergence of services – and BS in particular – as a manifestation of the structural change linked to the evolution of scientific and technological knowledge. We have provided empirical evidence for understanding the spatial concentration of services.

Although we would not claim to provide an exhaustive epistemological account of the role of knowledge in economics, this selective review has focused on the relationship between knowledge evolution and technical progress, which translate into changes in the structural sectoral composition of the economy. In revisiting some of the historical accounts of the link between knowledge and sector emergence from the British Industrial Revolution, the analysis in this chapter has focused on the rise of services in response to the debate currently revolving around the Knowledge Economy which has been linked to the increased tertiarization of economies.

Our main argument is that the contemporary increased complexity and volume of knowledge have brought about a shift in relative importance from the Mokyr (2002) *episteme* to *techne* and, along with a dramatically increased access to and standardization of epistemic knowledge due to ICTs, an ever-increasing specialization in narrowly based expertise (Witt, 2010). This led us to conclude that the main driving force behind the growth of BS and particularly KIBS, is intermediate demand.

From the perspective of the geography of structural change, the literature provides a spatial equivalent of our main argument in Hirschmann backward and forward linkages, a substantial ingredient of the classical Marshallian agglomeration economies applied to the case of BS.

Despite the increasing standardization and transferability of knowledge due to ICTs and the consequent process of production fragmentation and division of labour favouring the rise of BS, European evidence shows that BS tend to cluster in space and to localize close to their client industries. This suggests the importance of face-to-face contacts in the use of BS and is consistent with the view that KIBS do not provide a one-directional transfer of specialized information but are co-producers of knowledge in a process that involves their clients intimately (Muller and Doloreux, 2009). There is therefore an intrinsic value added for services to localize in proximity to their clients which goes beyond the traditional explanations based on the outsourcing of service functions out of manufacturing. This is all the more important when we look at the urbanization element of BS location patterns, which shows that, beyond intermediate demand, there is a strong element of spillovers among knowledge functions concentrated in human capital dense areas.

It is important to stress that we deliberately did not address all of the most recent debate on creative industries and creative class, since in our view some of these contributions are misleading in pointing to fuzzy knowledge concepts. Our intention was to provide a more historical account of knowledge dynamics and structural change.

Our future research agenda, in the context of this selected review, includes investigating whether our main argument can be confirmed empirically on a global scale. The process of tertiarization is spreading to countries with very different sectoral structures – such as India (Dasgupta and Singh, 2005) and would need to be addressed more at large.

Notes

1. 'Freeman puts an even greater emphasis on the historical evolution of distinct political–economy regimes associated with distinct techno-economic paradigms shaping the overall organization of knowledge accumulation and production under e.g. an electricity/internal-combustion/mass production mode vs. an ICT-driven one (cf. Freeman and Perez (1988), and Freeman and Louçã (2001) among others)' (Dosi 2007, p. 4).
2. 'The main point in writing Athena was that the material sphere of technology, production, efficiency in such mundane worlds as cotton mills, coal mines, water mills and shipyards must be understood as closely connected to the sphere of knowledge, ideas, experiments, mathematical proofs, and observation' (Mokyr 2007a, p. 1).
3. Note that nature is assumed to have fixed properties.
4. Knowledge selection in fact occurs at different levels: while the market selects the outcome of a technique, knowledge vehicles such as firms select the technique. Then the firms are selected, which determines which segments of knowledge are used and which are not (Mokyr, 2000). The literature on knowledge selection is vast and its review is beyond the scope of this chapter. However, Fleck (2000) focuses on the artefact rather than the technique, in order to distinguish between technological and cultural evolution (especially given the difficulties involved in mapping techniques and ideas/knowledge). Stankiewicz (2000) focuses the discussion on the whole cognitive system representing a technology, that is, the 'design space', attributing selection and variation only to the accumulation and transmission of knowledge, while Constant (2000) refers to the selection of information through recursive practices, that is reduced to reliable knowledge.
5. This is similar to a Bayesian process (Constant, 2000): successful reuse of the same bits of knowledge, in different technologies or artefacts, increases its reliability. What improves and survives becomes the *information*, the fit between the phenomenon observed and the idea tested. This recursive process does not imply that the knowledge that survives is ontologically true. Also, similar to Mokyr's evolution of knowledge, 'the critical roles interests, cultural pre-suppositions, negotiation, and contingent social factors play in technology [that has survived the recursive practice] are surely not denied' (Constant 1999, p. 263).
6. 'The Industrial Revolution was a collaborative effort of most of the Western economies, and the British may have had a comparative advantage in competence and microinventions and thus exported skilled craftsmen and mechanics (laws on the books prohibiting such movements notwithstanding), but they imported many of the best ideas' (Mokyr, 2010, p. 23).
7. Britain managed to maintain the high wages that had operated across Europe since the end of the black death when the population began to grow again.

8. The reasons for the difference in the price of capital have been well documented in Allen (2009; 2011).

9. This applies to the invention of the clock to measure longitude during navigation, an invention that cannot be said to have marked the industrial revolution but which gave rise to the use of mechanical wheels which became incorporated in most of the machines at the core of the industrial revolution.

10. Here the forces that induce the selection of knowledge sets are particularly relevant. See for example, the debate between Constant (1999) and Law and Singleton (2000), the reasons for the adoption of spinning technologies (Lazonick, 1979) and the invention and adoption of computer-based machine tools (Noble, 1984).

11. This view has dominated academic and policy debates in recent years, to the point that the 'Knowledge based Europe' has become part of the policy agenda.

12. It is beyond the scope of this chapter to review attempts to revisit the foundations of the theory of value by including knowledge (Jacques, 2000; Jaros and Sells, 2004). Here, we focus on the consequences of the knowledge- and technology-related processes of division of labour and the growth of services.

13. Mercantilists considered labour as an income generating activity and therefore – subject to taxes – as adding to the fiscal treasury. Regardless of the physical or immaterial type of the output, services produce income and therefore are 'productive' activities.

14. Marx's classification of service activities was based mainly on the social and economic relationships underlying the provision of services, rather than on the physical manifestation of such provision. It is interesting that Marx considered transport services to be part of industrial production and, therefore, part of the material sphere as well as a source of surplus value. Unlike transport, trade and banking were categorized as belonging to the sphere of *commercial and financial capital*; they produce neither value nor surplus value, they only add to profit. More specifically, these activities were not labelled unproductive because of their immateriality, a criterion that many of Marx's contemporaries applied; instead, they were seen as part of more a complex speculation as far as their role within the social reproduction of capital was concerned.

15. Baumol assumes that demand for services and goods, measured in constant prices, does not depend on income levels and that, at the aggregate level, the share of services in total output is constant over time and across countries. However, as the increase in (labour) productivity levels is lower in services than in manufacturing and combines with low productivity growth over time, the high-income countries will experience higher shares of employment in services. The cost–disease phenomenon consists of the fact that wages in services increase in line with average growth in the wage rates in the rest of the economy, leading to overall increases in the nominal shares of output in services. The presence of a cost disease shows that the changing structure of employment in services is due to the lack of productivity gains in services rather than to changing patterns of demand. The difficulty of achieving productivity gains in line with the rest of the economy, in turn, is a consequence of *technological stagnancy* in services compared to manufacturing sectors.

16. Biases in the measurement of services input and output are responsible for underestimations of innovation and economic performance. These problems were highlighted in the early 1990s by Griliches. His contribution, *Output Measurement in the Service Sector* (Griliches, 1992) is still considered the most exhaustive account of the measurement problems related to service activities.

17. See also Savona and Lorentz (2006) and Montresor and Vittucci Marzetti (2011) for different methodologies applied to I/O data.

18. In particular, we calculate the change in the share of manufacturing, FCB and other services as a part of total intermediate demand, final demand and gross output from the mid-1970s to the mid-2000s. Unfortunately we do not have comparable I/O tables for the

entire time period; therefore we use OECD I/O tables for the mid-1970s to 1990, and new Eurostat I/O tables for the period 1995–2005, and focus on four European countries (Denmark, Germany, France and the Netherlands).

19. Data on individual countries are available on request.

20. Specialization in BS is proxied by an index of Comparative Advantage (CA) in BS, calculated as the employment in BS in region i over total employment of region i divided by employment in BS for all regions, over total employment for all regions.

21. According to Hirschmann (1958, p. 100), quoted in Jones (1976) 'The input-provision, derived demand, or backward linkage effects, i.e. every non-primary economic activity, will induce attempts to supply through domestic production the inputs needed in that activity. The output-utilization or forward linkage effects, i.e., every activity that does not by its nature cater exclusively to final demands, will induce attempts to utilize its outputs as inputs in some new activities'.

22. We refer to the NACE 64, 72 and 74 (Communication services; Computer and related services; Other BS) as a share of total inputs and total outputs for several groups of sectors, based mainly on the Eurostat classifications (Agriculture and fishing; Mining and quarrying; Electricity gas and water and construction; Low-tech manufacturing; Medium-low-tech manufacturing; Medium-high-tech manufacturing; High-tech manufacturing; High-tech market Knowledge Intensive Services; other market KIS; non-market services; Financial intermediation). Data are computed for 2005 for a large group (27) of countries that includes all the countries of the European Union except Malta and Cyprus, and also includes Turkey and Norway. The analysis of variance indicates some regularities in the ranking of the industries grouped according to the Eurostat classification ($R^2 = 0.718$ and $R^2 = 0.619$, respectively, for the shares on inputs and on output.

23. Potential intermediate demand (INTDEM) is proxied by the weighted share of employment in manufacturing/services industries that are heavy users of BS, over total employment. In particular, we take a vector measuring the use of services in output for manufacturing/service sectors that are above average BS users and, for each region and year, we multiply this by total employment in the respective manufacturing/service sectors. The number is then divided by total employment in the region i in the year t: $INTDEM_{it} = \frac{\sum_{j=1}^{m} W_j E_{ijt}}{\sum_{j=1}^{n} E_{ijt}}$ where: i = region, j = sector, t = time, m = number of above average BS users manufacturing/service sectors, n = total number of sectors, E = employment, W = weight given by the average – across European countries – share of BS in total industry output computed from Eurostat symmetric I/O tables for 2000. The higher the indicator, the higher is regional employment in manufacturing/service sectors that are strong users of BS with respect to total regional employment for each year.

References

Abramovitz, M. and David, P.A. (2001) Two centuries of American macroeconomic growth. From exploitation of resource abundance to knowledge-driven development. SIEPR Discussion Paper 01-05, Stanford Institute for Economic Policy Research, Stanford University.

Acemoglu, D., Johnson, S., and Robinson, J.A. (2005) Institutions as a fundamental cause of long-run growth. In P. Aghion and S.N. Durlauf (eds), *Handbook of Economic Growth*, Volume 1A of *Economic Handbooks* (chapter 6, pp. 385–472). Amsterdam: Elsevier.

Acemoglu, D. and Robinson, J.A. (2006) Economic backwardness in political perspective. *American Political Science Review* 100: 115–131.

Acs, Z.J., Anselin, L. and Varga, A. (2002) Patents and innovation counts as measures of regional production of new knowledge. *Research Policy* 31: 1069–1085.

Aghion, P. and Howitt, P. (1992) A model of growth through creative destruction. *Econometrica* 60: 323–351.

Ahmad, S. (1966) On the theory of induced invention. *Economic Journal* 76: 344–357.

Allen, R.C. (2009) *The British Industrial Revolution in Global Perspective*. Cambridge: Cambridge University Press.

Allen, R.C. (2011) Why the industrial revolution was British: commerce, induced invention, and the scientific revolution. *The Economic History Review* 64: 357–384.

Antonelli, C. (1998) Localized technological change, new information technology and the knowledge-based economy: the European evidence. *Journal of Evolutionary Economics* 8: 177–198.

Archibugi, D. and Lundvall, B.-A. (eds) (2001) *The Globalising Learning Economy*. Oxford: Oxford University Press.

Arora, A. and Gambardella, A. (1994) The changing technology of technological change: general and abstract knowledge and the division of innovative labour. *Research Policy* 23: 523–532.

Baumol, W.J. (1967) Macroeconomics of unbalanced growth: the anatomy of an urban crisis. *American Economic Review* 57: 415–426.

Baumol, W.J. (2001) The growth of service industries. the paradox of exploding costs and persistent demand. In T. ten Raa and R. Schettkat (eds), *Paradox of the Services: Exploding Costs and Persistent Demand*. Cheltenham: E. Elgar.

Baumol, W.J., Blackman, S.A.B. and Wolff, E.N. (1985) Unbalanced growth revisited: asymptotic stagnancy and new evidences. *American Economic Review* 75: 806–816.

Baumol, W.J., Blackman, S.A.B. and Wolff, E.N. (1989) *Productivity and American Leadership*. Cambridge MA: MIT Press.

Baumol, W.J. and Bowen, W.G. (1966) *Performing Arts: The Economic Dilemma*. New York: Twentieth Century Found.

Bell, D. (1976) *The Coming of Post-Industrial Society: A Venture in Social Forecasting*. New York: Harper Colophon Books. Basic Books.

Berg, M. (2002) From imitation to invention: creating commodities in eighteenth-century Britain. *Economic History Review* 55: 1–30.

Berg, M. and Bruland, K. (eds.) (1998) *Technological Revolutions in Europe: Historical Perspectives*. Cheltenham: Edward Elgar.

Beyers, W.B. (2002) Services and the new economy: elements for a research agenda. *Journal of Economic Geography* 2: 1–29.

Cainelli, G., Evangelista, R. and Savona, M. (2006) Innovation and economic performance in services. a firm level analysis. *Cambridge Journal of Economics* 30: 435–458.

Ciarli, T. and Lorentz, A. (2010) Product variety and changes in consumption patterns: the effects of structural change on growth. Working Paper mimeo, Max Planck Institute of Economics.

Ciarli, T., Lorentz, A., Savona, M. and Valente, M. (2010) The effects of consumption and production structure on growth and distribution. A micro to macro model. *Metroeconomica* 61(1): 180–218.

Clark, C. (1940) *The Conditions of Economic Progress*. London: MacMillan.

Cohen, S.S. and Zysman, J. (1987) Manufacturing matters: the myth of the post-industrial economy. BRIE Working Paper. New York: Basic Books.

Constant, E.W. (1999) Reliable knowledge and unreliable stuff: on the practical role of rational beliefs. *Technology and Culture* 40: 324–357.

Constant, E.W. (2000) Recursive practice and the evolution of technological knowledge. In J.M. Ziman (ed.), *Technological Innovation as an Evolutionary Process* (chapter 16, pp. 219–233). Cambridge: Cambridge University Press.

Coombes, P.-P. (2000) Economic structure and local growth: France 1984–1993. *Journal of Urban Economics* 47: 329–343.

Cowan, Robin, D.P.A. and Foray, D. (2000) The explicit economics of knowledge codification and tacitness. *Industrial and corporate change* 9: 211–253.

Dasgupta, S. and Singh, A. (2005) Will services be the new engine of economic growth in India? Technical Report, Working Paper Series, n. 310 Centre for Business Research, University of Cambridge.

Delaunay, J.-C. and Gadrey, J. (1992) *Services in Economic Thought: Three Centuries of Debate*. Dordrecht: Kluwer Academic Publishers.

Doloreux, D. and Shearmur, R. (2011) Collaboration, information and the geography of innovation in knowledge intensive business services. *Journal of Economic Geography* 12 (1):
79–105.
Dosi, G. (1982) Technological paradigms and technological trajectories: a suggested interpretation of the determinants and directions of technical change. *Research Policy* 11(3): 147–162.
Dosi, G. (2007) Technological innovation, institutions and human purposefulness in socioeco-
nomic evolution: a preface to Christopher freeman "systems of innovation. selected essays
in evolutionary economics". LEM Papers Series 2007/18, Laboratory of Economics and
Management (LEM), Sant'Anna School of Advanced Studies, Pisa, Italy.
Duranton, G. and Puga, D. (2005) From sectoral to functional urban specialisation. *Journal of
Urban Economics* 57: 343–370.
Evangelista, R. (1999) *Knowledge and Investment. The Sources of Innovation in Industry.* Chel-
tenham UK: Edward Elgar.
Faggian, A. and McCann, P. (2009) Human capital and regional development. In R. Capello
and P. Nijkamp (eds), *Handbook of Regional Growth and Development Theories.* London:
Edward Elgar.
Fisher, A.G.B. (1945) *Economic Progress and Social Security.* London: MacMillan.
Fleck, J. (2000) Artefact ↔ activity: the coevolution of artefacts, knowledge and organization in
technological innovation. In J.M. Ziman (ed.), *Technological Innovation as an Evolutionary
Process* (chapter 18, pp. 248–266). Cambridge: Cambridge University Press.
Foray, D. (2006) *The Economics of Knowledge.* Cambridge MA, London: MIT Press.
Fourastié, J. (1949) *Le grand espoir du XX siécle.* Paris: PUF.
Francois, J.F. (1990) Producer services, scale, and the division of labor. *Oxford Economic Papers*
42: 715–729.
Francois, J.F. and Woerz, J. (2007) Producer services, manufacturing linkages, and trade. Tech-
nical report, Tinbergen Institute Discussion Paper, TI 2007-045/2.
Freeman, C. and Louçã, F. (2001) *As Time Goes By: From the Industrial Revolutions to the
Information Revolution.* New York: Oxford University Press.
Freeman, C. and Perez, C. (1988) Structural crises of adjustment: business cycles and investment
behaviour. In G. Dosi, C. Freeman, R. R. Nelson, G. Silverberg and L.L.G. Soete (eds),
Technical Change and Economic Theory (pp. 38–66). London: Pinter Publishers.
Fuchs, V.R. (1968) *The Service Economy.* New York: National Bureau of Economic Research.
Fuchs, V.R. (1977) The service industries and U.S. economic growth since World War II. NBER
Working Paper Series, 211, National Bureau of Economic Research.
Galor, O. (2010) The 2008 Lawrence R. Klein lecture comparative economic development:
insights from unified growth theory. *International Economic Review* 51: 1–44.
Gershuny, J. (1978) *After Industrial Society: The Emerging Self-Service Economy.* London:
Macmillan.
Glaeser, E.L. (1999) Learning in cities. *Journal of Urban Economics* 46: 254–277.
Glaeser, E.L., Kallal, H.D., Scheinkman, J.A. and Shleifer, A. (1992) Growth in cities. *Journal
of Political Economy* 100: 1126–52.
Godin, B. (2006) The knowledge-based economy: conceptual framework or buzzword? *Journal
of Technology Transfer* 31(1): 17–30.
Greif, A. (2006) *Institutions and the Path to the Modern Economy: Lessons from Medieval Trade.
Political economy of institutions and decisions.* New York: Cambridge University Press.
Griliches, Z. (1992) *Output Measurement in the Service Sector.* Chicago: University of Chicago
Press.
Guerrieri, P. and Meliciani, V. (2005) Technology and international competitiveness: the inter-
dependence between manufacturing and producer services. *Structural Change and Economic
Dynamics* 16: 489–502.
Henderson, V., Kuncoro, A. and Turner, M. (1995) Industrial development in cities. *Journal of
Political Economy* 103: 1067–90.
Hicks, J. (1932) *The Theory of Wages.* London: Macmillian.
Hirschmann, A.O. (1958) *Strategy of Economic Development.* New Haven, Connecticut and
London: Yale University Press.
Jacobs, J. (1969) *The Economy of Cities.* London: Random House.

Jacques, R. (2000) Theorising knowledge as work: the need for a 'knowledge theory of value'. In C. Prichard, R. Hull, M. Chumer and H. Willmott (eds), *Managing Knowledge: Critical Investigations of Work and Learning* (chapter Conclusion, pp. 199–215). London: Macmillan.

Jaros, S. and Sells, L. (2004) Jacques's (2000) call for a knowledge theory of value: implications for labour process theory. *Electronic Journal of Radical Organisation Theory* 8 (1): 1–17.

Jensen, M.B., Johnson, Bjorn, a. L.E., and Lundvall, B.-A. (2007) Forms of knowledge and modes of innovation. *Research Policy* 36: 680–693.

Johnson, A. (2005) Revisiting technology as knowledge. *Perspectives on Science* 13: 554–573.

Jones, L.P. (1976) The measurement of Hirschmanian linkages. *Quarterly Journal of Economics* 90: 323–333.

Kaldor, N. (1966) *Causes of the Slow Rate of Growth in the United Kingdom*. Cambridge: Cambridge University Press.

Kox, H.L.M. and Rubalcaba, L. (2007) Business services and the changing structure of European economic growth. Technical report, MPRA Paper n. 3750.

Kuznets, S. (1973) Modern economic growth: findings and reflections. *The American Economic Review* 63: 247–258.

Law, J. (1986) Editor's introduction: Power/knowledge and the dissolution of the sociology of knowledge. In J. Law (ed.), *Power, Action and Belief. A New Sociology of Knowledge?* (pp. 1–19). London: Routledge & Kegan Paul.

Law, J. and Singleton, V. (2000) Performing technology's stories: on social constructivism, performance, and performativity. *Technology and Culture* 41: 765–775.

Lazonick, W.H. (1979) Industrial relations and technical change: the case of the self-acting mule. *Cambridge Journal of Economics* 3: 231–62.

Lazonick, W.H. (1981) Production relations, labor productivity, and choice of technique: British and U.S. cotton spinning. *The Journal of Economic History* 41: 491–516.

Lee, C. (1994) The service industries. In R. Floud and D. McCloskey (eds), *The Economic History of Britain Since 1700*, second edition (Vol. 2, chapter 5, pp. 117–144). Cambridge: Cambridge University Press.

Lindert, P.H. (1994) Unequal living standards. In R. Floud and D. McCloskey (eds), *The Economic History of Britain Since 1700* (Vol. 1, chapter 14, pp. 357–387). Cambridge: Cambridge University Press.

Lundvall, B.-A. and Johnson, B. (1994) The learning economy. Princeton: *Journal of Industry Studies* 1: 23–42.

Machlup, F. (1980) *Knowledge and Knowledge Production* (Vol. 1). Princeton: Princeton University Press.

Marrano, M.G., Jonathan, H. and Gavin, W. (2009) What happened to the knowledge economy? ICT, intangible investment and Britain's productivity record revisited. *Review of Income and Wealth* 55: 686–716.

Marshall, A. (1920) *Principles of Economics*. London: Library of Economics and Liberty.

McCann, P. and van Oort, F. (2009) Theories of agglomeration and regional economic growth: a historical review. In N.P. Capello Roberta (ed.), *Handbook of Regional Growth and Development Theories* (chapter 1). London: Edward Elgar.

McCloskey, D.N. (2009) Science, bourgeois dignity, and the industrial revolution. MPRA Paper 22308.

Meliciani, V. and Savona, M. (2011) The determinants of regional specialisation in business services: Agglomeration economies, vertical linkages and innovation. SPRU Electronic Working Paper Series 193/2011, SPRU Science and Technology Policy Research, University of Sussex.

Metcalfe, J.S. (2002) Knowledge of growth and the growth of knowledge. *Journal of Evolutionary Economics* 12: 3–15, doi:10.1007/s00191-002-0107-y.

Metcalfe, J.S., Foster, J. and Ramlogan, R. (2006) Adaptive economic growth. *Cambridge Journal of Economics* 30: 7–32.

Miles, I., Kastrinos, N., Bilderbeek, R. and den Hertog, P. (1995) Knowledge intensive business services: users, carriers and sources of innovation. Working Paper, EIMS—European Innovation Monitoring System.

Mokyr, J. (1998) Induced technical innovation and medical history: an evolutionary approach. *Journal of Evolutionary Economics* 8: 119–137, doi: 10.1007/s001910050058.

Mokyr, J. (2000) Evolutionary phenomena in technological change. In J.M. Ziman (ed.), *Technological Innovation As an Evolutionary Process* (chapter 5, pp. 52–65). Cambridge: Cambridge University Press.

Mokyr, J. (2002) *The Gifts of Athena: Historical Origins of the Knowledge Economy.* Princeton: Princeton University Press.

Mokyr, J. (2007a) Knowledge, enlightenment, and the industrial revolution: reflections on The Gifts of Athena. *History of Science* 45: 185–196.

Mokyr, J. (2007b) The market for ideas and the origins of economic growth in eighteenth century Europe. *Tijdschrift voor Sociale en Economische geschiedenis* 4: 3–38.

Mokyr, J. (2009) *The Enlightened Economy: An Economic History of Britain, 1700-1850. New economic history of Britain.* New Haven: Yale University Press.

Mokyr, J. (2010) The contribution of economic history to the study of innovation and technical change: 1750–1914. In B.H. Hall and N. Rosenberg (eds), *Handbook of The Economics of Innovation* (Vol. 1, pp. 11–50). Amsterdam: North-Holland.

Mokyr, J. and Voth, H.-J. (2010) Understanding growth in Europe, 1700-1870: theory and evidence. In S. Broadberry and K.H. O'Rourke (eds), *The Cambridge Economic History of Modern Europe* (Vol. 1, 1700–1870, pp. 7–42). Cambridge: Cambridge University Press.

Montresor, S. and Vittucci Marzetti, G. (2011) The deindustrialization/tertiarisation hypothesis reconsidered. A sub-system application to the OECD7. *Cambridge Journal of Economics* 35(2): 401–421.

Muller, E. and Doloreux, D. (2009) What we should know about knowledge-intensive business services. *Technology in Society* 31: 64–72.

Muller, E. and Zenker, A. (2001) Business services as actors of knowledge transformation: the role of KIBS in regional and national innovation systems. *Research Policy* 30: 1501–1516.

Nelson, K. and Nelson, R. (2002) On the nature and evolution of human know-how. *Research Policy* 31: 719–733.

Noble, D.F. (1984) *Forces of Production. A Social History of Industrial Automation.* New York: Oxford University Press.

Oort, F., Oud, J. and Raspe, O. (2009) The urban knowledge economy and employment growth: a spatial structural equation modeling approach. *The Annals of Regional Science* 43(4): 859–877.

Peneder, M., Kaniovsky, S. and Dachs, B. (2003) What follows tertiarisation? Structural change and the role of knowledge-based services. *The Service Industry Journal* 23: 47–66.

Raspe, O. and Van Oort, F. (2006) The knowledge economy and urban economic growth. *European Planning Studies* 14: 1209–1234.

Rosenberg, N. (1974) Science, invention and economic growth. *The Economic Journal* 84: 90–108.

Rowthorn, R. and Ramaswamy, R. (1999) Growth, trade and deindustrialisation. Technical Report, IMF Staff Papers 46, 18-41.

Savona, M. and Lorentz, A. (2006) Demand and technology determinants of structural change and tertiarisation: an input-output structural decomposition analysis for four OECD countries. Working Papers, BETA.

Schmookler, J. (1966) *Invention and Economic Growth.* Cambridge: Harvard University Press.

Smith, A. (1960[1776]) *The Wealth of Nations.* New York: The Modern Library, Random House.

Stankiewicz, R. (2000) The concept of 'design space'. In J.M. Ziman (ed.), *Technological Innovation As an Evolutionary Process* (chapter 17, pp. 234–247). Cambridge: Cambridge University Press.

von Tunzelmann, G.N. (1995) *Technology and Industrial Progress: The Foundations of Economic Growth.* Aldershot: Edward Elgar.

Van Oort, F.G. (2007) Spatial and sectoral composition effects of agglomeration economies in the Netherlands. *Papers in Regional Science* 86: 5–30.

Witt, U. (2009) Novelty and the bounds of unknowledge in economics. *Journal of Economic Methodology* 16: 361–375.

Witt, U. (2010) Use of knowledge in society and their productive significance. Paper prepared for the symposium in honor of Stan Metcalfe, Max Planck Institute of Economics, Manchester.

Witt, U. and Zellner, C. (2009) How firm organizations adapt to secure a sustained knowledge transfer. *Economics of Innovation and New Technology* 18: 647–661.

Wood, P. (2006) The regional significance of knowledge-intensive services in Europe. *Innovation: The European Journal of Social Science Research* 19: 51–66.

Ziman, J.M. (1976) *The Force of Knowledge*. Cambridge: Cambridge University Press.

6

MULTILEVEL APPROACHES AND THE FIRM-AGGLOMERATION AMBIGUITY IN ECONOMIC GROWTH STUDIES

Frank G. van Oort, Martijn J. Burger, Joris Knoben and Otto Raspe

1. The Firm in Agglomeration Studies: The Missing Link?

Economic growth processes occur in urban areas and industrial clusters. Therefore, urban and regional planners, geographers and economists alike are interested in the forces that create, shape and maintain concentrations of economic activities. Since the early 1990s, a large body of empirical literature has emerged in the field of regional science and urban economics. This literature examines whether spatial circumstances give rise to agglomeration economies – external economies from which firms can benefit through co-location – that endogenously induce localized economic growth (Glaeser *et al.*, 1992; Henderson *et al.*, 1995; Combes, 2000; Rosenthal and Strange, 2003; Brülhart and Mathys, 2008). The literature argues that externalities or spillovers occur if an innovation or growth improvement implemented by a certain enterprise increases the performance of other enterprises without requiring the benefiting enterprise to pay (full) compensation. A particularly novel feature in this literature is the combination of traditional urban economics and regional science literature with new growth theory, as formulated by Romer (1986) and Lucas (1988). In their survey of the empirical literature on the benefits of agglomeration, Rosenthal and Strange (2004) point out that the elasticity of productivity to city and industry size typically ranges from 3% to 8%. However, a series of recent overview chapters and meta-analyses show that the effects of agglomeration economies on localized economic growth generally differ across sectors, space and time (Rosenthal and Strange, 2004; Van Oort, 2007; De Groot *et al.*, 2009; Melo *et al.*, 2009; Beaudry and Schiffauerova, 2009; Puga, 2010). Despite the complex and nuanced method of conceptually linking spillovers with growth and cities, an ever-growing body of empirical literature on urban externalities remains inconclusive on the exact agglomeration circumstances that optimally enhance growth. The missing link that leads to the ambiguity in the research results on agglomeration economies may be the relationship between agglomeration economies and individual firm performance. Although early studies examined the importance of firm-level performance in agglomerated contexts

Innovation, Entrepreneurship, Geography and Growth, First Edition.
Edited by Philip McCann and Les Oxley. Chapters © 2013 The Authors.
Book compilation © 2013 Blackwell Publishing Ltd. Published 2013 by Blackwell Publishing Ltd.

(Dicken and Malmberg, 2001; Taylor and Asheim, 2001), until recently, the firm-level has not been treated systematically in urban economics and spatial econometrics. Even in the strategic management literature, in which the core purpose is to explain differences in firm performance, this issue has received scant attention (McCann and Folta, 2008).

A remarkable issue in the literature relates to the fact that many studies understand spatially bounded externalities as related to an enterprise's geographical or network contexts rather than to internal firm performance. Relatively little is known about the importance of agglomeration economies to the performance of firms (Acs and Armington, 2004; Martin *et al.*, 2011). This gap is remarkable because the theories that underlie agglomeration economies are microeconomic in nature (Brakman *et al.*, 2009). Many empirical studies on agglomeration use aggregated data, with cities or city industries as the basic reference unit. These studies provide only limited insights and weak support for the effects of agglomeration economies on firm performance. Regional-level relationships are not necessarily reproduced at the firm level because information on the variance between firms is lost when aggregated regional-level data are used. Hence, even if regions endowed with a greater number of agglomeration economies grow faster, this conclusion cannot be generalized to firms. In the social sciences, this micro–macro problem is referred to as the 'ecological fallacy' (Robinson, 1950) or the 'cross-level fallacy' (Alker, 1969). In addition, agglomeration effects found in area-based studies may be purely compositional (Macintyre *et al.*, 1993). For example, the strategic management literature often argues that large firms are more likely to grow compared to small firms due to internal economies of scale. Hence, a location may grow rapidly due to the concentration of large firms rather than the localization of externalities or the external economies of scale. A similar issue is addressed in the work of Combes *et al.* (2008) and Mion and Naticchioni (2009) on spatial sorting and spatial wage disparities. Similarly, Baldwin and Okubu (2006) show that the agglomeration of productive firms may simply be the result of a spatial selection process in which more productive firms are drawn to dense economic areas. For this reason, it remains unclear whether geographical differences are an artifact of location characteristics (e.g. agglomeration economies) or are simply caused by differences in business and economic composition. This endogeneity problem makes it even more difficult to draw inferences about firms when using cities or regions as the lowest unit of analysis (Ottaviano, 2011). Continuous space modeling offers promising perspectives for solving these issues (Arbia, 2001; Duranton and Overman, 2005), but some aspects can be better addressed using multilevel modeling.

To overcome the apparent impasse in the measurement and interpretation of agglomeration externalities, microeconomic and behavioral conceptualizations are needed. In particular, recent concepts introduced in evolutionary economic geography and strategic management dynamics are promising for explaining growing firms and organizations in cities because they address the heterogeneity in the actors involved, spatial scale, selection and survival, and time and path dependency (Frenken *et al.*, 2007; McCann and Folta, 2008; McCann and Van Oort, 2009). Accompanying research methods that seriously consider micro–macro linkages of firms in their individual spatial and sectoral contexts are needed for this purpose as well (Duranton and Puga, 2005; Briant *et al.*, 2010). Recently, two strands of literature have focused on the micro–macro relationships of firms in their relevant contexts using multilevel analysis. On the one hand, urban economics and spatial econometrics consider the connection between hierarchical multilevel models and the standard spatial econometric specifications. There are limitations and difficulties with multilevel modeling in relation to spatial econometrics, such as the incorporation of spatial dependence within and between hierarchical levels of analysis and the relationship with sectoral heterogeneity (Corrado and Fingleton, 2012). On the other hand, strategic management studies increasingly introduce multilevel modeling to analyze the interaction between firm performance and (agglomerated) contexts (Beugelsdijk, 2007). Following social sciences, hierarchical random effects or multilevel modeling, which allows the micro level and macro level to be modeled simultaneously, is becoming an increasingly common practice in strategic management and organization studies. Goldstein (2003) and Moon *et al.* (2005) summarize recent overviews of area-based studies in relation to multilevel modeling.

In this chapter, we argue that addressing the micro–macro level heterogeneity and interrelationships – basically, questioning which types of firms profit from which types of agglomeration economies – is served by multilevel modeling. Furthermore, we argue that these insights help to clarify the agglomeration–performance ambiguity. We show that the relationship with sectoral heterogeneity or cross-level interactions can be addressed adequately. We highlight the potential of multilevel modeling in agglomeration and economic growth studies, stressing the cross-fertilization of current hierarchical modeling with the spatial econometrics literature. We do this by briefly introducing two case studies of multilevel models in a Dutch context of agglomeration economies and firm performance. These two case studies highlight the potentials and drawbacks of the research method for urban economics, economic geography and organization studies.

This chapter is further structured as follows. After introducing theories on agglomeration economies in urban economics and the strategic management literature in Section 2, we briefly introduce the logic and structure of multilevel modeling in Section 3. We then present the two case studies – first, a survival and growth model of newly established advanced producer service firms in the Netherlands (Section 4), and second, a study of firm-level productivity in Dutch cities (Section 5). In both cases, we link firm-level performance to agglomeration circumstances. In addition to mixed-hierarchical relations at different levels, the model of new business firm survival and growth also shows a cross-classified structure: firm-level variation is related to agglomeration, sectoral and cluster (combined agglomeration and sectoral) contexts. In the case study of firms' productivity, we hypothesize, based on the strategic management literature, that the relationship between firm performance and agglomeration is positively moderated by medium-sized firms, but not by small or large firms. Testing for this nonlinear heterogeneity using interaction effects in multilevel modeling is the main added value of the second case study. Section 6 concludes with a discussion of the usefulness of multilevel modeling in economic agglomeration studies.

2. The Macro to Micro Link in Agglomeration Economics and Organization Studies

2.1 *Agglomeration Economics*

The origin of the agglomeration economies concept can be traced to the end of the nineteenth century. At the *fin de siècle*, the neoclassical economist Alfred Marshall aimed to overturn Malthus' and Ricardo's pessimistic (but influential) predictions on the co-evolution of economic and population development. He introduced a form of localized aggregate increasing returns to scale for firms. In his seminal work, *Principles of Economics* (Book IV, Chapter X), Marshall (1890) mentioned a number of cost-saving benefits or productivity gains external to a firm. He argued that a firm could benefit from co-location with other firms engaged in the same type of business. Marshall considered these *agglomeration economies* to be uncontrollable and difficult to regulate as well as immobile and spatially constrained.

Marshall focused on a local specialist labor pool, the role of local knowledge spillover and the existence of nontraded local inputs. In contrast, Hoover (1948), Ohlin (1933) and Isard (1956) identified the sources of agglomeration advantages as internal economies of scale and external economies of scale in the form of localization and urbanization economies. The production cost efficiencies realized by serving large markets may lead to increasing returns to scale in a single firm. There is nothing inherently spatial in this concept, except that the existence of a single large firm in space implies a large local concentration of employment. External economies are qualitatively very different.

Due to firm size or a large number of local firms, a high level of local employment may allow for the development of external economies within a group of local firms in a sector. These are known as *localization economies*. The strength of these local externalities is assumed to vary, implying that they are stronger in some sectors and weaker in others (Duranton and Puga, 2000). The associated economies of scale comprise factors that reduce the average cost of producing outputs in that locality. Following Marshall (1890), a spatially concentrated sector can exert a pull on (and support) a large labor pool that includes workers with specialized training in the given industry. Obviously, this situation reduces search costs and increases flexibility in appointing and firing employees. Moreover, a concentration of economic activity in a given sector attracts specialized suppliers to that area, which, in turn, reduces transaction costs. Finally, agglomerated firms engaged in the same sector can profit from knowledge spillover because geographic proximity to other actors facilitates the diffusion of new ideas or improvements related to products, technology and organization.

In contrast, *urbanization economies* reflect external economies passed to enterprises as a result of savings from the large-scale operation of the agglomeration or city as a whole. Thus, they are independent of industry structure. Localities that are relatively more populous or places that are more easily accessible to metropolitan areas are also more likely to house universities, industry research laboratories, trade associations and other knowledge-generating institutions. The dense presence of these institutions, which are not solely economic in character but are also social, political and cultural, supports the production and absorption of knowledge, stimulating innovative behavior and differential rates of interregional growth (Harrison *et al.*, 1997). However, areas that are too densely populated may result in a dispersion of economic activities due to pollution, crime or high land prices. In this respect, one can speak of urbanization diseconomies.

Agglomeration economies are now thought to be more complex than Marshall originally suggested. Quigley (1998), for instance, describes additional features that are embedded in the categorization but not recognized for their individual value. These include scale economies or indivisibilities within a firm, the historical rationale for the existence of productivity growth in agglomerated industries. In consumption terms, the existence of public goods leads to urban amenities. Cities function as ideal institutions for the development of social contacts, which correspond to various kinds of social and cultural externalities. Moreover, agglomeration economies may provide greater economic efficiency growth due to potential reductions in transaction costs (Martin and Ottaviano, 1999). The growing importance of transaction-based explanations of local economic productivity growth is a logical outcome of the interaction between urban economies and knowledge-based service industries, and these explanations have become more important recently (Raspe and Van Oort, 2011).

Studies on urban economics and externalities have increasingly used firm-level data to assess the effect of agglomeration economies on firm performance. Audretsch and Dohse (2007) find that German firms located in a knowledge-based cluster grow faster than firms located in a region that is less endowed with knowledge resources. Renski (2011) obtains that industrial localization and regional industrial diversity have a positive on new businesses survival in the United States. The benefits of urbanization economies are, however, limited. Henderson (2003) considers the productivity effect of employment density in a plant's own county versus neighboring counties. Using industry and time dummies, he finds that a 10% increase in employment in a plant's own county increases the productivity of a plant by 0.8% in the high-tech industry. Using French firm-level data (both manufacturing and services), Martin *et al.* (2011) find that doubling the size of a firm's sector increases firm productivity by 5–10%. Baldwin *et al.* (2008) find similar results for the effect of a firm's industry size (in terms of buyer and supplier networks, labor market pooling and knowledge spillovers) on firm productivity in five broad manufacturing sectors in Canada. Andersson and Lööf (2011) find that Swedish firms located in larger regions are more productive and also become more productive. Although the relative lack of firm-level evidence in the agglomeration economics literature can mainly be ascribed to data limitations and confidentiality restrictions, its absence is nevertheless remarkable. The theories that underlie agglomeration economies are microeconomic in nature (Martin *et al.*, 2011). In other words, agglomeration economies do not directly foster regional economic growth; they do so only indirectly, through their effect on firm performance.

2.2 Agglomeration in Organization Studies

During the last two decades, in addition to the proliferation of research on geographical agglomerations, firm strategy researchers have paid increasing attention to the performance implications to firms of locating in agglomerations. Early research has concentrated on positive performance effects as incentives for firms to co-locate in an effort to explain the emergence of agglomerations (Tallman *et al.*, 2004; Bell, 2005; Arikan, 2009). More recently, researchers have begun to highlight possible negative performance effects (Shaver and Flyer, 2000; Arikan and Schilling, 2011; Knoben, 2011), and a sizable amount of empirical support for these effects has emerged. The ambiguity in research results concerning the relation between firm density, clustering and firm performance due to externalities is similar to the ambiguity in the current urban economics and regional science debates. The performance–agglomeration relationship requires research with better tools and better data to reflect the transfer mechanisms between firms and their absorptive capacities. Agglomerations are not homogenous, and they vary along several dimensions. However, research on the effect of agglomeration-level heterogeneity on the performance–agglomeration relationship has been far from conclusive (Beaudry and Schiffauerova, 2009). Furthermore, firm-level heterogeneity has been insufficiently studied in the context of the performance–agglomeration relationship (McCann and Folta, 2008). Overall, the possibility that different firms may be influenced differently by different dimensions of agglomeration remains unexplored in this body of literature.

A potential theoretical solution to address firm-level heterogeneity is to examine the interactions within (agglomerated) contexts. The strategic management approach to agglomeration economies is distinguished by its focus on explaining firm-level heterogeneity in the performance. This approach argues that agglomerated firms can realize the potential benefits of location in an agglomeration only to the extent that they are capable of using knowledge from co-located firms in combination with their own knowledge assets to create value (McCann and Folta, 2011). Kogut and Zander (1992) argue that firms vary significantly in such 'combinative capabilities'. It is suggested that these variations are related to three functions of firms. The first component of a firm's combinative capabilities is its 'organizing principles', defined as the firm's ability to coordinate different parts of the organization and transfer knowledge among them. Firm size is commonly thought to be the most important proxy for this concept. For very small firms, organizing principles reside fully with the entrepreneur or the manager of the firm, whereas for larger firms, 'organization' is increasingly achieved through impersonal means, such as standard operating procedures, routines and dedicated organizational structures. The second component of a firm's combinative capabilities is its existing knowledge base. The larger a firm's existing knowledge base, the better it can assess, access and internalize externally available knowledge. Thus, it is more likely that the net performance effect of agglomeration will be positive for the firm. The third component of a firm's combinative capabilities relates to the number of its localized connections. Firms actively and purposefully collaborate with other firms to obtain, exchange and mutually develop resources. The benefit of collaborating with other firms in the same region emerges from the fact that geographical proximity facilitates both planned and serendipitous face-to-face interactions, which foster the exchange of tacit knowledge (Knoben and Oerlemans, 2006). These ideas have rarely been tested empirically, which leads to the ambiguity in organizational studies regarding the agglomeration–firm performance relationship. Although these three factors are expected to have direct effects on firm performance, the state-of-the-art strategic management literature has focused on their moderating effects on the performance–agglomeration relationship using multilevel modeling.

3. The Multilevel Model

3.1 *From Macro to Micro*

The features of agglomeration economies described above may explain why regions characterized by an agglomeration of economic activities tend to exhibit higher economic growth (McCann and Van Oort, 2009). Despite the focus in the empirical literature on the relationship between agglomeration economies and regional growth as a macro-level phenomenon, the underlying theory of agglomeration contains both macro- and micro-level propositions (see Rosenthal and Strange, 2004). Although these propositions begin and end at the urban or regional level, they recede at the level of the individual firm. Coleman (1990) explored this fact in his bathtub model (also known as the 'Coleman boat'), concluding that system-level phenomena (e.g. agglomeration) influence system outcomes (e.g. regional economic performance) through their effect on firms' orientations and performance. In this respect, performance differences between regions cannot be perceived as a direct result of macro-economic differences between regions. Instead, they are a by-product of firms' individual behaviors.

Firms are interested in seeking agents whose production function is partly determined by the region or city in which they are embedded. This phenomenon is influenced by the opportunities (agglomeration economies) and constraints (agglomeration diseconomies) present in this external environment (Granovetter, 1985; Grabher, 1993). In turn, differences in opportunities and constraints across regions generate differences in firm performance, and

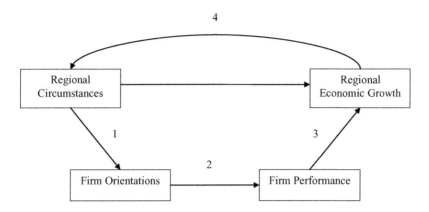

Figure 1. Macro- and Micro-level Propositions: Effects of Regional Circumstances on Regional Economic Growth.

hence, in regional performance. Firms optimize their own performance but do not strive for regional growth. This phenomenon is more explicitly described as follows (see Figure 1):

1. The region in which a firm is embedded generates opportunities and economic constraints for firms located in that region through agglomeration economies and agglomeration diseconomies (macro-to-micro transition).
2. Firms with more economic opportunities and fewer economic constraints (Proposition 1) tend to perform better in terms of their survival chances, employment growth and productivity growth (purposive action).
3. Regions containing successful firms (Propositions 1 and 2) exhibit higher economic growth. Regional performance is conceptualized as the weighted sum of the firms' performances (micro-to-macro transition).
4. Regional performance affects regional circumstances, resulting in a feedback loop. In this fashion, the model can be linked to the evolutionary development of regions.

Two features of this theoretical model call for clarification. First, a firm's external environment consists not only of its location (physical environment) but also other components, such as the sector in which the firm is embedded. For example, firms nested within the same sector share the same technologies and are affected by the same labor market policies and product life cycle. Second, not all opportunities and constraints facing a firm are related to macro-level properties, such as initial firm size, age or entrepreneurship. However, even when constraints and resources are firm-based, the extent to which their effect is independent of the external environment remains debatable. In our two case studies, we focus on the first two propositions and examine the extent to which the macro–micro link exists in agglomeration economics.

3.2 *The Multilevel Framework*

Hierarchical or multilevel modeling allows the micro level and macro level to be modeled simultaneously. Following Jones (2004), there are two distinct advantages to multilevel models. First, multilevel models offer a natural way to assess contextuality, or the extent to which a link exists between the macro level and the micro level. Applying multilevel analysis to empirical work on agglomeration begins from the simple observation that firms sharing the same external environment are more similar in their performance than firms that do not share the same external environment because of shared agglomeration externalities. Thus, we can assess the extent to which variance in the survival and growth rates of new establishments (case study 1, see Section 4) or firm-level productivity (case study 2, see Section 5) can be attributed to between-firm variance, between-area variance, or between-sector variance (McGahan and Porter, 1997). With multilevel analysis, we are able to assign variability to the appropriate context (Bullen *et al.*, 1997). Second, multilevel analysis allows us to incorporate unobserved heterogeneity into the model by including random intercepts and allowing relationships to vary across contexts through the inclusion of random coefficients. Whereas 'standard' regression models are designed to model the mean, multilevel analyses focus on modeling variances explicitly. This kind of complexity can be captured in a multilevel framework through the inclusion of random coefficients (Snijders and Bosker, 1999).

Hox (2002) and Goldstein (2003) provide introductions to multilevel or random-effect regression modeling. The model assumes that we have data from J groups, with a different number of respondents n_j in each group. On the respondent level, we have the outcome of respondent i in group j, variable Y_{ij}. There is an explanatory variable X_{ij} at the respondent level and one group-level explanatory variable Z_j. To model these data, a separate regression model is formulated in each group:

$$Y_{ij} = \beta_{0j} + \beta_{1j}X_{ij} + e_{ij}. \tag{1}$$

The variation of the regression coefficients β_j is modeled by a group-level regression model:

$$\beta_{0j} = \gamma_{00} + \gamma_{01}Z_j + \mu_{0j}, \tag{2}$$

and

$$\beta_{1j} = \gamma_{10} + \gamma_{11}Z_j + \mu_{1j}. \tag{3}$$

The individual-level residuals e_{ij} are assumed to have a normal distribution with mean zero and variance σ_e^2. The group-level residuals $\mu_{0j} + \mu_{1j}$ are assumed to have a multivariate normal distribution with an expected value of zero, and they are assumed to be independent from the residual errors e_{ij}. The variance of the residual errors μ_{0j} is specified as σ_e^2, and the variances of the residual errors μ_{0j} and μ_{1j} are specified as $\sigma_{\mu 0}^2$ and $\sigma_{\mu 1}^2$. We write this model as a single regression model by substituting equations (2) and (3) into equation (1). Substitution and rearranging terms give

$$Y_{ij} = \gamma_{00} + \gamma_{10}X_{ij} + \gamma_{01}Z_j + \gamma_{11}X_{ij}Z_j + \mu_{0j} + \mu_{1j}X_{ij} + e_{ij}. \tag{4}$$

The segment $\gamma_{00} + \gamma_{10}X_{ij} + \gamma_{01}Z_j + \gamma_{11}X_{ij}Z_j$ in equation (4) contains all of the fixed coefficients; it is the fixed (or deterministic) part of the model. The segment $\mu_{0j} + \mu_{1j}X_{ij} + e_{ij}$ in equation (6) contains all of the random error terms; it is the random (or stochastic) part of the model. The term $X_{ij}Z_j$ is an interaction term that appears in the model due to modeling the varying regression slope β_{1j} of the respondent-level variable X_{ij} with the group-level variable Z_j.

Even if the analysis includes only variables at the lowest (individual) level, standard multivariate models are not appropriate. Multilevel models are needed because grouped data violate the assumption of independence of all observations (Corrado and Fingleton, 2012). The amount of dependence can be expressed as the intraclass correlation (ICC) ρ. In the random-effect model, the ICC is estimated by specifying an empty model, as follows:

$$Y_{ij} = \gamma_{00} + \mu_{0j} + e_{ij}. \tag{5}$$

This model does not explain any variance in Y. It only decomposes the variance of Y into two independent components: σ_e^2, which is the variance of the lowest level errors e_{ij}, and $\sigma_{\mu 0}^2$, which is the variance of the highest level errors μ_{0j}. Using this model, the (ICC) ρ is given by the equation

$$\rho = \sigma_{\mu 0}^2 / (\sigma_{\mu 0}^2 + \sigma_e^2). \tag{6}$$

Our outcome variable Y_{ij} is the firm performance, measured as productivity. On the regression line (3), β_{0j} is the usual intercept, β_{1j} is the usual regression coefficient (slope) for the explanatory variable and e_{ij} is the usual residual error term. The subscript j is for the region, and the subscript i is for individual firms. The difference with a usual regression model is that we assume that each region j has a different intercept coefficient β_{0j} and a different slope coefficient β_{1j} (because the intercept and slope vary across the regions, they are often referred to as random coefficients; see Hox, 2002).

4. Case Study 1: New Firm Survival and Growth in Advanced Producer Services

4.1 Agglomeration in the Advanced Producer Service Sector

To examine the relationship between agglomeration economies and firm performance, in this first case study, we concentrate on the survival and employment growth of new establishments in the advanced producer services sector in the Netherlands. An advantage of focusing on new establishments is that these establishments are less constrained by previous decisions, such as past capital installments, which influence how they value the marginal worker and whether new employment is created (Rosenthal and Strange, 2003). In the absence of many establishment-level variables, we avoid the endogeneity problems that are often present in analyses by using data on incumbent establishments.

The existing empirical literature clearly hypothesizes that new establishments benefit from agglomeration. Questioning whether agglomeration externalities bestow new entrepreneurial start-ups with any competitive advantage. Geroski (1995) argues that the growth and survival prospects of new firms depend on their ability to learn from their environment and to link changes in their strategic choices to the changing configuration of that environment. In line with Audretsch and Mata (1995), we hypothesize that survival, and subsequently, growth processes following entry are at least as important as the entry process itself. The post-entry performance of establishments reveals the selection process of markets.

Our selection of economic activities focuses on new establishments in advanced producer services sectors.[1] Advanced business services can profit extensively from agglomeration externalities because advanced business services are among the most concentrated economic sectors in Europe (Brülhart and Traeger, 2005) and these kinds of activities involve the creation, accumulation and dissemination of knowledge. Advanced producer services are characterized by their heavy reliance on professional knowledge, both codified (explicit) and tacit (implicit).

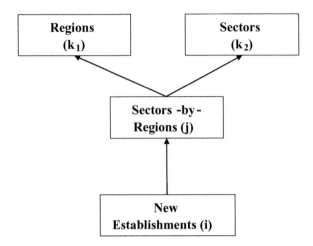

Figure 2. A Mixed Hierarchical and Cross-Classified Model of the External Environment of New Establishments.

4.2 *A Mixed Hierarchical and Cross-Classified Model*

Multilevel analysis, as presented in a stylized way in Section 3, is concerned with modeling hierarchically nested structures (e.g. firms located in the same region are also located in the same country due to the nesting of the two levels). However, the external environment of a firm may consist of elements that have a nonhierarchical nesting structure because they are grouped along more than one dimension or they cut across hierarchies (Goldstein, 2003). For example, sectors are not nested in regions, and vice versa. These different facets of the external environment may explain variations in firm performance (Corrado and Fingleton, 2012).

In our model, we distinguish between four classifications, first in regions (40 NUTS-3 regions in the Netherlands), second in sectors (19 sectors in the advanced producer services), third in sectors-by-regions ($40 * 19 = 781$ clubs) and fourth in establishments of firms (46,038 newly founded establishments, 27,133 of which survive and grow in the first five years of existence). Firms may be affected by the region (agglomeration) in which they are located. As indicated in Section 2, these location factors may be general (urbanization economies, in which all establishments in a given location are exposed to these factors) or sector-specific (localization economies, in which these factors are restricted to a subset of firms nested within a given sector in that location). However, firms may also be affected by the classification of sectors or 'clubs' (sector–location combinations, see Gordon and McCann, 2000). Thus, we disentangle the general location factors and the nation-wide sector-specific factors from the sector-specific factors that are spatially bounded. To illustrate this, we use a mixed hierarchical and cross-classified model (presented in Figure 2). We have a three-level model (with four classifications) with a random intercept for firms at the lowest level and random intercepts for regions ($k1$), sectors-by-regions (j) and sectors ($k2$) at the higher levels. More formally, we estimate the following base probit model for the probability of survival $y_{ij(k1,k2)}$ of new establishments in the advanced producer services:

$$y_{ij(k1,k2)} = Binomial(n_{ij(k1,k2)}, \mu_{ij(k1,k2)})$$

$$probit(\mu_{ij(k1,k2)}) = X_{ij(k1,k2)}\beta_0 + u_{0j(k1,k2)} + v_{0k1} + v_{0k2}$$

$$\text{where } u_{0j(k1,k2)} \sim N\left(0, \sigma^2_{u0j(k1,k2)}\right), \; v_{0k1} \sim N\left(0, \sigma^2_{v0k1}\right), \; v_{0k2} \sim N\left(0, \sigma^2_{v0k2}\right),$$

$$(7)$$

in which the probability of survival or growth of new firms $\mu_{ij(k1,k2)}$ is explained by the single fixed intercept term $X_{ij(k1,k2)}\beta_0$, which is the average survival or growth rate of new firms in the advanced producer services. The three separate random terms $u_{0j(k1,k2)} + v_{0k1} + v_{0k2}$ are related to the intercept and mirror the remaining residual variation at the higher levels. This differs from a typical regression model in that we assume that each sector-by-region j, region $k1$ and sector $k2$ have a different intercept. Note the mixed-hierarchical and cross-classified structure here: the indexing structure $\mu_{ij(k1,k2)}$ refers to the ith firm in the jth club, which is nested in region k_1 and sector k_2. This null model allows us to understand how to attribute variation in the probability of new establishment survival and growth to various contexts.

As indicated in Section 3.2, the variance partition coefficient (VPC) measures the extent to which the probability of survival and growth of new establishments in the same club, region or sector resemble one another relative to those from new establishments in different clubs, regions or sectors. This figure may also be interpreted as the proportion of the total residual variation in survival that is due to differences between clubs, regions or sectors. For example, the VPC for regions represents the percent of variation explained by the region-level differences for firm i in club j and sector $k2$.

$$\text{VPC}_{k1} = \sigma^2_{v0k1} / \left(\sigma^2_{u0j(k1,k2)} + \sigma^2_{v0k1} + \sigma^2_{v0k2}\right) \qquad (8)$$

In equation (8), the term $\sigma^2_{u0j(k1,k2)}$ is the between-club variance, σ^2_{v0k1} is the between-region variance and σ^2_{v0k2} is the between-sector variance. We assume that the probit distribution for the firm-level residual implies a variance of 1 (Goldstein, 2003).

4.3 Adding Predictor Variables and Cross-Level Interactions

To determine the extent to which agglomeration variables explain the partitioned variability, we can add predictor variables to these classifications. More specifically, the predictors (or fixed parameters) we add here contain measures related to firm characteristics, sector-by-region characteristics and region characteristics. Because we are mainly interested in the effects of regional and sector-by-region characteristics on firm performance, we include sector fixed effects (δ_{k2}) by including sector dummies. More formally,

$$y_{ij(k1,k2)} = Binomial\left(n_{ij(k1,k2)}, \mu_{ij(k1,k2)}\right)$$

$$probit\left(\mu_{ij(k1,k2)}\right) = X_{ij(k1,k2)}\beta_0 + \beta_{10}X_{1ij(k1,k2)}$$

$$+ \sum_{j=1}^{q} \beta_{q0}X_{qj(k1,k2)} + \sum_{k1=1}^{r} \beta_{r0}X_{rk1} + \delta_{k2} + u_{0j(k1,k2)} + v_{0k1}. \qquad (9)$$

where $u_{0j(k1,k2)} \sim N(0, \sigma^2_{u0j(k1,k2)})$, $v_{0k1} \sim N(0, \sigma^2_{v0k1})$.

In equation (9), the segment $\beta_{10}X_{1ij(k1,k2)} + \sum_{j=1}^{q} \beta_{q0}X_{qj(k1,k2)} + \sum_{k1=1}^{r} \beta_{r0}X_{rk1}$ contains the predictor variables X at the firm, club and region levels that enter the analysis. The subscripts

q and r indicate the number of predictor variables included at the club and regional levels, respectively (please note that with respect to the establishment level, we only include initial firm size X_1. The β refer to the associated regression slope terms.

Equation (9) is a random intercept model. Only the intercept varies across clubs and regions. However, parameter estimates may also vary across different subpopulations. For example, the effects of localization and urbanization economies may vary over small and large firms. This can be modeled using a cross-level interaction between firm size (X_1) and the respective agglomeration economies. Including firm size as predictor variable at the firm level, we obtain the following equation:

$$y_{ij(k1,k2)} = \text{Binomial}\,(n_{ij(k1,k2)},\, \mu_{ij(k1,k2)})$$

$$\text{probit}(\mu_{ij(k1,k2)}) = X_{ij(k1,k2)}\beta_0 + \beta_{10}X_{1ij(k1,k2)} + \sum_{j=1}^{q} \beta_{q0}X_{qj(k1,k2)} + \sum_{k1=1}^{r}\beta_{r0}X_{rk1} + \delta_{k2}$$

$$+ \sum_{j=1}^{q}\beta_{q10}X_{1ij(k1,k2)}X_{qj(k1,k2)} + \sum_{k1=1}^{r}\beta_{r10}X_{1ij(k1,k2)}X_{rk1} + u_{ij(k1,k2)}X_{1ij(k1,k2)}$$

$$+ v_{1k1}X_{1ij(k1,k2)} + u_{0j(k1,k2)} + v_{0k1},\tag{10}$$

where $u_{0j(k1,k2)} \sim N(0, \sigma^2_{u0j(k1,k2)})$, $v_{0k1} \sim N(0, \sigma^2_{v0k1})$.

In equation (10), $\sum_{j=1}^{q}\beta_{q10}X_{1ij(k1,k2)}X_{qj(k1,k2)} + \sum_{k1=1}^{r}\beta_{r10}X_{1ij(k1,k2)}X_{rk1}$ now represents the cross-level interactions between firm size and the club-level variables and between firm size and the region-level variables, respectively, whereas $u_{1j(k1,k2)}X_{1ij(k1,k2)} + v_{1k1}X_{1ij(k1,k2)} + u_{0j(k1,k2)} + v_{0k1}$ represents the random part of the model. The expressions $u_{1j(k1,k2)} + v_{1k1}$ are the random slope parameters that make the effect of firm size on the probability of survival or growth dependent on the club and region in which the firm is embedded. The cross-level interactions that aim to explain the random slopes can be interpreted as the variation of the effect of the club and region variables across small and larger firms. In the remainder of the case study, we focus on the interaction between firm size and the different agglomeration economies. However, it should be noted that the range of possible interactions is not limited to these variables.

4.4 *Data and Variables*

Data on employment at the firm level were obtained from the LISA (*National Informa-tion System of Employment*) database, an employment register that covers all establishments in the Netherlands for the period 1996–2006. Our first dependent variable, *SURVIVAL* (2000–2006), is a Boolean dummy variable measured at the level of the establishment, which takes the value 1 if a new establishment in 2000 or 2001 survived the first five years of its existence. There are 46,038 new firms in the dataset. Our second dependent variable, *EMPLOYMENT GROWTH*, is a Boolean dummy variable measured at the level of the firm that takes the value 1 if a firm that was newly established in 2000/2001 (and surviving) grows in terms of an increase in the number of employees in the first five years of its existence. There are 27,133 surviving and growing firms in the dataset. As indicated in the theoretical framework of agglomeration economies, we focus on two types of agglomeration economies. *LOCALIZATION ECONOMIES*, or sector-specific scale economies, are defined at the sector-by-region level and measured as the concentration of

Table 1. VPCs for the Survival and Employment Growth of New Producer Service Firms.

	Model 1 Survival	Model 2 Employment growth
VPC (firm) – between-firm variance	90.9%	93.7%
VPC (club) – between-club variance	1.3%	0.8%
VPC (region) – between-region variance	3.3%	2.5%
VPC (sector) – between-sector variance	4.5%	3.0%
Total	100%	100%
N	46,038	27,133

own-sector employment in the region under observation. *URBANIZATION ECONOMIES*, or economies available to all firms in a region, are defined at the region level and measured by the concentration of total employment, which arises from urban size and density. We control at the firm level for *INITIAL FIRM SIZE*, measured as the natural logarithm of the number of employees in the year the firm was founded. Size represents the economies of scale available to a new establishment. By explicitly differentiating between internal and external economies of scale, we account for compositional effects. At the club level, we control for market structure with the variable *COMPETITION*. This is measured as the natural logarithm of the number of entries and exits in the regional sector between 2000 and 2006 divided by the number of firms in 2000 (compare Glaeser *et al.*, 2000). Finally, at the regional level, the controls are *R&D EXPENDITURES*, measured as the natural logarithm of the R&D expenditures of firms, research institutes and government agencies in 2000, and *HUMAN CAPITAL* stock in a region, measured as the natural logarithm of the percentage of the workforce that was highly educated (ISCED 5-6) in 2000.

4.5 Modeling Strategy

We estimate six models. First, we estimate two random intercept probit models (equation (7)) for survival and employment growth without including predictor variables. The VPCs are derived from these models (equation (8)), which serve as a tool to indicate the extent to which location matters by explicitly disentangling the between-location variance from the between-firm and between-sector variance. These cross-classified probit models are estimated using the Markov Chain Monte Carlo algorithm using Gibbs sampling. Second, we estimate two random intercept probit models (equation (10)) to assess the importance of the different types of agglomeration economies on new firm survival and employment growth. Third, we estimate two random coefficient models to assess whether the effect of agglomeration economies varies across firms of different sizes.[2]

Table 1 shows the proportion of the total residual variation in new firm survival and employment growth in the advanced producer services sector that is due to differences between clubs, regions, or (sub)sectors. We see that firm performance (survival and growth) is mainly affected by internal characteristics. More than 90% of the total variance is between-firm variance. The between-region variance is approximately 3%, whereas the between-club variance is approximately 1%. Hence, the location effect explains approximately 4% of the variation in firm performance. Although the external environment explains a relatively

Table 2. Multilevel Probit on New Firm Survival and Employment Growth.

	Model 3 – *PROBIT* survival	Model 4 – *PROBIT* employment growth
Fixed part		
Intercept	0.153 (0.659)	−1.739 (0.509)***
Initial establishment size (ln)	0.013 (0.007)*	0.302 (0.010)***
Localization economies (ln)	0.094 (0.053)*	0.014 (0.027)
Competition (ln)	−0.085 (0.054)	−0.125 (0.045)***
Urbanization economies (ln)	0.277 (0.102)***	0.174 (0.074)**
Human capital (ln)	−0.129 (0.146)	−0.034 (0.132)
R&D expenditures (ln)	−0.064 (0.035)*	0.019 (0.027)
Random part		
u_{ojk1}	0.013 (0.002)	0.006 (0.003)
v_{ok1}	0.023 (0.006)	0.013 (0.004)
Sector fixed effects	Yes	Yes
Mundlak correction	Yes	Yes
Observations	46,038	27,133

$*p < 0.10$, $**p < 0.05$, $***p < 0.01$; standard errors between parentheses.

small part of the variation in firm performance, the region contributes to firm performance. The region represents a solitary factor that accounts for the enormous diversity of firms. Because we defined agglomeration economies as both regional (urbanization economies) and club-related (localization economies), we conclude that these externalities 'explain' approximately 3–5% of the variance in firm performance of new firms.

4.6 Agglomeration Economies, New Firm Survival and Employment Growth

Table 2 shows the results of our further model estimates. Model 3 is the probit model on survival, and model 4 the probit model on unconditional employment growth for the new firms that survived in the first five years of existence.[3] With respect to firm size and survival opportunities (due to downscaling possibilities), we find a small positive and significant effect. On average, a 1% increase in firm size increases the likelihood of survival by 0.012 percentage points. The effect we obtain may be small because our 'sample' of new firms mainly consists of smaller firms and the heterogeneity of size in relation to survival is relatively low. However, with respect to the employment growth of new firms, we find a much larger and significant relationship: a 1% increase in size increases the likelihood of survival by 0.32 percentage points. This is in line with arguments on the 'economies of scale' in the literature, which emphasize that small firms must overcome cost disadvantages (in contrast to larger firms). 'Internal economies of scale' cause a reduction in per-unit costs over the number of units produced, efficiency advantages, and hence, growth potential.

We now turn to the effect of the agglomeration economies on new firm performance in the advanced producer services sector. From the previous section, we see evidence of a 'solitaire spatial effect'. However, the effect of location on firm performance is complex. First, the concentration of own-sector employment (localization economies) has a small, positive effect on new firm survival but no effect on the unconditional employment growth. A 1% increase in own-sector employment increases the probability of survival by 0.09 percentage points. The urban density effect, stemming from urbanization economies, has a much higher impact on new firm performance in the advanced producer services. New firms located in dense urban regions experience higher survival rates and employment growth. A 1% increase in urban density increases the probability that a firm in the advanced producer services sector will survive the first five years by 0.28 percentage points and increases the probability of employment growth in the first five years by 0.17 percentage points. We conclude that new firms in the advanced producer services sector have fewer difficulties surviving in cities. Moreover, when they succeed and survive, their growth rates are significantly higher due to this 'concentration of total employment' effect.

4.7 *Varying Effects of Agglomeration across Small and Large Firms*

Focusing on the effect of agglomeration externalities, we analyze whether there is a positive relationship between agglomeration economies and firm performance in terms of new firm survival and employment growth. This relationship might not be fixed in all regions ('fixed' meaning that it does not vary over regions). We argue that some firms (based on firm-specific characteristics) profit more than others, or that externalities only appear for some types of firms. In this section, we test for 'cross-level interaction effects', interactions between variables measured in hierarchically structured data on different levels (Hox, 2002). We focus on initial firm size and analyze the possibility that agglomeration economies are mainly effective for larger start-ups.

It appears that initial firm size has a significant slope variance (the basic underlying condition for the existence of cross-level interaction effects). Table 3 shows the results of the random coefficient models, in which we allowed for the possibility that the effect of initial firm size can vary from region to region (regions have different slopes), including an interaction effect on size and localization and urbanization economies. The random part in Table 3 shows that the covariance between the region's intercept and slope is significant and *positive*. This positive covariance suggests that a higher intercept is associated with a higher slope. In other words, larger firms perform better in some regions, or their smaller counterparts perform less well in other regions. Concerning survival, we find that the interaction effects between initial establishment size and localization and urbanization economies are significant and positive. This means that *larger* start-ups profit more from own industry and urban density. We find the opposite for employment growth: the interaction effect between initial establishment size and localization economies is significant but *negative*, whereas the interaction effect between initial establishment size and urbanization economies is not significant. The first finding means that *smaller* start-ups profit more from proximity to a concentration of own-sector employment than do their larger counterparts. New firms with differing start-up sizes do not profit differently from urbanization economies in relation to employment growth.

The first case study focuses on the determinants of the survival and growth of new firms in the advanced producer services sector in the Netherlands. Employing a mixed hierarchical and cross-classified probit regression, we introduce a model of firm survival and growth that is specific to the characteristics of the internal and external environment of a firm. This external environment may consist of several components, such as the firm's location, sector or club (location-by-sector). This case study shows that 1) the location effect can be carefully disentangled from the firm and sector effect and 2) we can analyze whether

Table 3. Multilevel Probit on New Firm Survival and Employment Growth.

	Model 5 – *PROBIT* survival	Model 6 – *PROBIT* employment growth
Fixed part		
Intercept	−0.041 (0.636)	−1.483 (0.476)***
Initial establishment size (ln)	−0.138 (0.131)	0.157 (0.182)*
Localization economies (ln)	0.083 (0.054)	0.023 (0.027)
Competition (ln)	−0.087 (0.054)	−0.095 (0.043)**
Urbanization economies (ln)	0.254 (0.098)***	0.173 (0.064)**
Human capital (ln)	−0.181 (0.138)	0.046 (0.120)
R&D expenditures (ln)	−0.064 (0.033)*	0.007 (0.024)
Est. size *localization economies	0.022 (0.013)*	−0.031 (0.018)*
Est. size *urbanization economies	0.051 (0.021)**	–
Random part		
u_{ojk1}	0.015	0.005
	(0.003)	(0.003)
U_{1jk1}	0.009	0.024
	(0.002)	(0.005)
v_{0k1}	0.033	0.021
	(0.008)	(0.006)
v_{1k1}	0.006	0.007
	(0.002)	(0.003)
Sector fixed effects	Yes	Yes
Mundlak correction	Yes	Yes
Observations	46,038	27,133

*$p < 0.10$, **$p < 0.05$, ***$p < 0.01$; standard errors between parentheses.
Insignificant cross-level interaction were omitted from the analysis.

firms benefit from agglomeration economies asymmetrically. Similar insights are difficult to obtain with other estimation methods.

5. Case Study 2: Agglomeration, Organization and Productivity of Firms

5.1 Nonlinear Heterogeneity in Micro–Macro relations

In our second case study, we present a multilevel analysis that extends the arguments regarding the agglomeration performance relationship with insights from the strategic management literature. Specifically, we argue that agglomerations are heterogeneous along two spatial dimensions, urbanization and localization (level of specialization). Similar to the previous case study, it is hypothesized that these dimensions give rise to orthogonal performance implications for firms. In line with the hypotheses postulated in Section 2.2, we test whether a firm's combinative capabilities, as manifested in its organizing principles – which are measured for this chapter, rather simply, by firm size – are related to firm productivity in agglomerated contexts. We again test our hypotheses by estimating multilevel models, this time with nonlinear interaction effects between the agglomeration and firm-level variables, using survey data from a sample of Dutch firms. The results suggest that the effects of different dimensions of agglomeration on firm performance are strongly and nonlinearly moderated by a firm's combinative capabilities. The moderation effect is not uniform across either the two different agglomeration dimensions or the different sizes of firms.

A central concept in strategic management theories concerns a firm's ability to coordinate different parts of the organization and transfer knowledge among them (Kogut and Zander, 1992; McCann and Folta, 2011). Size plays a significant role in a firm's organizing principles. For small firms, organizing principles are located in the entrepreneur or the manager of the firm, whereas for larger firms, 'organization' is increasingly achieved through impersonal means, such as standard operating procedures, routines and dedicated organizational structures. The literature suggests that inertia and rigidity are associated with larger firm size as well (Miller and Chen, 1994). Due to the complexity of large firms, actions between large numbers of people must be coordinated and managed, resulting in institutionalized and rigid rules and procedures. These structures may reduce large firms' openness to their environment as well as their flexibility, consequently preventing them from finding and effectively integrating externally available resources into their existing resources. The literature also emphasizes the inability of very small firms to internalize externally available resources (Deeds and Rothaermel, 2003). Full reliance on one or several individuals to assess, access and internalize externally available resources without procedures, routines or dedicated units to aid such processes is likely to result in missed opportunities and the lack of capability to utilize external resources.

The above arguments suggest that when a firm is too large or too small, it is unlikely to fully benefit from the positive performance effects of agglomeration. For such firms, we expect the net agglomeration effect to be negative. We thus hypothesize that the relationship between firm performance and agglomeration is positively moderated by medium-sized firms but not by small or large firms. Testing this nonlinear heterogeneity using interaction effects in multilevel modeling is the main added value of this second case study.

5.2 Data and Variables

At the firm level, we use data from an establishment-level survey that was conducted in 2005 in the Netherlands. We opted for a survey in this case study rather than relying on secondary data because our research goal requires detailed productivity data at the establishment level (rather than the consolidated firm level) from a wide range of industries and size classes. Existing databases fail to meet these requirements. The survey targeted firms in the manufacturing and business services industries. We excluded retail and customer-related services because these predominantly follow the distribution of the population and are therefore unlikely to exhibit distinct and geographically differentiated patterns of agglomeration.

Within the manufacturing and business services industries in the selected regions, we used a random stratified sample from the LISA database (see Section 4.4), taking into account firm size, industry and region (i.e. municipalities).[4] Ultimately, the size of the sample was 28,637 firms. The survey was targeted at directors or owners at the establishment level. After a round of reminders, the response rate was approximately 7% ($N = 2009$). The final sample is representative of the stratification by region, size and industry. Table 4 outlines the population and response rates.

Previous research on the relationship between agglomeration effects and firm performance utilized a wide variety of performance indicators. Some of these measures are highly context-dependent. Performance measures that are frequently used in cross-industry studies are employment growth and productivity (Beaudry and Schiffauerova, 2009). Employment

Table 4. Geographical Breakdown of Population and Survey Response.

Region	# Municipalities sampled	# Firms sampled	Response (%)
Amsterdam	16	5980	399 (6.7%)
Rotterdam	28	4818	357 (7.4%)
Groningen	12	2128	167 (7.8%)
Eindhoven	16	3763	289 (7.7%)
Apeldoorn	14	2217	162 (7.3%)
Arnhem	24	3259	271 (8.3%)
The Hague	13	3117	185 (5.9%)
Utrecht	13	3355	179 (5.3%)
TOTAL	136	28,637	2009 (7.0%)

growth, however, has been criticized as a performance measure for well-performing firms investing in labor-saving innovations, particularly in the manufacturing industries. We adopt the level of productivity of the firm, defined as the added value of a firm per employee, as our performance measure. The firm's added value is determined as the yearly gross turnover in 2004 minus purchases for that year (all intermediate goods and service needed in the production process of the firm). The added value includes the firm's taxes, subsidy, wages and profits. Productivity is determined by dividing the added value at the firm level by the number of employees of the firm (again measured for 2004).

Our size measure is designed to capture our collection of highly heterogeneous firms. We used the gross sales of the firm in the 2004 as our size measure. This measure is commonly considered the most applicable size measure in cross-industry research (Cohen and Klepper, 1996). Job density was used as an indicator of urbanization externalities stemming from a large concentration of economic activity. We used density rather than the absolute number of jobs to correct for differences in geographical size between municipalities. Urbanization economies were thus measured by a density indicator reflecting the number of total jobs per square kilometer within the responding firm's municipality. Economies of specialization were measured by the location quotient for the region and industry in which the responding firm was active (based on its two-digit SIC code) in the year 2002. In all models, we included industry fixed effects to control for differences between industries that are not captured by our main effects. We included industry dummies at the two-digit SIC level.

5.3 *Modeling Results*

The results are presented in Table 5. Model 1 shows two firm-level characteristics with a direct effect on firm performance. It shows that the performance effect is positive, but with diminishing returns for firm size. Model 2 reveals that the two region-level variables (i.e. urbanization and specialization) have no effect on firm productivity when examining their direct effect in isolation. Model 3 illustrates that the findings of models 1 and 2 remain unchanged when firm- and region-level variables are included simultaneously. Model 4, however, shows that the picture changes drastically when cross-level interaction effects are included. The model fit improves significantly at both the firm and the region level, and many interesting effects are revealed. Due to their nonlinear nature, these interaction effects

Table 5. Hierarchical Multilevel Regression Models of Firm Productivity.

Variable	Model 1	Model 2	Model 3	Model 4
Firm-level variables				
Size	0.30*** (0.02)		0.30*** (0.03)	0.34*** (0.02)
Size^2	−0.21*** (0.00)		−0.21*** (0.00)	−0.05*** (0.01)
Region-level variables				
Urbanization		0.08 (0.05)	0.06 (0.04)	0.10** (0.05)
Specialization		0.12 (0.07)	−0.01 (0.07)	0.07 (0.07)
Cross-level interaction effects				
Size*Urbanization				−0.04** (0.02)
Size^2*Urbanization				−0.02** (0.00)
Size*Specialization				−0.11** (0.04)
Size^2*Specialization				−0.03*** (0.01)
Constant	10.97*** (0.21)	10.38*** (0.35)	10.66*** (0.32)	10.45*** (0.32)
Observations	2009	2009	2009	2009
Number of regions	128	128	128	128
Industry fixed effects	Yes	Yes	Yes	Yes
R-squared region level	55.4%	27.7%	60.2%	62.7%
R-squared firm level	13.1%	1.1%	13.3%	15.2%
Log-likelihood	7948.19	8190.25	7916.14	7865.91

[a]Standard errors in parentheses.
*$p < 0.100$; **$p < 0.050$; ***$p < 0.001$.

are extremely difficult to interpret based on Table 5. Therefore, the combinations of firm- and region-level variables for which significant interaction effects were found are presented in Figures 3 and 4.

Figure 3 presents the interaction effect between urbanization and firm size. Figure 3a presents the productivity effects of the range of combinations between the two variables, and Figure 3b presents the relationship between urbanization and performance for three selected levels of firm size. The figure clearly reveals that the relation between urbanization and performance is qualitatively different for different levels of firm size. In line with our hypothesis, the relationship is positive for medium-sized firms but negative for small and large firms. The relationship is significantly more negative for small firms compared to

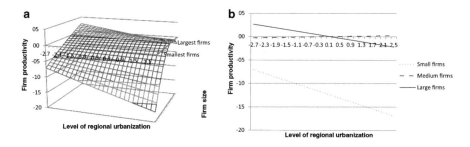

Figure 3. Multilevel Interaction Between Firm Size and Urbanization Effects.

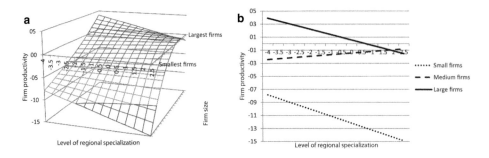

Figure 4. Multilevel Interaction Between Firm Size and Specialization Effects.

large firms. Figure 4 presents the interaction effect between specialization and firm size. Again, in line with our hypothesis, the relationship between the agglomeration effect and firm productivity is positive for medium-sized firms but negative for small and large firms. However, in this instance, the strength of the negative relation does not significantly differ between large and small firms. If some firms experience a negative performance effect and others experience a positive effect from co-location and agglomeration, the total regional effect is dependent on the composition and structure of the region. This explains why, on a regional level, as noted in Section 1, outcomes of agglomeration economies and growth potentials can be ambiguous.

6. Conclusion

A large body of empirical literature examines whether spatial circumstances give rise to agglomeration economies, external economies from which firms can benefit through co-location, which endogenously induce localized economic growth. Many empirical studies show that agglomeration economies may be one source of the uneven distribution of economic activities and economic growth across cities and regions. At the same time, little is known about the importance of agglomeration economies for the performance of firms. This absence is remarkable because the theories that underlie agglomeration economies are microeconomic in nature. Agglomeration economies do not directly foster regional economic growth; they do so indirectly through their effect on firm performance.

In this chapter, we have shown that multilevel analysis provides an analytical tool to assess the extent to which a link exists between the macro level and the micro level. As Corrado and Fingleton (2012, p. 29) note, 'Hierarchical models are almost completely absent from the spatial econometrics literature (and vice versa are spatial econometric models mostly absent from the multilevel literature, for an exception see Steenbeek *et al.*, 2012), but hierarchical models represent one major alternative way of capturing spatial effects, focusing on the multilevel aspects of causation that are a reality of many spatial processes. Recognition of the different form of interactions between variables that affect each individual unit (firm) of the system and the groups they belong to has important empirical implications'. Multilevel models offer a natural way to assess contextuality. Applying multilevel analysis to empirical work on agglomeration begins with the simple observation that firms sharing the same external environment are more similar in their performance than firms that do not share the same external environment. This is due to shared agglomeration externalities. Thus, we assessed the extent to which variance in the survival and growth rates of new firms (case study 1) and firm-level productivity (case study 2) can be attributed to between-firm variance, between-area variance, or between-sector variance. Using multilevel analysis, we are able to assign variability to the appropriate context. Multilevel analysis allows us to incorporate unobserved heterogeneity into the model by including random intercepts and allowing relationships to vary across contexts through the inclusion of random coefficients. Whereas 'standard' regression models are designed to model the mean, multilevel analysis focuses on modeling variances explicitly. For example, the effect of urbanization and local-ization externalities may vary across small and large firms (case study 2) or across sectors simultaneously with spatial levels (case study 1). This kind of complexity can be captured in a multilevel framework through the inclusion of random coefficients.

Our two case studies show that cross-level interactions and cross-classified (multiple mem-bership) variants of the multilevel model have considerable advantages over other estimation methods (e.g. spatial econometrics) in capturing the firm- and context-level heterogeneity in firm performance. However, there are some limitations to the use of multilevel analysis in spatial research. Most importantly, multilevel analysis does not fully account for the spatial dependence present in data in that it does not allow for the effect of neighboring regions on the performance of a firm. Spatial spillover effects between regions may be highly relevant, and failing to account for these effects may underestimate the importance of 'space' in the performance of firms (Corrado and Fingleton, 2012). For example, R&D and human capital are well known for their spatial spillover effects. Viable solutions would be to include spa-tially weighted independent variables in the model (e.g. Florax and Folmer, 1992), to use a conditional autoregressive multilevel model (e.g. Breslow and Clayton, 1993) or to employ a spatial multiple membership model (e.g. Browne *et al.*, 2001). Combining such empirical strategies with a micro–macro framework will advance the literature on agglomeration eco-nomics in its effort to determine the extent to which the agglomerated environment of firms is important for their performance.

Notes

1. The sectors in advanced producer services in our study include publishing, banks and insurance, financial services, real estate activities, rental and leasing, computer services, information services, accounting, legal services, market research, advertising, management consulting, architectural and engineering activities, telecommunications, office administra-tion and business support activities.
2. Models 3–6 are estimated using a restricted iterative generalized least-squares estimation (RIGLS) and a second-order PQL estimation (Breslow and Clayton, 1993; Goldstein and Rasbash, 1996). The standard model assumes that the establishment-level predictor variables are uncorrelated with the club- and regional-level error terms and the club-level predictor variables are uncorrelated with the regional-level error terms. However, both theoretically and empirically, such an assumption is difficult to meet. Not correcting for this would lead to inconsistent parameter estimates. As shown by Snijders and Berkhof (2007), the correlation between the lower level predictor variables and higher level error terms can be easily removed by including club- or region-level means of the lower level predictor variables in the regression model, a procedure known as the Mundlak (1978) correction. Hence, our multilevel probit models are augmented with this correction.

3. Because we estimated survival and growth, the latter analysis faces the problem of panel attrition by nonsurvival. Firms that do not survive inhibit information on the missing-dependent variable. Possible disturbances in the estimations of the growth coefficients related to this selection bias occur when characteristics of nonsurvival are related to firm growth. An effective way to control for this selection bias is to apply a *two-step Heckman procedure*, including a correction factor that reflects the effects of all unmeasured characteristics related to firm survival and captures the part of the nonsurvivors effect that is related to growth. The use of an *instrument* variable in the survival analysis is highly relevant. This variable should relate to nonsurvival, but not to growth. Because both phenomena are often considered 'in line with one another', it is difficult to find appropriate instruments. We tested for the average regional number of bankruptcies (1994–2006), a sectoral 'new economy' variable (Audretsch and Dohse, 2007), and for individual-level *size-quadrat* specifications. One can hypothesize that they have an effect on survival, but not on growth per se (Raspe and Van Oort, 2011). The test gave us insight into the fact that controlling for selection bias does not improve the models significantly (although the instruments can be significant, the correction factor is not significant or is only slightly significant). Because the focus in our chapter is on the multilevel research framework and multilevel modeling (variance decomposition insights), we have chosen not to present the Heckman models. Instead, we only show the results of the probit multilevel regressions without correction for panel attrition.

4. In our sample, we included only firms with more than one employee. The reason for this choice was that the Netherlands is characterized by an extremely large number of self-employed people without personnel (well over a million in a labor force of less than eight million) who register their 'businesses' at their home addresses. However, these self-employed people do not truly own a business establishment; rather, they work for (sometimes several) larger organizations. The reasons for registering as self-employed are largely related to tax and social security benefits. As such, including this group of firms in our sample would bias our results.

References

Acs, Z. and Armington, C. (2004) The impact of geographic differences in human capital on service firm formation rates. *Journal of Urban Economics* 56: 244–278.

Alker, H.R. (1969) A typology of ecological fallacies. In M. Dogan and S. Rokan (eds), *Quantitative Ecological Analysis* (pp. 69–86). Cambridge, MA: MIT Press.

Andersson, M. and Lööf, H. (2011) Agglomeration and productivity: evidence from firm-level data. *Annals of Regional Science* 46: 601–620.

Arbia, G. (2001) Modelling the geography of economic activities in a continuous space. *Papers in Regional Science* 80: 411–423.

Arikan, A.T. (2009) Interfirm knowledge exchanges and the knowledge creation capability of clusters. *Academy of Management Review* 34: 658–676.

Arikan, A.T. and Schilling, M.A. (2011) Structure and governance in industrial districts: implications for competitive advantage. *Journal of Management Studies* 48: 772–803.

Audretsch, D.B. and Dohse, D. (2007) Location: a neglected determinant of firm growth. *Review of World Economics* 143: 79–107.

Audretsch, D.B. and Mata, J. (1995) The post-entry performance of firms: introduction. *International Journal of Industrial Organization* 14: 413–419.

Baldwin, R. and Okubu, T. (2006) Heterogeneous firms, agglomeration economies and economic geography. *Journal of Economic Geography* 6: 323–346.

Baldwin, R., Beckstead, D., Brown, W.M. and Rigby, D.L. (2008) Agglomeration and the geography of localization economies in Canada. *Regional Studies* 42: 117–132.

Beaudry, C. and Schiffauerova, A. (2009) Who's right, Marshall or Jacobs? The localization versus urbanization debate. *Research Policy* 38: 318–337.

Bell, G.G. (2005) Clusters, networks, and firm innovativeness. *Strategic Management Journal* 26: 287–296.

Beugelsdijk, S. (2007) The regional environment and a firm's innovative performance: a plea for a multilevel interactionist approach. *Economic Geography* 83: 181–199.

Brakman, S., Garretsen, H. and Van Marrewijk, C. (2009), *The New Introduction to Geographical Economics*. Cambridge, MA: Cambridge University Press.

Breslow, N.E. and Clayton, D.G. (1993) Approximate inference in generalised linear models. *Journal of the American Statistical Association* 88: 9–25.

Briant, A., Combes, P.P. and Lafourcadem, M. (2010) Dots to boxes: do the size and shape of spatial units jeopardize economic geography estimations? *Journal of Urban Economics* 67: 287–302.

Browne, W.J., Goldstein, H. and Rasbash, J. (2001) Multiple membership multiple classification (MMMC) models. *Statistical Modelling* 1: 103–124.

Brülhart, M. and Mathys, N.A. (2008) Sectoral agglomeration economies in a panel of European regions. *Regional Science and Urban Economics* 38: 348–362.

Brülhart, M. and Traeger, R. (2005) An account of geographic concentration patterns in Europe. *Regional Science and Urban Economics* 35: 597–624.

Bullen, N., Jones, K. and Duncan, C. (1997) Modelling complexity: analysing between-individual and between-place variation – a multilevel tutorial. *Environment and Planning A* 29: 585–609.

Cohen, W.M. and Klepper, S. (1996) Firm size and the nature of innovation within industries: the case of process and product R&D. *The Review of Economics and Statistics* 78: 232–243.

Coleman, J.S. (1990) *Foundations of Social Theory*. Cambridge, MA: Harvard University Press.

Combes, P.P. (2000) Economic structure and local growth: France 1984–1993. *Journal of Urban Economics* 47: 329–355.

Combes P.P., Duranton, G. and Gobillon, L. (2008) Spatial wage disparities: sorting matters. *Journal of Urban Economics* 63: 723–742.

Corrado, L. and Fingleton, B. (2012) Where is the economics in spatial econometrics? *Journal of Regional Science*, 52: 210–239.

Deeds, D.L. and Rothaermel, F.T. (2003) Honeymoons and liabilities: the relationship between age and performance in research and development alliances. *Journal of Product Innovation Management* 20: 468–484.

De Groot, H.F.L., Poot, J. and Smit, M.J. (2009) Agglomeration externalities, innovation and regional growth: theoretical reflections and meta-analysis. In R. Capello and P. Nijkamp (eds), *Handbook of Regional Growth and Development Theories* (Chapter 14). Cheltenham, UK: Edward Elgar.

Dicken, P. and Malmberg, A. (2001) Firms in territories: a relational perspective. *Economic Geography* 77: 345–363.

Duranton, G. and Overman, H.G. (2005) Testing for localization using micro-geographic data. *Review of Economic Studies* 72: 1077–1106.

Duranton, G. and Puga, D. (2000) Diversity and specialisation in cities: why, where and when does it matter? *Urban Studies* 37: 533–555.

Duranton, G. and Puga, D. (2005) From sectoral to functional urban specialization, *Journal of Urban Economics* 57: 343–370.

Florax, R. and Folmer, H. (1992) Specification and estimation of spatial linear panel models: Monte Carlo evaluation of pre-test estimators. *Regional Science and Urban Economics* 22: 402–432.

Frenken, K., Van Oort, F.G. and Verburg, T. (2007) Related variety, unrelated variety and economic growth. *Regional Studies* 41: 685–697.

Geroski, P.A. (1995) What do we know about entry? *International Journal of Industrial Organization* 13: 421–440.

Glaeser, E.L. (2000) The new economics of urban and regional growth. In: G.L. Clark, M.P. Feldman and M.S. Gertler (eds), *The Oxford Handbook of Economic Geography* (pp. 83–98). Oxford: Oxford University Press.

Glaeser, E.L., Kallal, H.D., Scheinkman, A. and Shleifer, A. (1992) Growth in cities. *Journal of Political Economy* 100: 1126–1152.

Goldstein, H. (2003) *Multilevel Statistical Models*, 3rd edn. London: Edward Arnold.

Goldstein, H. and Rashbash, J. (1996) Improved approximations for multilevel models with binary responses. *Journal of the Royal Statistical Society A* 159: 505–513.

Gordon, I.R. and McCann, P. (2000) Industrial clusters: complexes, agglomeration, and/or social networks? *Urban Studies* 37: 513–532.

Grabher, G. (1993) Rediscovering the scoial in the economics of interfirm relations. In G. Grabher (ed.), *The Embedded Firm. On the Socioeconomics of Interfirm Relations* (pp. 1–33). London: Routledge.

Granovetter, M.S. (1985) Economic action and social structure: the problem of embeddedness. *American Journal of Sociology* 81: 481–510.

Harrison, B., Kelley, M.R. and Gant, J. (1997) Innovative firm behavior and local milieu: exploring the intersection of agglomeration, firm effects, and technological change. *Economic Geography* 72: 233–258.

Henderson, J.V. (2003) Marshall's scale economies. *Journal of Urban Economics* 53: 1–28.

Henderson, J.V., Kuncoro, A. and Turner, M. (1995) Industrial development in cities. *Journal of Political Economy* 103: 1067–1085.

Hoover, E.M. (1948) *The Location of Economic Activity*. New York: McGraw Hill.

Hox, J.J. (2002) *Multilevel Analysis: Techniques and Applications*. Mahwah, NJ: Erlbaum.

Isard, W. (1956) *Location and Space-Economy*. Cambridge, MA: MIT Press.

Jones, K. (2004) An introduction to statistical modelling. In B. Somekh and C. Lewin (eds), *Research Methods in the Social Sciences* (pp. 236–251). London: Sage.

Knoben, J. (2011) The geographical distance of relocation search: an extended resource based perspective. *Economic Geography* 87: 371–392.

Knoben, J. and Oerlemans, L.A.G. (2006) Proximity and inter-organizational collaboration: a literature review. *International Journal of Management Reviews* 8: 71–89.

Kogut, B. and Zander, U. (1992) Knowledge of the firm, combination capabilities and the replication of technology. *Organization Science* 3: 383–397.

Lucas, R.E. (1988) On the mechanics of economic development. *Journal of Monetary Economics* 22: 3–42.

Macintyre, S., MacIver, S. and Sooman, A. (1993) Area, class and health: should we be focusing on places or people? *Journal of Social Policy* 22: 213–234.

Marshall, A. (1890) *Principles of Economics*. London: MacMillian.

Martin, P. and Ottaviano, J.P. (2001) Growth and agglomeration. *International Economic Review* 42: 947–968.

Martin, P., Mayer, T. and Mayneris, F. (2011) Spatial concentration and firm-level productivity in France. *Journal of Urban Economics* 69: 182–195.

McCann, B.T. and Folta, T.B. (2008) Location matters: where we have been and where we might go in agglomeration research. *Journal of Management* 34: 532–565.

McCann, B.T. and Folta, T.B. (2011) Performance differentials within geographic clusters. *Journal of Business Venturing* 26: 104–123.

McGahan, A.M. and Porter, M.E. (1997) How much does industry matter really? *Strategic Management Journal* 18: 15–30.

McCann, P.and Van Oort, F.G. (2009) Theories of agglomeration and regional economic growth: a historical review. In R. Capello and P. Nijkamp (eds), *Handbook of Regional Growth and Development Theories* (pp. 19–32). Cheltenham: Edward Elgar.

Melo, P.C., Graham, D.J. and Noland, R.B. (2009) A meta-analysis of estimates of agglomeration economies. *Regional Science and Urban Economics* 39: 332–342.

Miller, D. and Chen, M.J. (1994) Sources and consequences of competitive inertia – a study of the United-States airline industry. *Administrative Science Quarterly* 39: 1–23.

Mion, G. and Naticchioni, P. (2009) The spatial sorting and matching of skills and firms. *Canadian Journal of Economics* 42: 28–55.

Moon, G., Subramanian, S.V., Jones, K., Duncan, C. and Twigg, L. (2005) Area-based studies and the evaluation of multilevel influences on health outcomes. In A. Bowling and S.

Ebrahim (eds), *Handbook of Health Services Research – Investigation, Measurement and Analysis* (pp. 262–296). Berkshire: Open University Press.

Mundlak, Y. (1978) On the pooling of time series and cross-section data. *Econometrica* 46: 69–85.

Ohlin, B. (1933) *Interregional and International Trade*. Cambridge, MA: Harvard University Press.

Ottaviano, G.P. (2011) 'New' new economic Geography: firm heterogeneity and agglomeration economies. *Journal of Economic Geography* 11: 231–240.

Puga, D. (2010) The magnitude and causes of agglomeration economies. *Journal of Regional Science* 50: 203–219.

Quigley, J.M. (1998) Urban diversity and economic growth. *Journal of Economic Perspectives* 12: 127–138.

Raspe, O. and Van Oort, F.G. (2011) Growth of new firms and spatially bounded knowledge externalities. *Annals of Regional Science* 46: 495–518.

Renski, H. (2011) External economies of localization, urbanization and industrial diversity and new firm survival. *Papers in Regional Science* 90: 473–502.

Robinson, W.S. (1950) Ecological correlations and the behavior of individuals. *Sociological Review* 15: 351–357.

Romer, P.M. (1986) Increasing returns and long-run growth. *Journal of Political Economy* 94: 1002–1037.

Rosenthal, S.S. and Strange, W.C. (2003) Geography, industrial organization, and agglomeration. *Review of Economics and Statistics* 85: 377–393.

Rosenthal, S.S. and Strange, W.C. (2004) Evidence on the nature and sources of agglomeration economies. In J.V. Henderson and J.F. Thisse (eds), *Handbook of Regional and Urban Economics: Cities and Geography* (Vol. 4, pp. 2119–2179). Amsterdam: North Holland.

Shaver, J.M. and Flyer, F. (2000) Agglomeration economies, firm heterogeneity, and foreign direct investment in the United States. *Strategic Management Journal* 21: 1175–1193.

Snijders, T.A.B. and Bosker, R.J. (1999) *Multilevel Analysis: An Introduction to Basic and Advanced Multilevel Modelling*. London: Sage.

Snijders, T.A.B. and Berkhof, J. (2007) Diagnostic checks for multilevel models. In J. De Leeuw and E. Meijer (eds), *Handbook of Multilevel Analysis* (pp. 139–173). New York: Springer.

Steenbeek, W., Volker, B., Flap, H. and Van Oort, F.G. (2012) Local business as attractors or preventers of neighborhood disorder. *Journal of Research in Crime and Delinquency*, forthcoming.

Tallman, S., Jenkins, M., Henry, N. and Pinch, S. (2004) Knowledge, clusters, and competitive advantage. *Academy of Management Review* 29: 258–271.

Taylor, M. and Asheim, B. (2001) The concept of the firm in economic geography. *Economic Geography* 77: 315–328.

Van Oort, F.G. (2007) Spatial and sectoral composition effects of agglomeration economies. *Papers in Regional Science* 86: 5–30.

7

A RELATIONAL APPROACH TO THE GEOGRAPHY OF INNOVATION: A TYPOLOGY OF REGIONS

Rosina Moreno and Ernest Miguélez

1. Introduction

Agents do not create in isolation. Indeed, the production of innovation relies on the recombination of existing knowledge and ideas. Employees within a firm and across its different departments create and recombine ideas through a process of collective learning that is structured within the organization (March, 1991; Lorenz, 1996). Organizations produce innovations by combining existing knowledge that goes beyond the limits of their boundaries. In short, firms turn to external sources of ideas (Rosenkopf and Almedia, 2003) and their ability to recombine and exploit such knowledge is pivotal to boost their competitive advantage (Dosi, 1988; Singh and Agrawal, 2011). Cassiman and Veugelers (2006), amongst others, have consistently shown that complementarities between firms' internal R&D activities and their external knowledge acquisition are strong predictors of performance.

Recognition of the critical role of knowledge flows, knowledge diffusion and knowledge recombination dates back to the well-known Marshallian externalities. Several decades later, endogenous growth models (Lucas, 1988; Romer, 1990; Grossman and Helpman, 1991) put knowledge spillovers at the forefront of the mainstream research agenda. During the 1990s, empirical analysis from the geography of innovation (Jaffe, 1986, 1989; Jaffe *et al.*, 1993; Feldman, 1994; Feldman and Audretsch, 1999) and new economic geography models (Martin and Ottaviano, 1999) emphasized the localized pattern of knowledge spillovers and their role in explaining both the high spatial concentration of economic activity and spatial differences in economic growth. Central to this reasoning is the assumption that corporate and public R&D investment spills over to third parties in the form of an externality, but 'the ability to receive knowledge spillovers is influenced by distance from the knowledge source' (Audretsch and Feldman, 1996, p. 630).

Recently, scholars have started to claim that excessively close actors may have little to exchange after a certain number of interactions (Boschma and Frenken, 2010). Indeed, the production of ideas requires the combination of different, although related, complementary

Innovation, Entrepreneurship, Geography and Growth, First Edition.
Edited by Philip McCann and Les Oxley. Chapters © 2013 The Authors.
Book compilation © 2013 Blackwell Publishing Ltd. Published 2013 by Blackwell Publishing Ltd.

pieces of knowledge to be most effective. However, at some point, co-located agents may start to combine and recombine local knowledge that eventually becomes redundant and less valuable. As a result, processes of lock-in may begin to occur (David, 1985; Arthur, 1989). Conversely, firms looking for external sources of knowledge that lie beyond their own boundaries may find that the knowledge they require is available beyond the boundaries of the region (Bergman and Maier, 2009). This strategic behaviour increases the probability of gaining *first mover* advantages in the market for the focal firm (Bergman and Maier, 2009) and consequently for the region. Hence, if there are strong internal connections between firms within a given region, but weak external connections to other sources of knowledge, 'there is the risk of localism, which implies that a regional economy is unable to acquire and master external knowledge and is hence likely to be less innovative' (Fratsei and Senn, 2009, p. 17). Thus, it is important to balance internal and external, local and nonlocal interactions, to ensure a satisfactory amount of adoption and creation of knowledge.

We build our empirical strategy on this idea and develop a method that tries to quantify to what extent actors in regions can access sources of knowledge that lie beyond the confines of their cluster. This puts regions in a better strategic position to potentially use extra-regional ideas in the production of innovations. In so doing, we expect to increase our understanding of why some regional economies become locked into nondynamic development paths, whereas others seem able to reinvent themselves continuously (Martin and Sunley, 2006).

To the best of our knowledge, little attention has been paid to this issue from an academic or policy-making perspective. The case of Europe is a paradigmatic example. Despite recent empirical evidence and the importance European policy makers place on interregional connections to build a coherent and integrated European Research Area (European Commission, 2007, 2010), policy reports do not tend to consider the external dimensions of regional innovation (e.g. the Regional Innovation Scoreboard, 2009). We strongly believe that connections to external sources of knowledge are as important for regions as their scientific and technological base. Consequently, we aim to fill this knowledge gap.

In this chapter, we describe a method for constructing a synthetic indicator able to identify the regions in the best (and worst) position to access sources of knowledge from beyond their boundaries. To do this, we feed from various research streams – geography of innovation, regional economics, innovation economics and regional innovation systems (RIS) literature – and we survey and discuss the most recent conceptual and empirical contributions. On the basis of this review, we conceptually model the ways in which organizations and other actors in regions access external-to-the-region pieces of knowledge. We suggest that two different regimes are at work: (1) informal interactions and unintentional relations arising from serendipitous encounters between actors who lie in close spatial proximity and (2) formal, intentional relations based on coordinated and well-defined linkages between actors who might, or might not, be in close spatial proximity. Hence, we characterize regions in terms of the ways in which they can potentially access external knowledge. In short, our research will provide a method for quantifying regions' exposure to external knowledge through these two patterns.

On the basis of the proposed method, we aim to develop a typology of regions according to their position in these two dimensions: regions in a superior potential position to build informal connections with the outside world above the average, but lacking formal, intentional linkages (*clustering regions*); regions with numerous formal relations but potentially few informal connections (*globalizing regions*); regions that do not have an advantageous positions in either of these two dimensions (*noninteractive regions*) and finally, regions with values above the mean in both indices (*knowledge networking regions*). We apply our approach to a group of NUTS2 regions in 31 European countries (EU-27 plus Iceland, Liechtenstein, Norway and Switzerland).

The outline of the chapter is as follows: Section 2 reviews some relevant conceptual and empirical studies on the idea that agents access external-to-the-region knowledge to avoid regional lock-in. In this section, we bring together dispersed, but related, literature. Section 3 develops in more detail our conceptual model of connectivity through the two dimensions outlined above, and examines in depth the concept of 'knowledge networking regions'. Section 4 describes the empirical approach taken here. Section 5 summarizes some remarkable findings and Section 6 presents conclusions and policy implications.

2. Review of Theoretical and Empirical Literature

2.1 *Physical Space and Knowledge Flows*

Most geography of innovation scholars have reiterated that the role of physical proximity in enhancing knowledge creation is critical to understand the uneven distribution of economic and innovation activities across space, as well as the major spatial differences in growth rates between regions, even within the same country. To recap, empirical studies in the geography of innovation (Jaffe, 1986, 1989; Jaffe *et al.*, 1993; Feldman, 1994; Feldman and Audretsch, 1999) and economic geography (Martin and Ottaviano, 1999) literature have established that knowledge produced by a firm is only partially appropriated by the producer itself, whereas part of this knowledge spills over to other firms and institutions, reducing in this way innovation costs of these other organisations, as shown by endogenous growth models (Romer, 1986, 1990; Lucas, 1988). Face-to-face interactions between employees (Allen, 1977; Krugman, 1991b), frequent meetings, monitoring of competitors (Porter, 1990), spin-offs, trust building (Glaeser *et al.*, 2002) and the like, which are essential to the effective exchange of ideas, have been indistinctly taken to explain the mechanisms by which knowledge spills over as an externality. Due to the nature of these mechanisms and the highly contextual features of the knowledge that is transferred, knowledge barters are assumed to occur amongst members of a co-located community and, therefore, knowledge is considered to be spatially sticky.

To sum up, the hypotheses hold that a firm's insertion into a given cluster provides it with advantages that are not available to firms outside the cluster. Co-location creates an 'industrial atmosphere' (Marshall, 1920; Becattini, 1979) or 'local buzz' (Storper and Venables, 2004), where information flows, knowledge transfers and learning opportunities take place continuously in both organized and accidental meetings (Bathelt *et al.*, 2004). A key point is that little effort is needed to participate in the buzz, that is, flows are more or less automatically received by those who share the physical space (*op. cit.*).

Critical to this line of argument is the explicit differentiation between tacit knowledge and codified/explicit knowledge. Tacit knowledge is highly contextual, difficult to transfer and share across long distances and therefore better transmitted in the form of meetings and face-to-face interactions (Breschi and Lissoni, 2001a,b) that are facilitated most by co-location (Breschi *et al.*, 2010). Codified/explicit knowledge may travel frictionless across the space by means of information and communication technologies. Tacit knowledge is therefore relatively immobile, which implies that actors can only share it when they have a similar social context. This social context is also assumed to be bound in space (Gertler, 2003).

These are undoubtedly pivotal elements within the literature. However, an important point has been made by several scholars from innovation economics and organizational science. In their view, two contradictory arguments explain the diffusion of knowledge and its spatial stickiness (Torré, 2008): (1) tacit knowledge is a public good and its appropriateness escapes the control of its producers, who cannot prevent others from benefitting from it and (2) because it is highly contextual, tacit knowledge needs frequent interactions to be transmitted. Objections to this contradictory logic have led researchers to show that co-location favours the transmission of knowledge, instead, via market mechanisms and pecuniary externalities across members of the same epistemic community, including local networks (vertical and horizontal) and local mobility of the labour force. These transmission methods have nothing to do with pure knowledge externalities (Almeida and Kogut, 1997, 1999; Zucker et al., 1998; Rychen and Zimmermann, 2008; Torré, 2008; Breschi and Lissoni, 2009; Camagni and Capello, 2009). Thus, spatial proximity is not a necessary or sufficient condition for knowledge to flow across agents (Boschma, 2005). In contrast, social and other forms of non-spatial proximity, which are in the very nature of the relationships between members of the same epistemic community, are essential. As a result, highly contextual knowledge might not be as spatially sticky as is usually assumed in the geography of innovation literature, if other types of proximity are also at work. As we will discus in more detail in Section 3, the reality probably lies somewhere between these two approaches. Thus, pure localized knowledge externalities may still play a role (Iammarino and McCann, 2006), especially in the early stages of an industry life cycle (Audretsch and Feldman, 1996).

2.2 From Localization to a Balanced Internal–External Mix of Knowledge Flows

Indeed, an increasing number of academics have called into question the widely accepted assumption that knowledge flows are localized. This assumption, they argue, might have limited our understanding of the ways in which knowledge flows across space (Coe and Bunnell, 2003). Certainly, recent empirical evidence casts doubts on the orthodox viewpoint outlined earlier. Some studies have started to explore the influence of extra-local knowledge sources on firms' innovative performance, although the results are ambiguous. For instance, in their analysis of the Boston biotech community, Owen-Smith and Powell (2004) showed that although membership to local networks, rather than centrality within these networks, was a conduit to better company performance, central positions in geographically dispersed networks increased firms' patent volume. Thus, 'being situated at the intersection of numerous formal pipelines enhances firm-level knowledge outputs' (op. cit., p. 16). Gittelman (2007) suggested that geographical proximity matters for innovation, but opportunities for learning by interacting also exist beyond regions' boundaries in the case of US biotech firms. Indeed, he estimated that distant research teams received more citations of their output than teams formed in closer proximity. In parallel, Gertler and Levite (2005) found that the most successful Canadian biotech firms are externally oriented. Thus, patenting Canadian biotech firms are more likely to have foreign partners in their collaborative projects than their non-patenting counterparts. This suggests that the best places for biotech innovators are not only those with a strong 'local buzz', but also regions that are well connected extra-locally.

Trippl et al. (2009) analysed the software cluster in Wien. It was found that the local context remains highly relevant as a source of knowledge and information, but extra-local connections (national and European customers, suppliers, competitors and service companies) also play an important role. The authors concluded that the interplay between local, national and global seems to drive innovation-oriented firms in the software industry. Similar conclusions were drawn in Giuliani and Bell (2005) for the case of a Chilean wine cluster. According to the authors, two types of behaviour characterize knowledge dynamics in this cluster: (1) although local linkages are prominent, they are highly selective, rather than unstructured and unplanned and (2) for some firms, learning links are partially or almost exclusively found outside the cluster. Further examples are case studies by Asheim and Isaksen (2002), who analysed three Norwegian clusters (shipbuilding, mechanical engineering and electronics). They found external-to-the-region contacts to be crucial in the innovation process of firms. As the authors pointed out, firms in clusters tend to exploit both place-specific resources and external knowledge sources to increase their innovation rates. Similar conclusions were made by Vang and Chaminade (2007) in a study of Toronto's film industry and by Belussi *et al.* (2010) in a chapter on life science firms in the Emilia Romana region (Italy).

In a similar vein, Rosenkopf and Almedia (2003) convincingly argued that, despite the larger pools of knowledge available at local level, firms need to search for knowledge sources beyond their geographical and technological vicinity as the distant context may offer particularly useful ideas and insights for recombination. Using data on patents, citations, interfirm alliances and labour mobility, the aforementioned authors evaluated various knowledge inflows at different spatial scales. Despite their claims, the positive effects of distant relationships (in the form of alliances and mobility) were not supported by the data. Simonen and McCann (2008) drew similar conclusions in a different context. Their study on interfirm labour mobility in a sample of Finish firms shows that labour inflows from the same area are positively related to firms' innovative performance. Meanwhile, outside-the-region inflows are only related to firms' performance when the incoming worker belongs to high-tech sectors that are similar to the focal firm. Boschma *et al.* (2009) found similar results for Swedish firms. They argued that the positive effects of employee inflows might depend on the skills portfolio of the incumbent workers and on whether or not they come from the firm's geographical area. Therefore, they split inflows according to the employees' skills (i.e. similar, related and unrelated skills). They found that both related and unrelated skills had a positive effect when incumbent workers come from the firm's own area, whereas only related skill inflows had a positive impact in the case of extra-local workers. Their explanation is based on the following logic: incumbent workers with very similar skills to the receiving firm do not add any value to its current knowledge base, whereas workers with different, but related, skills do contribute to firms' performance even if they move in from a different spatial context.

This empirical evidence goes hand in hand with an increasing number of claims from prominent academicians who have raised concerns in this area. Thus, several scholars have lately stressed the need for firms to network with extra-local knowledge pools to overcome potential situations of regional 'entropic death', 'lock-in' or 'over-embeddedness' (Camagni, 1991; Grabher, 1993; Uzzi, 1996; Boschma, 2005). These claims have contributed to a lively current debate amongst research streams about the conditions in which tacit knowledge can be transmitted at a distance and go beyond a region's confines, as well as the extent of such transmission. Indeed, it has been argued that two very close actors may have little knowledge to exchange and that innovative production usually requires the combination of dissimilar, but related, complementary knowledge (Boscham and Iammarino, 2009; Boschma and Frenken, 2010).[1] Thus, as time passes and local interactions lead to the combination and recombination of the same pieces of knowledge, organizations end up stuck in strong social structures that tend to resist social change (Boschma and Frenken, 2010; Morrison *et al.*, 2011) and prevent them from recognizing opportunities in new markets and technologies (Lambooy and Boschma, 2001). Thus, 'distant contexts can be a source of novel ideas and expert insights useful for innovation processes (...). Firms therefore develop global pipelines not only to exchange products or services, but also to benefit from outside knowledge inputs and growth impulse' (Maskell *et al.*, 2006, p. 998). As already asserted in the social network literature, nonredundant rather than repeated ties are the most apposite to increase knowledge flows and innovation (Granovetter, 1973; Burt, 1992).

Truly dynamic regions in the era of the knowledge economy are therefore characterized not only by dense local learning and interaction, but also by the ability to identify and establish inter-regional and international connections to outside sources of ideas (Gertler and Levitte, 2005; Maskell *et al.*, 2006). Thus, certain actors within dynamic regions can build connections with more or less remote actors, to form nonredundant ties that bring new knowledge into a given local network (Burt, 1992). These actors function as knowledge gatekeepers, setting up global bridges between the local network and outside sources of knowledge (Glucker, 2007). Thus, they introduce knowledge variation into the regional economy, which can prevent the region from entering nondynamic development paths. In sum, regions that host globally connected organizations end up being more successful than others (Bergman and Maier, 2009).

Analogously, the RIS literature (Autio, 1998; Cooke *et al.*, 2000) has generally looked at regions in an isolated manner, that is, without any specific consideration of inter-relationships across regional systems or on larger spatial scales. However, recent contributions within this stream have also started to tackle this issue (Tödtling and Trippl, 2005). Indeed, external links provide access to ideas and technologies that are not endogenously generated within the regional system, which is actually far from being self-sustained (*op. cit.*). In consequence, recent works have suggested the concept of 'Open RIS' (Belussi *et al.*, 2010).

Following on from part of these theoretical and empirical contributions, Bathelt *et al.* (2004) envisage a conceptual model that is concerned with the coexistence between a vibrant 'local buzz' and a number of 'pipelines' that provide access to relevant pools of knowledge outside the 'buzz'. These authors hint at the fact that in reality firms build pipelines to benefit from knowledge hotspots around the world, and do not build their knowledge stock solely from local interactions (Bahlmann *et al.*, 2008). The logic in Bathelt's *et al.* (2004) implies that[2]: (1) new (tacit) knowledge is created around the globe and firms that can access it through global pipelines gain competitive advantage; (2) this knowledge acquired from abroad may spill over or be transferred within the local cluster through the local network of a firm or individual; consequently (3) there is a kind of trade-off between 'a too much inward-looking and a too much outward-looking' structure of grabbing knowledge (Bathelt *et al.*, 2004, p. 46) and (4) there are limits to the number of pipelines a firm can manage at the same time, and therefore it is better to have several firms managing a set of pipelines than for one large firm that manage a high, but limited, number of pipelines. Pioneering contributions along these lines were made, however, by Hägerstrand (1965), who distinguished between contagious and hierarchical patterns of information diffusion. In the contagious diffusion regime, information flows first at close proximity from the originating source, then with effort at greater distances. According to the hierarchical regime, information first diffuses from relatively large cities to other equal-sized cities, even those at large physical distances, between which communication infrastructures are supposed to be more developed. Maggioni *et al.* (2007) and Maggioni and Uberti (2011) took these insights into account and developed an extensive research agenda based on the distinction between unintended cross-regional spatial spillovers and intentional relations based on aspatial networks. Their logic is straightforward: knowledge is created in central organizations that tend to co-locate. Subsequently, knowledge is diffused either through a trickle down process of spatial contagion of neighbouring regions (by means of face-to-face interactions and other 'unintended' means) or through aspatial networks structured in the form of contractual agreements between organizations that connect clusters, irrespective of the spatial distance between them.

Tödtling *et al.* (2006) and Trippl *et al.* (2009) use a broader set of dimensions to classify the ways in which knowledge flows within and between clusters and regions. For these authors, knowledge diffusion processes can be summarized by differentiating between two dimensions. The first dimension distinguishes between traded and untraded interdependencies (following Storper, 1997) on the basis of whether or not there is monetary or similar compensation. The second dimension distinguishes between static and dynamic knowledge exchanges, that is, transfers of pieces of already available knowledge or barters that involve interactive learning processes between agents, respectively (see also Capello, 1999).

As we will see in more detail in Section 3, our conceptual framework is based on these early contributions, although some differences will be worth mentioning.

2.3 *Do Regions 'Pipe' External Knowledge? Some Evidence at Regional Level*

Within regional science, the number of studies that address cross-regional relationships and their impact on economic outcomes has sharply increased in the last 25 years. A clear example is the growing number of chapters that apply spatial econometric techniques at regional level. These chapters have been more or less concerned with estimating cross-regional knowledge externalities in knowledge production function (KPF) frameworks (Acs *et al.*, 1994; Anselin *et al.*, 1997; Bottazzi and Peri, 2003). Indeed, as stated by prominent scholars, there is no reason to assume that knowledge stops flowing because of regional borders (Krugman, 1991a; Audretsch and Feldman, 2004). Therefore, spatial econometric techniques and the spatial weight matrix have notably improved the way such externalities are measured (Autant-Bernard and Massard, 2009). Admittedly, this approach is no more than a corollary of the traditional localized knowledge spillovers story, although it considers that externalities may spread to regions in the immediate vicinity.

Other studies within this stream have tried to go one step further. Moreno *et al.* (2005) and Parent and LeSage (2008), amongst others, have exploited the concept of technological proximity between regions *vis-à-vis* spatial proximity in estimates of cross-regional externalities. Their underlying logic relies on the idea that knowledge externalities flow easily amongst the members of epistemic communities of scientists and technicians in highly specialized technological fields, irrespective of their geographical location, due to the fact that they share a specific knowledge background and common jargon and codes. Similarly, Kroll (2009) and Ponds *et al.* (2010) have built weight matrices using collaborative research data across regions to proxy the social distance between them at aggregate level. In this way, they show the importance of reflecting nonspatial, more meaningful measures of proximity across regions in estimations of the effects of cross-regional knowledge flows on regional innovative performance. The aforementioned study by Maggioni *et al.* (2007) follows a similar approach, as spatial contagious effects *vis-à-vis* network effects in the form of research collaborations are estimated in a spatial KPF framework. However, their approach reveals that when the spatial weight matrix is subtracted from the network matrix and a pure social matrix is considered on its own, important spatial effects are unaccounted for.

Despite these and other contributions, the literature on cross-regional knowledge diffusion and regional innovation is relatively scant, apart from studies on the purely spatial approach. Likewise, supra-national organizations' policy reports on regional innovation do not tend to consider that extra-regional linkages are part of the regional innovation performance, either from an input or output perspective. For instance, the latest Regional European Scoreboard (2009) takes into account a number of regional innovation indicators, such as human capital, R&D expenditure, ICT penetration, employment in high technologies and patents. However, it does not include indicators concerning a region's degree of openness to external sources of knowledge, in neighbouring or distant regions, that may have a definite impact on regional innovative output and, subsequently, on economic development. By means of principal component analysis, the Regional Innovation Monitor (European Commission, 2011) produces a typology of innovative regions using several indicators, including public and private R&D, patents and population with tertiary education. None of these indicators appraise a region's capacity to access and use external knowledge in its innovation processes. Similar approaches are followed by the Global Innovation Index (INSEAD, 2011), the OECD (Marsan and Maguire, 2011) and Navarro *et al.* (2009). Only recently, in its annual assessment of the performance of regions (OECD, 2009), the OECD included co-patenting with external-to-the-region inventors as an indicator of knowledge sharing.

Similarly, regional innovation datasets (OECD[3] or Eurostat[4]) barely reflect the relational dimensions of regions as entities that establish relationships through their actors that usually go beyond the regions' boundaries and are beneficial for their innovative performance, as they are their human capital or R&D efforts.

In consequence, we believe that the approaches that are currently used to assess the innovation performance of regions are far too simplistic. Our research project tries to fill this gap by proposing a method for computing a composite indicator that evaluates the extent to which regions can access external pieces of knowledge and information, either by a process of informal barters between agents located in neighbouring regions or by means of formal linkages with outsiders. Subsequently, our strategy will provide a taxonomy of regions that is based on the mechanisms for accessing external knowledge: formal versus informal interactions.

3. Towards the 'Knowledge Networking Region'

The above review helps us to build a conceptual framework for the 'knowledge networking region' notion, which we develop in the present section. Again, our primary aim in this chapter was to develop a simple method for appraising the external dimension of regional knowledge production. In doing so, we obtain an instrument for classifying regions into different tiers, according to their capacity to access external sources of knowledge and innovation. To achieve this, we distinguish between two ways in which regional agents access external knowledge. As outlined earlier, the approach chosen at this stage resembles that of Bathelt *et al.* (2004) and Maggioni *et al.* (2007). Thus, actors access external knowledge pools by means of two distinct patterns, that is

- an informal, nonintentional and serendipitous pattern of knowledge interactions that take place between agents located in spatial proximity and
- a formal, intentional and conscious pattern of linkage formation between actors, irrespective of their geographical location.

Later, these two patterns are illustrated in detail. Note that our distinction has nothing to do with the usual classifications, such as *tacit* (assimilated to informal) verus *codified* (assimilated to formal) knowledge. Again, the tacit property has been widely advocated as the reason why knowledge of this type is easily transmitted by means of face-to-face contacts, and therefore co-location is required (Breschi and Lissoni, 2001a,b). However, several authors stress that even when knowledge is totally codified, what is required is a tacit understanding of the message that is transmitted, which is a property of the epistemic community and may have little to do with the territory in which the knowledge is produced (Cowan *et al.*, 2000; Steinmueller, 2000; Breschi and Lissoni, 2001a,b). Note also that our attention is totally focused on the dichotomy between informal/formal mechanisms, rather than whether the linkages are in neighbouring regions or not. In this way, we allow for cross-regional formal knowledge flows between contiguous regions. Finally, amongst the formal cross-regional linkages considered, we include collaborations between actors, as in many previous studies. However, we also include geographical mobility of highly skilled labour and access to codified knowledge located outside the region. Bearing this in mind, we will now describe in detail the logic behind each of the patterns of regional capacity to access external knowledge.

3.1 *Informal Pattern of Knowledge Diffusion*

Co-location brings people together, facilitates contacts for information and enhances the exchange of knowledge. In other words, agents who are spatially concentrated benefit from knowledge externalities. In this case, the producer of a given piece of knowledge cannot internalize all its effects and part of it spills over to other agents, who do not compensate the initial producer. These kinds of knowledge flows occur via informal face-to-face interactions, monitoring of competitors, advisor–student relationships and so on. Just being in a location is enough to contribute to and benefit from continuous flows of information and updates, gossip, news, rumours and recommendations (Gertler, 1995; Bathelt *et al.*, 2004).

As we discussed in previous sections, empirical studies tend to confirm that knowledge externalities are geographically bound, in which no other forms of proximity are necessarily involved. The transfer of knowledge takes place without explicit coordination between agents. Thus, firms near knowledge sources show better innovative performance than firms located elsewhere (Audretsh and Feldman, 1996). In many instances, the administrative boundaries of a region do not coincide with the boundaries of the 'local buzz'. When the sender and the receiver of the externality are not located (sometimes by chance) in the same region, spillovers across regions occur.

As already stated, the spatial economics and econometrics literature has long dealt with the estimation of cross-regional knowledge externalities in a KPF framework (Acs *et al.*, 1994; Anselin *et al.*, 1997, amongst many others). For instance, well-known studies on

Europe have estimated the spatial scope of knowledge spillovers to be around 250–300 km (Bottazzi and Peri, 2003; Moreno *et al.*, 2005).[5]

Needless to say, the informal pattern of interaction described here does not measure knowledge externalities *per se*. In fact, knowledge spillovers are invisible (Krugman, 1991a), although they may sometimes leave a chapter trail (Jaffe *et al.*, 1993). The variables chosen in our analysis only let us assess the extent to which each region is well positioned to endorse informal interactions and serendipitous encounters that may encourage knowledge diffusion between actors of neighbouring regions. What is actually measured, as in the literature, is the potential for localized spillovers (D'Este and Iammarino, 2010). Whether or not knowledge indeed flows across regions is an interesting question, which goes beyond the scope of this analysis.[6] The following variables could be used to proxy the advantageous position of regions that may receive knowledge flows from informal interactions:

- R&D expenditure in neighbouring regions: R&D is well established as being the greatest source of new knowledge (Arrow, 1962) and a source of spatial informal knowledge exchanges through pure externalities (Jaffe, 1986, 1989). Thus, cross-regional R&D externalities have been widely investigated (Anselin *et al.*, 1997; Bottazzi and Peri, 2003; Bode, 2004).
- Patent applications in neighbouring regions: Patent applications have been used as an indicator of R&D productivity at regional level. Therefore, patent applications in neighbouring regions can be used as an indicator of potential informal access to knowledge from innovation outputs (Autant-Bernard and LeSage, 2011).
- Human capital in neighbouring regions: Theoretical and empirical contributions have shown the existence of human capital externalities (Lucas, 1988; Rauch, 1993; Moretti, 2004), arguing that skilled individuals tend to be more productive when they are surrounded by their peers. Although studies regarding cross-regional informal flows from human capital stocks are less preponderant, human capital externalities may well go beyond the boundaries of the administrative region.

3.2 *Formal Pattern of Knowledge Exchange*

In recent years, several authors have pointed out that, even at close spatial proximity, knowledge flows are not automatically received just by 'being there', as previous literature tends to assume. Rather, knowledge flows follow specific transmission channels, which are mainly based on market interactions (Breschi and Lissoni, 2001a,b). In some instances, actors look for external-to-the-firm pieces of knowledge in knowledge pools that lie beyond the boundaries of their own region. Thus, some members of a region can activate linkages with these pools. As reviewed in Section 2, such linkages are pivotal to access external pieces of ideas and information that would otherwise not be available for the local cluster.

These members therefore play the role of 'knowledge gatekeepers'. This figure is derived from the concept of 'technological gatekeeper', proposed by Allen (1977). Knowledge gatekeepers make a conscious effort to establish formal linkages with knowledge hotspots outside the region, irrespective of the geographical distance. Contrary to informal knowledge diffusion mechanisms, the links that are built are not automatic and participation in them is not free. Their establishment requires a costly process. Gatekeepers take the role of global bridges (Glucker, 2007) that link the 'local buzz' with external knowledge sources, thus covering 'structural holes' between networks (Burt, 1992). For a knowledge gatekeeper to be effective for the region as a whole, it has to be inserted in global networks and well embedded in the 'local buzz' through which the incoming insights are diffused. If this is the case, the more connected a gatekeeper is with external partners, the more potentially connected the region will be with distant pools of knowledge, and therefore the higher the probability of gaining competitive advantages in the market, both for the focal firm and for the entire region (Bergman and Maier, 2009).

This knowledge transfer, which can take place across large distances (although not exclusively), requires other forms of proximity to be effective. Other dimensions of proximity (such as social, cognitive, institutional and organizational) are key in understanding interactive learning and diffusion of knowledge between partners that are located at a distance (Boschma, 2005).[7]

Naturally, a large number of connections between agents and external sources of knowledge do not ensure that the knowledge will enter and spread into the region. Ultimately, this will depend on the absorptive capacity of the gatekeeper (Cohen and Levinthal, 1990) and, more importantly, on whether or not this gatekeeper is willing to share its knowledge within the 'local buzz'. If the connected agents behave as external stars (Morrison *et al.*, 2011), then the region as a whole will not benefit from their external connections.

Like Bathelt *et al.* (2004) and Maggioni *et al.* (2007), we believe that alliances between organizations are critical to build 'pipelines' with outsiders. However, as in Boschma *et al.* (2009), we extend the formation of external linkages to the issue of the geographical mobility of knowledge workers who embody tacit knowledge (see also Coe and Bunnell, 2003; Rosenkopf and Almedia, 2003). The capacity of particular agents to connect with external sources of codified knowledge is also considered. In sum, the following measures may proxy for these formal linkages:

- Cross-regional co-patents: Networks of inventors are a source of potential knowledge flows, as individuals connected within a collaborative framework are more willing to learn from each other than isolated inventors (Breschi and Lissoni, 2004, 2009; Cowan and Jonard, 2004; Singh, 2005; Gomes-Casseres *et al.*, 2006).
- Inflows of inventors: Mobility may also favour knowledge diffusion. The movement of skilled individuals across locations contributes to knowledge mobilization throughout the space. Skilled workers take their knowledge with them and share it in a workplace with their new employer and colleagues. In return, they acquire knowledge from their new colleagues and, in general, promote new combinations of knowledge (Laudel, 2003; Trippl and Maier, 2010).
- Citations made to outside-the-region patents: We use this proxy as it indicates the extent to which regional actors rely on already codified sources of knowledge that go beyond regional boundaries. Patent citations have been used widely in studies of innovation to measure the scope of knowledge flows (Jaffe *et al.*, 1993, Peri, 2005).

3.3 *A Simple Typology*

In short, up to six variables (three for each regime) are assembled to approximate the extent to which a region can take advantage of cross-regional knowledge diffusion.

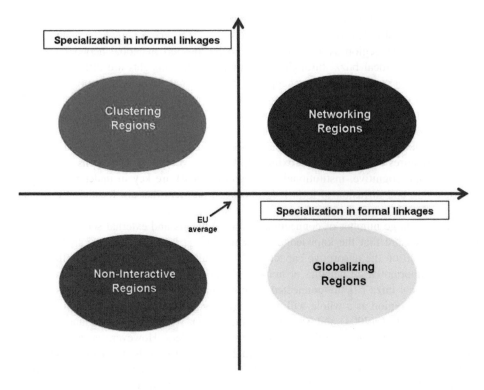

Figure 1. A Typology of Regions According to the Type of Linkages to External Sources of Knowledge.

The computation of the two subindices will shed some light on each region's specialization pattern, in terms of its level of connectivity with external knowledge. Combinations of regions' specialization in one regime or the other will produce the following typology:

- Clustering regions: Regions showing higher than average values for potential informal linkages but lower than average values for formal linkages.
- Globalizing regions: Regions characterized by lower than average values for informal linkages but higher than average values for formal linkages.
- Noninteractive regions: Regions showing lower than average values for both indicators.
- Knowledge networking regions: Regions showing higher than average values for both synthetic indicators – informal and formal linkages.

Figure 1 graphically summarizes the suggested typology. In a nutshell, 'knowledge networking regions' are regions that are in a relatively advantageous position to receive and access external pools of knowledge through the two patterns illustrated in the previous sections.

4. Empirical Approach

Below, we summarize the result of applying the method outlined in the previous section to a group of 287 NUTS2 regions belonging to 31 European countries (EU-27 plus

Iceland, Liechtenstein, Norway and Switzerland). See the Appendix for the complete list of countries.

4.1 Variable Construction

With respect to the construction of the indicator of a region's capacity to access knowledge through informal interactions we consider the following variables:

- R&D expenditure in neighbouring regions (R&D expenditure weighted by a predefined spatial weight matrix): average value of R&D expenditure in the neighbouring regions.
- Patent applications in neighbouring regions (patent applications weighted by a predefined spatial weight matrix): average value of patent applications in the neighbouring regions.
- Human capital in neighbouring regions (percentage of population aged 15 and over with tertiary education over the total population, weighted by a predefined spatial weight matrix): average value of human capital in the neighbouring regions.

The spatial weight matrix taken from the spatial econometrics toolkit will help us to construct this subindicator. This is a nonstochastic square matrix that captures an *ad hoc* intensity of the interdependencies between each couplet of regions, where $W = \{w_{ij}\}$, leading to a definition of 'neighbouring'. The most usual definition of neighbouring is the first-order physical contiguity, that is, if two regions share the same administrative border $w_{ij} = 1$, and $w_{ij} = 0$ otherwise. In this chapter, we use a more complex version of this matrix, which takes the physical distance between regions' centroids, instead of contiguity, as a neighbouring criterion and introduces strong spatial decay, giving far more importance to short-distance neighbours than to long-distance neighbours. Concretely, we define $w_{ij} = \exp(-0.01d_{ij})$, where d_{ij} is the Euclidean distance, in kilometres, between the centroids of region i and region j. Following Bottazzi and Peri (2003), a cut-off of 300 km is introduced.[8]

The proxies used to construct the indicator that capture formal interactions include:

- Co-patents with other regions: the valued degree centrality of cross-regional co-patents. The number of patents co-authored with inventors from outside the region. When a patent involves inventors whose addresses are in different regions, we assume that cross-regional collaborations took place. We 'full-count' all the collaborations across regions, irrespective of the number of inventors reported in each patent. For each patent with multiple inventors, all possible pairs of regions ij were created.
- Inflows of skilled workers: valued in-degree centrality of cross-regional inflows of inventors. Number of inflows of inventors from other regions. A 'mobile' inventor is broadly defined as an individual who moves across different regions, irrespective of whether the focal individual changes his employer or not. Mobility is computed through observed changes in the inventor's region of residence, as reported in the patent documents.[9] Admittedly, in this manner we only capture mobility if the inventor applies for a patent before or after a move, which probably underestimates real mobility. We compute the movement in time between the origin and the destination patent, but only if there is a maximum lapse of 5 years between them.
- Cross-regional patent citations: valued in-degree centrality of cross-regional patent citations. Number of citations made to patents of other regions.

The socio-matrix, taken from social network analysis (SNA), is used to build the variables that make up this indicator. This is a tabular representation in matrix form that measures social relationships between the members of a network. Networks are formed by actors, or nodes (regions in our case), which are connected to one another by means of relations or ties. These connections form relationships between nodes that can be represented in the socio-matrix, whose elements capture the intensity of the relationship between node i and node j. Relations in a network might be undirected when the relationships are symmetric, or directed when the direction of the relation between a given pair of points does matter. In addition, the relations between nodes might be binary (1 when a relationship exists, and 0 otherwise) or valued (the intensity of the relationship matters and numerical values are 'attached' to each of the lines). One of the most important point measures in SNA is that of degree centrality. The aim is to detect the most central (i.e. the most popular) actor within the structure. This is defined as simply the number of incumbent linkages that a given node has. When networks are directed, the degree centrality may include separately in-degree centrality (the number of edges directed to the vertex) and out-degree centrality (the number of edges that the vertex directs to other vertices).

Using the different variables suggested and the corresponding instruments, we compute a single measure that allows us to assert whether or not a given region is a knowledge networking region. In addition, we obtain a composite indicator for the formal linkages dimension and another for informal linkages.

Both synthetic indicators corresponding to each dimension are developed following the procedure used in the European Innovation Scoreboard (2009). Specifically, because the indicator variables we are using for the two different categories of linkages can be highly volatile and have skewed data distributions (where most regions show low performance levels and a few regions show exceptionally high performance levels), data will be modified first using a square root transformation. Second, based on the square root values, rescaled values are obtained by subtracting the minimum value and then dividing by the difference between the maximum and minimum value. The maximum rescaled score is thus equal to 1 and the minimum rescaled score is equal to 0.[10] For each kind of linkage (informal and formal) a composite indicator is calculated as the unweighted average of the rescaled scores for all indicators within the respective dimension. In sum, knowledge networking regions are regions above the European average in terms of specialization on both types of linkages.

4.2 *Data Sources*

The raw data corresponding to informal knowledge diffusion variables (R&D expenditure, patents and human capital) were assembled by CRENoS, using manifold data sources: Eurostat, OECD REGPAT database, ISTAT and the Institut National de la Statistique et des Études Économiques. A summary of data sources can be found in Table 1, where the time span considered for each variable is also reported.

The data source for the formal knowledge exchange variables was the OECD REGPAT database (January 2010 edition). The OECD citations database (January 2010 edition) was used for the cross-regional citations. A socio-matrix was built for each of the variables, and degree centrality (or in-degree centrality) measures were calculated.

Population data from Eurostat was used to normalize all six measures to the size of the region (see Table 1 again).

Table 1. Description of the Variables Used for the Synthetic Indicators.

Variable	Description	Sources	Years considered	Weight
Variables used for the construction of the synthetic indicator on spatial linkages				
R&D exp. per capita in the neighbouring regions	Average value of the millions of Euros spent on RD activities over population in the closest neighbouring regions: $w_{ij} = \exp(-0.01 \cdot d_{ij})$, cut-off 300 km	Compiled by CRENoS using Eurostat, ISTAT and Institut National de la Statistique et des Études Économiques	2006–2007	1/3
Patent activity per capita in the neighbouring regions	Average number of patents released over population in the closest neighbouring regions: $w_{ij} = \exp(-0.01 \cdot d_{ij})$, cut-off 300 km	Compiled by CRENoS using the OECD REGPAT database	2005–2006	1/3
Human capital in the neighbouring regions	Percentage of population aged 15 and over with tertiary education in the closest neighbours: $w_{ij} = \exp(-0.01 \cdot d_{ij})$, cut-off 300 km	Compiled by CRENoS using Eurostat	2005–2007	1/3
Variables used for the construction of the synthetic indicator on aspatial linkages				
Co-patents per capita	Number of patent co-authored with inventors from outside the region over population	Compiled by AQR using the OECD REGPAT database	2002–2004	1/3
Inflows of inventors per capita	Number of inflows of inventors coming from other regions over population	Compiled by AQR using the OECD REGPAT database	2002–2004	1/3
Cross-regional citations per capita	Number of citations made to patents from other regions over population	Compiled by CRENoS using the OECD REGPAT and citations database	2002–2004	1/3

We are completely aware of the caveats of using patent data in economic analysis. For instance, it is well known that not all inventions are patented, they do not have the same economic impact and not all patented inventions are commercially exploitable (Griliches, 1991). In addition, it is known that firms frequently patent for strategic reasons, to build up a patent portfolio to improve their position in negotiations or their technological reputation (Verspagen and Schoenmakers, 2004). Equally, the socio-matrices that were built reflect, to some extent, either the innovation capacity of regions, the degree of decentralization of innovation activity in the different national states or the different sectoral specializations in regions, which in turn determine the regional propensity to apply for patents (pharmaceuticals and biotech firms have an above average patent propensity).[11] Bearing these shortcomings in mind, we still find the empirical analysis worthwhile.

5. Results

We built both subindicators using the procedure described earlier. Figure 2 shows the scatter plot of the subindicators that were computed. Clearly, a strong positive relationship arose, as the correlation coefficient is 0.73. Note that the majority of the regions were either noninteractive (113) or knowledge networking regions (118). Meanwhile, only 41 regions were clustering regions and 15 were globalizing regions. Clearly, there seems to be a relationship between both subindices. We believe that this relationship is not accidental. Whether or not there is a causal relationship between the two subindices or the direction of this causality are interesting questions, which are beyond the scope of this analysis, although.

Figure 3 maps the spatial distribution of the four categories of regions considered. A short description of each type of region is given below, based on Figures 2 and 3.

5.1 Clustering Regions

We computed that 41 regions out of 287 could be labelled as clustering regions. These are regions that are located in relatively close proximity to other highly innovative regions (in terms of R&D, patents and human capital), and therefore can potentially receive informal knowledge flows governed by physical distance. However, and more importantly, these regions lack a critical number of formal, intentional knowledge linkages with external sources of knowledge. Amongst them, we identified regions in the centre of Spain and north of Italy, some French regions close to Paris and Germany, some regions in the north and west of England, part of Ireland and the regions of southern Norway. To sum up, the Clustering regions seem to belong to the EU15 and are close to core regions that are both informally and formally specialized. Broadly speaking, they are low-to-medium technologically advanced regions that, by happy chance, are located physically near to knowledge poles and are therefore dragged into innovative activities by their innovative neighbours.

5.2 Globalizing Regions

We computed that 15 regions out of 287 were labelled as globalizing regions. These regions are well connected by formal linkages to external areas, despite being relatively physically isolated from other innovative regions. Broadly speaking, these regions tend to perform notably better than clustering regions in terms of innovation activity. The list includes one

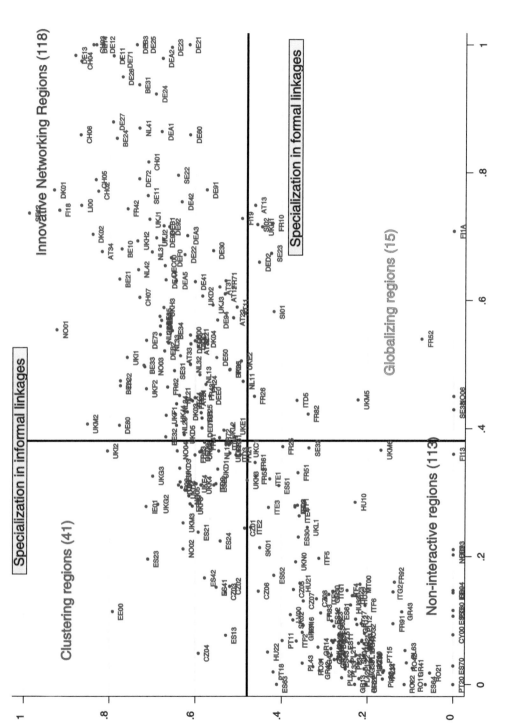

Figure 2. Scatter Plot of European Regions. Formal Linkages versus Informal Linkages.

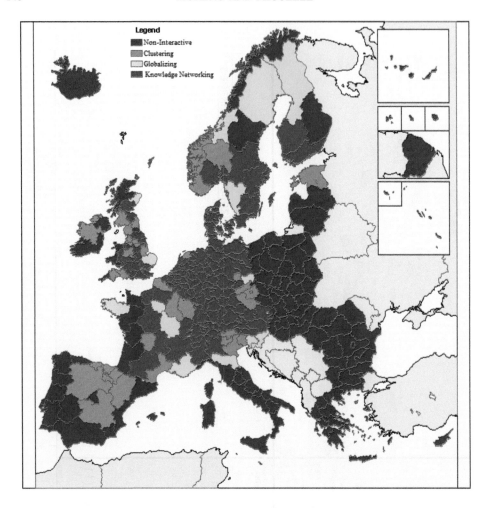

Figure 3. Typology of Regions Depicted on a Map.

German region (Dresden), four French regions (Île de France, Bourgogne, Provence-Alpes-Côte d'Azur and Bretagne), two British regions (East Anglia and North Eastern Scotland), Emiglia Romana in Italy, Trondelag in Norway, Wien in Austria, Pohjois Suomi in Finland, two Swedish regions (Vaestsverige and Örve Norrland) and two Slovenian regions (Zahodna Slovenija and Vzhodna Slovenija). Note that 2 of these 15 regions contain important capital cities, for example Paris and Wien. This kind of region acts more intensely as a regional knowledge hub, because it is connected to external knowledge sources by means of formal relations, and enables actors in nearby regions to access knowledge by means of a contagious process of informal interactions. This is particularly true for the two aforementioned capitals.

5.3 *Noninteractive Regions*

We computed that 113 regions out of 287 were noninteractive regions. These regions, which lack potential access to external knowledge by means of formal and informal linkages, are mainly those belonging to the New Entrant countries and some specific regions in southern European countries (all of Portugal and Greece, most of Spain except the central area and the south of Italy).

5.4 *Knowledge Networking Regions*

Networking regions are concentrated in the centre of Europe and in the Scandinavian countries. These regions are physically located close to high performing regions, so they are potentially in an advantageous position to benefit from informal knowledge diffusion mechanisms. However, they also act as knowledge hubs that are formally connected to external knowledge pools. As we can see, this subsample consists of 118 regions out of 287, which are mostly located in Germany, the Netherlands, Belgium, Denmark, southern Sweden, southern Finland, Switzerland, northern Italy, southeast England and part of France. Therefore, apart from three northern Italian regions, no other region in Southern or Eastern Europe appears on the list. This supports a clear core–periphery pattern in the geographical distribution of the regions that in one way or another rely on external sources of knowledge for the development of innovation. Therefore, broadly speaking, knowledge networking regions are those that are better positioned to benefit more from spatial knowledge diffusion, through different regimes and at different spatial scales and from the construction of the European Research Area.

5.5 *Robustness Analysis*

Here we list a number of robustness checks that we have performed for the calculation of the two subindicators presented so far. The results (the number and type of regions in each category) do not vary to a large extent. Consequently, most of the results are not presented here to save space. However, they can be provided by the authors on request. A few of the maps resulting from these checks are shown in Figure 4 below.

First, we recalculated the informal linkages composite indicator using different weight matrices. Concretely, less complex matrices were used, such as a first-order contiguity matrix (Figure 4A), an inverse distance matrix and a squared inverse distance matrix (Figure 4B). Any significant variation must be set apart (as expected, the first-order contiguity weight matrix slightly shifted the typological classification of some of the regions, which reflects the heterogeneous size of European NUTS2 regions).

Second, we recalculated the formal linkages indicator by subtracting all the linkages made with regions contiguous to the focal region (Figure 4C), regions whose centroid lies within 300 km of the centroid of the focal region, regions belonging to the same NUTS1 as the focal region and regions belonging to the same country as the focal region (Figure 4D). Even though a few changes were observed, the general picture remains the same.

6. Concluding Remarks and Policy Implications

In the previous sections, we described a detailed method to construct a composite indicator and two subindices that examine the ways in which actors in regions may access external-to-the-region pools of different and complementary knowledge. In motivating our approach, we extensively surveyed an instrumental list of theoretical and empirical studies across different disciplines and subdisciplines. These studies have more or less dealt with the mechanisms through which knowledge diffuses, especially across space and between

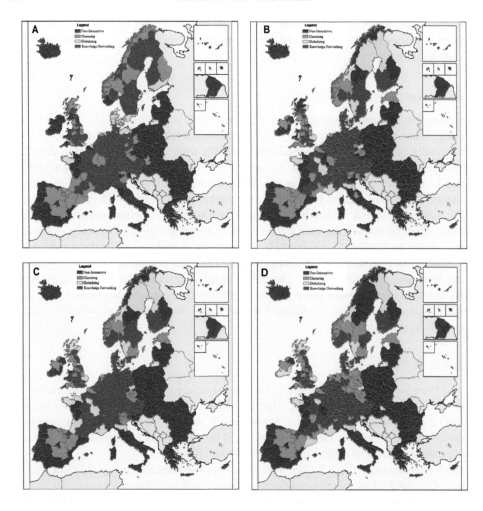

Figure 4. Typology of Regions Depicted on a Map. Robustness Analysis. (A) First-Order Contiguity Weight Matrix. (B) Inverse of the Squared Distance Weight Matrix. (C) Formal Linkages between Contiguous Regions Excluded. (D) Formal Linkages within Countries Excluded.

different locations. Based on our method, we also provided a typology of regions that captures their diversity in terms of their degree of openness to external sources of knowledge. Finally, the NUTS2 regions of 31 European countries were used to apply our novel approach and derive preliminary conclusions and policy implications from the results.

Despite increasing evidence of the role of knowledge diffusion across different geographical areas and the importance of this phenomenon for regional innovation, our review showed that mainstream research and policy makers barely consider this issue when they assess the innovative performance of cities, regions or countries. We believe that connections to external sources of knowledge are as important for regions as their scientific and technological base, and policies that specifically focus on this issue might be required. For years, regional policy programs have aimed to strengthen the local cluster knowledge base and its social preconditions for innovation (Rodríguez-Pose and Crescenzi, 2008). Here, we call into question this narrow approach and propose that the external dimension of regions is also relevant. Because this dimension has been quietly overlooked so far, policy makers lack a critical pillar for the development of RIS. However, as stressed in Bathelt *et al.* (2004), the 'local buzz' basically takes care of itself, whereas external linkages specifically require institutional and infrastructure support. This inquiry was an attempt to open up a future research agenda within the literature to improve our understanding of the external dimension of RIS and consequently develop a battery of policies on this issue.

Next, our empirical approach provided a typology of four distinct types of regions according to their degree of openness to external sources of knowledge and their specialization in the different ways in which actors in these regions may access external knowledge, that is, formal and informal linkages. This diversity of regions suggests that specific policies should be applied to each type of region, not only according to their innovative performance and social preconditions, but also according to the ways in which they connect with outsiders. This typology also translates into a ranking, which could serve as a guideline for regions to identify other areas with similar development conditions that have achieved a better rank and whose best practices could serve as a benchmark for implementing similar policies elsewhere.

Finally, our study also provides elements that could help firms' localization policies. As stressed in Gertler and Levitte (2005), firms' location decisions are influenced by the endogenous characteristics of regions and by opportunities to benefit from linkages worldwide, through which they can access manifold knowledge pools.

Acknowledgments

The views expressed in this article are those of the authors and do not necessarily reflect those of the World Intellectual Property Organization. Part of this work was carried out while Ernest Miguélez was visiting the Rotman School of Management at the University of Toronto (Toronto, Canada). The use of the School's facilities is gratefully acknowledged. Roberta Capello, Jordi Suriñach and the participants of the 51st European Regional Science Association Conference (Barcelona, 1 September 2011), Special Session on "Knowledge, Innovation and Economic Geography", provided insights on earlier versions of this project, which were of great help. We are also grateful to the Special Issue Editors, Philip McCann, Raquel Ortega-Argilés, and Les Oxley. Some of the data used in this project were compiled by CRENoS. Finally, we also acknowledge financial support from the Ministerio de Ciencia e Innovación, ECO2008–05314 and ECO2011–30260-C03–03, the Knowledge, Innovation, Territory (KIT) – Programme ESPON 2013 (2010–2013), and Ernest Miguelez from the Ministerio de Educación, AP2007–00792. However, any mistakes or omissions are ours.

Notes

1. Note that, as stressed in Boschma and Iammarino (2009, p. 295), 'extra-regional knowledge that is complementary, but not similar, to existing competences in the region will particularly enhance interactive learning. (...). If the external knowledge is unrelated, the industrial base of the region cannot absorb it and is unlikely to benefit from it. When the external knowledge is the same (...), it can be absorbed locally, but the new knowledge will not add much to the existing local knowledge base'. As we will show later on, our empirical application does not consider this distinction, which is left for future extensions.

2. Note that in their model they allow the scope of the 'local buzz' to go beyond the limits of the administrative region into neighbouring regions that might totally or partially belong to this same 'buzz'. In contrast, 'pipelines' are established with actors located at a distance. Moreover, whereas information inflows within the 'local buzz' do not require a major effort as they are more or less automatically received, the construction of 'pipelines' requires a conscious, intentional commitment to identify potential partners and build formal relations.

3. http://stats.oecd.org/Index.aspx?datasetcode=REG_DEMO_TL2.

4. http://epp.eurostat.ec.europa.eu/portal/page/portal/region_cities/regional_statistics/data/main_tables.

5. These estimations imply that spillovers are very likely to cross administrative borders, even at the level of NUTS2 regions and in countries in which this aggregation level translates into large regions, such as Spain.

6. Yet, the ability of actors within regions to absorb, understand and take advantage of incoming spillovers might also be dependent on their absorptive capacity (Cohen and Levinthal, 1990).

7. See also previous studies by the French School of Proximity (for a thorough review of this literature, see Carrincazeaux *et al.*, 2008).

8. Other distance decays have been tried, such as 0.02, 0.03, 0.04, 0.05, 0.06, 0.07, 0.08, 0.09 and 0.10.

9. Note that a single ID for each inventor and anyone else involved is missing. Hence, to compile the mobility history of inventors, we need to identify them individually by name and surname, as well as via other useful information contained in the patent document. Data cleaning and parsing, name matching and name disambiguation are the different stages undertaken to single out who is who in these patents, see Miguélez and Gómez-Miguélez (2011).

10. To determine the maximum and minimum scores in the normalization process, we exclude outliers. Positive outliers are identified as values that are higher than the average plus two times the standard deviation. Negative outliers are identified as values that are lower than the average minus two times the standard deviation.

11. See Ter Wall and Boschma (2009) for a discussion of additional shortcomings of using patents in regional analysis, and Lenzi's (2010) awareness of the use of inventors identified through patents.

References

Acs, Z.J., Audretsch, D.B. and Feldman, M.P. (1994) R&D spillovers and recipient firm size. *Review of Economics and Statistics* 76(2): 363–367.

Allen, T.J. (1977) *Managing the Flow of Technology: Technology Transfer and the Dissemination of Technological Information within the R&D Organization.* Cambridge, Massachusetts: MIT Press.

Almeida, P. and Kogut, B. (1997) The exploration of technological diversity and the geographic localization of innovation. *Small Business Economics* 9(1): 21–31.

Almeida, P. and Kogut, B. (1999) Localisation of knowledge and the mobility of engineers in regional networks. *Management Science* 45(7): 905–917.

Anselin, L., Varga, A. and Acs, Z. (1997) Local geographic spillovers between university research and high technology innovations. *Journal of Urban Economics* 42(3): 422–448.

Arthur, W.B. (1989) Competing technologies, increasing returns, and lock-in by historical events. *Economic Journal* 99: 116–131.

Arrow, K.J. (1962) The economic implications of learning by doing. *Review of Economic Studies* 29(3): 155–173.

Asheim, B.T. and Isaksen, A. (2002) Regional innovation systems: the integration of local 'sticky' and global 'ubiquitous' knowledge. *Journal of Technology Transfer* 27(1): 77–86.

Audretsch, D.B. and Feldman, M.P. (1996) R&D spillovers and the geography of innovation and production. *The American Economic Review* 86(3): 630–640.

Audretsch, D.B. and Feldman, M.P. (2004) Knowledge spillovers and the geography of innovation. In V. Henderson and J. Thisse (eds), *Handbook of Urban and Regional Economics* (pp. 2713–2740). Amsterdam: Elsevier.

Autant-Bernard, C. and LeSage, J.P. (2011) Quantifying knowledge spillovers using spatial econometric models. *Journal of Regional Science* 51(3): 471–496.

Autant-Bernard, C. and Massard, N. (2009) Underlying mechanisms of knowledge diffusion. IAREG Working Paper 4.7.

Autio, E. (1998) Evaluation of RTD in regional system of innovation. *European Planning Studies* 6(2): 131–140.

Bahlmann, M.D., Huysman, M.H., Elfring, T. and Groenewegen, P. (2008) Global pipelines or global buzz? A micro-level approach towards the knowledge-based view of clusters. VU University Amsterdam, Serie Research Memoranda 0002.

Bathelt, H., Malberg, A. and Maskell, P. (2004) Clusters and knowledge: local buzz, global pipelines and the process of knowledge creation. *Progress in Human Geography* 28(1): 31–56.

Becattini, G. (1979) Dal 'settore' industriale al 'distretto' industriale. Alcune considerazioni sull'unità d'indagine dell'economia industriale. *Rivista di economia e politica industriale* 5(1): 7–21.

Belussi, F., Sammarra, A. and Sedita, S.R. (2010) Learning at the boundaries in an "Open Regional Innovation System": a focus on firms' innovation strategies in the Emilia Romagna life science industry. *Research Policy* 39(6): 710–721.

Bergman, E.M. and Maier, G. (2009) Network central: regional positioning for innovative advantage. *The Annals of regional Science* 43(3): 615–644.

Bode, E. (2004) The spatial pattern of localized R&D spillovers: an empirical investigation for Germany. *Journal of Economic Geography* 4(1): 43–64.

Boschma, R. (2005) Proximity and Innovation: a Critical Assessment. *Regional Studies* 39(1): 61–74.

Boschma, R. and Frenken, K. (2010) The spatial evolution of innovation networks. A proximity perspective. In R. Boschma and R. Martin (eds), *The Handbook of Evolutionary Economic Geography* (pp. 120–135). Cheltenham: Edward Elgar.

Boschma, R., Eriksson, R. and Lindgren, U. (2009) How does labour mobility affect the performance of plants? The importance of relatedness and geographical proximity. *Journal of Economic Geography* 9(2): 169–190.

Boschma, R.A. and Iammarino, S. (2009) Related variety, trade linkages and regional growth. *Economic Geography* 85(3): 289–311.

Bottazzi, L. and Peri, G. (2003) Innovation and spillovers in regions: evidence from European patent data. *European Economic Review* 47(4): 687–710.

Breschi, S. and Lissoni, F. (2001a) Localised knowledge spillovers vs. innovative millieux: knowledge "tacitness" reconsidered. *Papers in Regional Science* 80(3): 255–273.

Breschi, S. and Lissoni, F. (2001b) Knowledge spillovers and local innovation systems: a critical survey. *Industrial and Corporate Change* 10(4): 975–1005.

Breschi, S. and Lissoni, F. (2004) Knowledge networks from patent data: methodological issues and research targets. In H. Moed, W. Glänzel and U. Schmoch (eds), *Handbook of Quantitative Science and Technology Research: The Use of Publication and Patent Statistics in Studies of S&T Systems* (pp. 613–643). Berlin: Springer Verlag.

Breschi, S. and Lissoni, F. (2009) Mobility of skilled workers and co-invention networks: an anatomy of localized knowledge flows. *Journal of Economic Geography* 9(4): 439–468.

Breschi, S., Lenzi, C., Lissoni, F. and Vezzulli, A. (2010) The geography of knowledge spillovers: the role of inventors' mobility across firms and in space. In R. Boschma and R. Martin (eds), *The Handbook of Evolutionary Economic Geography* (pp. 353–369). Cheltenham: Edward Elgar.

Burt, R.S. (1992) *Structural Holes: The Social Structure of Competition.* Cambridge, Massachusetts: Harvard University Press.

Camagni, R. (1991) *Innovation Networks: Spatial Perspectives.* London: Belhaven-Pinter.

Camagni, R. and Capello, R. (2009) Knowledge-base economy and knowledge creation: the role of space. In U. Fratesi and L. Senn (eds), *Growth and Innovation of Competitive Regions: The Role of Internal and External Connections* (pp. 145–166). Berlin: Springer-Verlag.

Capello, R. (1999) Spatial transfer of knowledge in high-technology milieux: learning vs. collective learning processes. *Regional Studies* 33(4): 353–365.

Carrincazeaux, C., Lung, Y. and Vicente, J. (2008) The scientific history of the French School of Proximity: interaction- and Institution-based approaches to regional innovation systems. *European Planning Studies* 16(5): 617–628.

Cassiman, B. and Veugelers, R. (2006) In search of complementarity in innovation strategy: internal R&D and external knowledge acquisition. *Management Science* 52(1): 68–82.

Coe, N.M. and Bunnell, T. (2003) Spatializing' knowledge communities: towards a conceptualisation of transnational innovation networks. *Global Networks* 3(4): 437–456.

Cohen, W.M. and Levinthal, D.A. (1990) Absorptive capacity: a new perspective on learning and innovation. *Administrative Science Quarterly* 35(1): 128–152.

Cooke, P., Boekholt, P. and Tödtling, F. (2000) *The Governance of Innovation in Europe.* London: Pinter.

Cowan, R. and Jonard, N. (2004) Network structure and the diffusion of knowledge. *Journal of Economic Dynamics and Control* 28(8): 1557–1575.

David, P.A. (1985) Clio and the Economics of QWERTY. *American Economic Review* 75(2): 332–337.

D'Este, P. and Iammarino, S. (2010) The spatial profile of university-business research partnerships. *Papers in Regional Science* 89(2): 335–350.

Dosi, G. (1988) Sources, procedures and microeconomic effects of innovation. *Journal of Economic Literature* 26(3): 1120–1171.

European Commission (2007) Green Paper. The European research area: new perspectives. COM(2007) 161.

European Commission (2010) A vision for strengthening world-class research infrastructures in the ERA. Report of the Expert Group on Research Infrastructures.

European Commission (2011) Regional innovation monitor. Innovation patterns and innovation policy in european regions – trends, challenges and perspectives. Project No. 0932. Enterprise and Industry Directorate-General.

Feldman, M.P. (1994) Knowledge complementarity and innovation. *Small Business Economics* 6(5): 363–372.

Feldman, M.P. and Audretsch, D. (1999) Innovation in cities: science-based diversity, specialization and localized competition. *European Economic Review* 43(2): 409–429.

Fratesi, U. and Senn, L. (2009) Regional growth, connections and economic modelling: an introduction. In U. Fratesi and L. Senn (eds), *Growth and Innovation of Competitive Regions: The Role of Internal and External Connections* (pp. 3–28). Berlin: Springer-Verlag.

Gertler, M.S. (1995) 'Being there': proximity, organization, and culture in the development and adoption of advanced manufacturing technologies. *Economic Geography* 71(1): 1–26.

Gertler, M.S. (2003) Tacit knowledge and the economic geography of context, or the indefinable tacitness of being (there). *Journal of Economic Geography* 3(1): 75–99.

Gertler, M.S. and Levite, Y.M. (2005) Local nodes in global networks: the geography of knowledge flows in biotechnology innovation. *Industry and Innovation* 12(4): 487–507.

Gittelman, M. (2007) Does geography matter for science-based firms? Epistemic communities and the geography of research and patenting in biotechnology. *Organization Science* 18(4): 724–741.

Giuliani, E. and Bell, M. (2005) The micro-determinants of meso-level learning and innovation: evidence from a Chilean wine cluster. *Research Policy* 34(1): 47–68.

Glaeser, E., Laibson, D. and Sacerdote, B. (2002) An economic approach to social capital. *Economic Journal* 112(483): 437–458.

Glückler, J. (2007) Economic geography and the evolution of networks. *Journal of Economic Geography* 7(5): 619–634.

Gomes-Casseres, B., Hagedoorn, J. and Jaffe, A.B. (2006) Do alliances promote knowledge flows? *Journal of Financial Economics* 80(1): 5–33.

Grabher, G. (1993) The weakness of strong ties: the lock-in of regional development in the Ruhr area. In G. Grabher (ed.) *The Embedded Firm* (pp. 255–277). London: Routledge.

Granovetter, M.S. (1973) The strength of weak ties. *The American Journal of Sociology* 78(6): 1360–1380.

Griliches, Z. (1991) Patent statistics as economic indicators: a survey. NBER Working Papers 3301.

Grossman, G.M. and Helpman, E. (1991) *Innovation and Growth in the Global Economy*. Cambridge, Massachusetts: MIT Press.

Hagerstrand, T. (1965) Aspects of the spatial structure of social communication and the diffusion of information. *Papers of the Regional Science Association* 16(1): 27–42.

Iammarino, S. and McCann, P. (2006) The structure and evolution of industrial clusters: transactions, technology and knowledge spillovers. *Research Policy* 35(7): 1018–1036.

INSEAD (2011) Global Innovation Index 2011, INSEAD.

Jaffe, A.B. (1986) Technological opportunity and spillovers of R&D: evidence from firms' patents, profits, and market value. *American Economic Review* 76(5): 984–1001.

Jaffe, A.B. (1989) Real effects of academic research. *American Economic Review* 79(5): 957–970.

Jaffe, A.B., Trajtenberg, M. and Henderson, R. (1993) Geographic localisation of knowledge spillovers as evidenced by patent citations. *Quarterly Journal of Economics* 108(3): 577–598.

Kroll, H. (2009) Spillovers and proximity in perspective: a network approach to improving the operationalisation of proximity. Working Papers Firms and Regions No. R2/2009, Fraunhofer ISI.

Krugman, P. (1991a) *Geography and Trade*. Cambridge, Massachusetts: MIT Press.

Krugman, P. (1991b) Increasing returns and economic geography. *Journal of Political Economy* 99(3): 483–499.

Lambooy, J.G. and Boschma, R.A. (2001) Evolutionary economics and regional policy. *Annals of Regional Science* 35(1): 113–133.

Laudel, G. (2003) Studying the brain drain: can bibliometric methods help? *Scientometrics* 57(2): 215–237.

Lenzi, C. (2010) Technology mobility and job mobility: on the use of patent data for inventors' career analysis, unpublished manuscript.

Lorenz, E. (1996) Collective learning processes and the regional labour market, unpublished research note, European Network on Networks, Collective Learning and RTD in Regionally-Clustered High-Technology SMEs.

Lucas, R.E. (1988) On the mechanics of economic development. *Journal of Monetary Economics* 22(1): 3–42.

Maggioni, M.A. and Uberti, T.E. (2011) Networks and geography in the economics of knowledge flows. *Quality and Quantity* 45(5): 1031–1051.

Maggioni, M.A., Nosvelli, M. and Uberti, T.E. (2007) Space versus networks in the geography of innovation: a European analysis. *Papers in Regional Science* 86(3): 471–493.

Marsan, G.A. and Maguire, K. (2011) Categorisation of OECD regions using innovation-related variables. Organisation for Economic Co-operation and Development (OECD) regional development working paper, March 2011.

Maskell, P., Bathelt, H. and Malmberg, A. (2006) Building global knowledge pipelines: the role of temporary clusters. *European Planning Studies* 14(8): 997–1013.

March, J.G. (1991) Organizational consultants and organizational research. *Journal of Applied Communication Research* 19(1–2): 20–31.

Marshall, A. (1920) *Principles of Economics*. Londres: Macmillan.

Martin, P. and Ottaviano, G. (1999) Growing locations: industry location in a model of endogenous growth. *European Economic Review* 43(2): 281–302.

Martin R. and Sunley, P. (2006) Path dependence and regional economic evolution. *Journal of Economic Geography* 6(4): 395–437.

Miguélez, E. and Gómez-Miguélez, I.G. (2011) Singling out individual inventors from patent data, IREA Working Paper, May 2011.

Moreno, R., Paci, R. and Usai, S. (2005) Spatial spillovers and innovation activity in European regions. *Environment and Planning A* 37(10): 1793–1812.

Moretti, E. (2004) Human capital externalities in cities. In V. Henderson and J. Thisse (eds), *Handbook of Urban and Regional Economics* (pp. 2243–2291). Amsterdam: Elsevier.

Morrison, A., Rabellotti, R. and Zirulia, F.L. (2011) When do global pipelines enhance knowledge diffusion in clusters?. Papers in Evolutionary Economic Geography (PEEG) 1105, Utrecht University.

Navarro, M., Gibaja, J.J., Bilbao-Osorio, B. and Aguado, R. (2009) Patterns of innovation in EU-25 regions: a typology and policy recommendations. *Environment and Planning C: Government and Policy* 27(5): 815–840.

Organizational Consultants and Organizational Research (2009) *OECD Regions at a Glance 2009*. Paris: Organizational Consultants and Organizational Research, doi: 10.1787/reg_glance-2011-en.

Owen-Smith, J. and Powell, W.W. (2004) Knowledge networks as channels and conduits: the effects of spillovers in the Boston biotechnology community. *Organization Science* 15(1): 5–21.

Parent, O. and LeSage, J.P. (2008) Using the variance structure of the conditional autoregressive spatial specification to model knowledge spillovers. *Journal of Applied Econometrics* 23(2): 235–256.

Peri, G. (2005) Determinants of knowledge flows and their effect on innovation. *The Review of Economics and Statistics* 87(2): 308–322.

Ponds, R., Van Oort, F.G. and Frenken, K. (2010) Innovation, spillovers and university-industry collaboration: an extended knowledge production function approach. *Journal of Economic Geography* 10(2): 231–255.

Porter, M.E. (1990) *The Competitive Advantage of Nations*. London: Macmillan.

Rauch, J.E. (1993) Productivity gains from geographic concentration of human capital: evidence from the cities. *Journal of Urban Economics* 34(3): 380–400.

Regional Innovation Scoreboard (2009) Regional Innovation Scoreboard, Pro Inno Europe. Inno Metrics.

Rodríguez-Pose, A. and Crescenzi, R.(2008) Reseacrh and development, spillovers, innovation systems, and the genesis of regional growth in Europe. *Regional Studies* 42(1): 51–67.

Romer P.M. (1986) Increasing returns and long-run growth. *Journal of Political Economy* 94(5): 1002–1037.

Romer P.M. (1990) Endogenous technological change. *Journal of Political Economy* 98(5): 71–102.

Rosenkopf, L. and Almeida, P. (2003) Overcoming local search through alliances and mobility. *Management Science* 49(6): 751–766.

Rychen, F. and Zimmermann, J.B. (2008) Clusters in the global knowledge-based economy: knowledge gatekeepers and temporary proximity. *Regional Studies* 42(6): 767–776.

Simonen, J. and McCann, P. (2008) Firm innovation: the influence of R&D cooperation and the geography of human capital inputs. *Journal of Urban Economics* 64(1): 146–154.

Singh, J. (2005) Collaborative networks as determinants of knowledge diffusion patterns. *Management Science* 51(5): 756–770.

Singh, J. and Agrawal, A.K. (2011) Recruiting for ideas: how firms exploit the prior inventions of new hires. *Management Science* 57(1): 129–150.

Steinmueller, W.E. (2000) Will new information and communication technologies improve the 'codification' of knowledge? *Industrial and Corporate Change* 9(2): 361–376.

Storper, M. (1997) *The Regional World*. New York and London: The Guilford Press.

Storper, M. and Venables, A. (2004) Buzz: face-to-face contact and the urban economy. *Journal of Economic Geography* 4(4): 351–370.

Ter Wal, A.L.J. and Boschma, R. (2009) Applying social network analysis in economic geography: framing some key analytic issues. *The Annals of Regional Science* 43(3): 739–756.

Todtling, F. and Trippl, M. (2005) One size fits all?: towards a differentiated regional innovation policy approach. *Research Policy* 34(8): 1203–1219.

Todtling F., Lehner P. and Trippl, M. (2006) Innovation in knowledge intensive industries: the nature and geography of knowledge links. *European Planning Studies* 14(8): 1035–1058.

Torre A. (2008) On the role played by temporary geographical proximity in knowledge transmission. *Regional Studies* 42(6): 869–889.

Trippl, M. and Maier, G. (2010) Knowledge spillover agents and regional development. *Papers in Regional Science* 89(2): 229–233.

Trippl, M., Tödtling, F. and Lengauer, L. (2009) Knowledge sourcing beyond buzz and pipelines: evidence from the Vienna software sector. *Economic Geography* 85(4): 443–462.

Uzzi, B. (1996) The sources and consequences of embeddedness for the economic performance of organizations. *American Sociological Review* 61(4): 674–698.

Vang, J. and Chaminade, C. (2007) Cultural clusters, global-local linkages and spillovers: theoretical and empirical insights from an exploratory study of toronto's film cluster. *Industry & Innovation* 14(4): 401–420.

Verspagen, B. and Schoenmakers, W. (2004) The spatial dimension of patenting by multinational firms in Europe. *Journal of Economic Geography* 4(1): 23–42.

Zucker, L.G., Darby, M.R. and Armstrong, J. (1998) Geographically localized knowledge: spillovers or markets? *Economic Inquiry* 36(1): 65–86.

Appendix: List of countries (and number of regions in each one)

Austria, AT (9), Belgium, BE (11), Bulgaria, BG (6), Switzerland, CH (1), Cyprus, CY (1), Czech Republic, CZ (8), Germany, DE (39), Denmark, DK (5), Estonia, EE (1), Spain, ES (19), Finland, FI (5), France, FR (26), Greece, GR (13), Hungary, HU (7), Ireland, IE (2), Iceland, IS (1), Liechtenstein, LI (1), Italy, IT (20), Lithuania, LT (1), Luxemburg, LU (1), Latvia, LV (1), Malta, MT (1), the Netherlands, NL (12), Norway, NO (7), Poland, PL (16), Portugal, PT (7), Romania, RO (8), Sweden, SE (8), Slovenia, SI (2), Slovakia, SK (4), United Kingdom, UK (12).

8

AN 'INTEGRATED' FRAMEWORK FOR THE COMPARATIVE ANALYSIS OF THE TERRITORIAL INNOVATION DYNAMICS OF DEVELOPED AND EMERGING COUNTRIES

Riccardo Crescenzi and Andrés Rodríguez-Pose

1. Introduction

The unprecedented pace of the process of technological change and the progressive 'globalization' of innovation systems are making the territorial dynamics of innovation, on one hand, more complex to analyse and, on the other, progressively more interconnected across continents, countries and regions. This changing scenario poses a number of challenges for scholars, practitioners and policy makers alike to develop progressively more sophisticated frameworks of understanding able to capture the complexity of the on-going processes. The ultimate aim is to develop adequate policy tools to spread the benefits of existing processes and mitigate their potential drawbacks in both developed and developing countries.

In this context, the advancement of both theoretical and empirical literature in a number of fields of the social sciences – not only in economic geography and geographical economics, but also in international business studies and technology studies – has suggested that the insights on the innovation process that can be produced by a single discipline in isolation are partial and inconclusive. There is thus an increasing consensus on the need for 'integrated' interdisciplinary eclectic approaches to the genesis of innovation for both positive and normative purposes. In addition, in light of the increasing degree of interconnectedness between regional economies, such a framework should provide consistent insights on the experiences of developed and developing countries to enable mutual learning and policy transfer.

This chapter aims to contribute to this debate in two different ways. First, it intends to show how different streams of literature on the genesis of innovation at the territorial level can be productively cross-fertilized into an '*integrated*' and eclectic conceptual framework of understanding. Second, it makes use of this framework to re-interpret a large body of empirical literature in a comparative perspective and investigate in a systematic fashion the similarities and dissimilarities in the territorial innovation dynamics of developed and emerging countries.

Innovation, Entrepreneurship, Geography and Growth, First Edition.
Edited by Philip McCann and Les Oxley. Chapters © 2013 The Authors.
Book compilation © 2013 Blackwell Publishing Ltd. Published 2013 by Blackwell Publishing Ltd.

The review of the literature in a comparative perspective will show how an integrated framework can contribute to overcome the existing conceptual and empirical barriers that have limited the capacity of developed and developing countries to learn from each other's experiences, limiting the transfer of successful policy tools. In addition, making use of both quantitative and qualitative information within a theory-driven conceptual framework allows to rise above the limitations of both 'scoreboard' approaches, which rely exclusively on the comparison of basic quantitative indicators, and of comparative case studies that remain limited in terms of generality and conceptual foundations. Finally, the approach facilitates identifying areas where more research is needed to support policy making in different contexts.

To show how different strands of literature on the genesis of innovation at the territorial level can be cross-fertilized into a joint 'meso-level' conceptual framework, the chapter is divided into three further sections. Section 2 briefly reviews the existing meso-level innovation literature with the aim of singling out the components of an 'integrated' conceptual framework. The Section 3 discusses the capability of this framework to account for 'real world' regional developmental dynamics in both developed and developing countries more accurately than alternative approaches. The Section 4 concludes with some considerations on the 'value added' and implications of this approach.

2. The Conceptual Foundations of an 'Integrated Framework' for the Comparative Analysis of Innovative Dynamics

The comparative analysis of innovative performance at the territorial level calls for an appropriate analytical framework. Such a framework should possess a number of important features that would make it a suitable foundation for comparative analysis and, eventually, for policy transfer. It should not only be a tool for the detection of the factors of success in leading regions/countries, but a full-embracing conceptualization of the determinants of regional innovation in both core and peripheral areas, developed and developing countries. Let us briefly review some key contributions to the literature on the territorial determinants of innovation to identify the potential 'building blocks' of an 'integrated' framework for comparative territorial analysis of innovation dynamics.

2.1 *Link Between R&D Investments and Innovation*

By adopting the relationship between innovative efforts and the generation of new ideas/knowledge as its milestone, this conceptual framework would be a suitable foundation for both quantitative and qualitative comparative analyses of regional and local innovative dynamics. The relationship between local innovative efforts and knowledge output is grounded in endogenous growth theory (Romer, 1990; Aghion and Howitt, 1992; Cheshire and Magrini, 2000), the knowledge production function approach (Griliches, 1986; Audretsch and Feldman, 1996a,b; Audretsch, 2003) and the 'technology-gap theory' of technological development (Fagerberg, 1988). The latter explicitly assumes the interaction of two 'conflicting' forces: innovation (which generates the technology gap) and imitation or diffusion (which tend to reduce it) as the motors of the process of long-term technological development. The capability of countries and regions to catch-up with the technological leaders depends on their 'technological congruence' and on their indigenous 'social infrastructure'. It is the capacity to single out these two fundamental forces behind the process of technological development and their explicit link with internal socio-institutional characteristics that makes Fagerberg's approach particularly suitable for our comparative framework. It fundamentally represents the attempt of the 'formal analytical' economic literature to incorporate the Schumpeterian legacy into progressively more sophisticated and comprehensive frameworks that embed innovation into a complex set of other economic processes.

The 'systems of innovation approach', on one hand, and the literature on localized knowledge spillovers and the spatial dimension of the process of innovation, on the other, have tried to move beyond the linear relationship between R&D and innovation by conceptualizing the role of more 'qualitative/intangible' conditioning factors and offering what their proponents deem to be a more realistic view of the process of technological development in time (institutions supportive of innovative dynamics are seen as the result of long-term processes of social learning) and space. These contributions have flourished outside the economics 'mainstream' and have frequently made use of 'appreciative' approaches and qualitative methods for their empirical analyses. As a consequence, their insights have remained neglected by quantitative comparative exercises involving quantitative indicators, in the same way as the 'generality' of linear approaches has been lacking in case study-based analyses.

2.2 *Systems of Innovation Conditions*

The 'systems of innovation' approach provides fundamental insights into the dynamics of the process of innovation not only by harmoniously 'embedding' innovation into its socioeconomic context, but also by effectively integrating proximity, local synergy and interaction (Camagni, 1995; Camagni and Capello, 2003) and the importance of 'interorganization networks, financial and legal institutions, technical agencies and research infrastructures, education and training systems, governance structures and innovation policies' (Iammarino, 2005, p. 499) into the innovative process. A growing number of researchers are also attempting to recalibrate regional innovation system (RIS) frameworks for emerging country perspectives (Scott and Garofoli, 2007; Lundvall *et al.*, 2009; Padilla-Perez *et al.*, 2009 provide useful overviews). Recalibrating RIS to emerging country conditions is essential as, first, in these countries development in the formal economy partly depends on the performance of the broader, informal innovation system – social capital and networks, institutions and governance capacity (Lundvall *et al.*, 2009). Second, their 'innovation experiences' need to be understood as part of the globalization of both production and R&D that has been occurring since the 1970s (Mitra, 2007; Bruche, 2009). As Yeung (2009) points out, the task is to explain innovation under globalization: as Saxenian and Sabel (2008) argue, research needs to explain the specific 'puzzle' of rapid development of high-tech hubs in countries without the consistent quality of institutions generally thought necessary for growth.

These interactions between (local) actors are intrinsically unique and hard to measure and compare across different systems. However, recent developments in the regional systems of innovation literature have acknowledged the idiosyncratic nature of these factors whereas, at the same time, placed them into broader frameworks that make them suitable for comparative analysis. This is, for example, the case of the 'evolutionary integrated view of the regional systems of innovation' (Iammarino, 2005) which is based on the identification of meso-level 'structural regularities from past knowledge accumulation and learning' (Iammarino, 2005, p. 503). The macro national-level institutions that provide the broad framework conditions for the genesis of innovation interact with the microlevel behaviour of firms, research centres and universities giving rise to highly localized meso-level conditions: a series of 'external conditions in which externalized learning and innovation occur' (Cooke, 1997, p. 485), which can be identified across innovation systems and on which comparative analysis can be based. This set of localized conditions act as the unique combination 'of innovative and conservative components, that is, elements that favour or deter the development of successful RIS' (Rodríguez-Pose, 1999, p. 82) in every space. An important leap in the usability of these concepts for comparative analysis has come from their operational translation into a set of 'measurable' features of the regional realm, directly dealing with concrete constraints in terms of availability of comparable and reliable data. This is the case of the analyses based on 'social filter indices': composite indicators based on the theory-driven selection of proxies for the 'structural preconditions' for the establishment of fully functional systems of innovation (Rodríguez-Pose and Crescenzi, 2008). The social filter index approach focuses on three main aspects of social structure: educational achievement (Lundvall, 1992; Malecki, 1997); the productive employment of human resources (Gordon, 2001) and demographic structure and dynamism (Rodríguez-Pose, 1999).

The use of the 'social filter index' makes it possible to capture such factors in a more parsimonious fashion for comparative analysis, identifying broad regularities in 'innovation-prone' regions across a large number of cases (Crescenzi and Rodríguez-Pose, 2009). This approach is particularly helpful when looking at both developed and emerging countries in a comparative perspective, because it cuts through differences that flow from being at different stages in the development process. However, as it will be discussed later, this literature has also made it clear that the social filter index – although multidimensional in nature – should not be interpreted in isolation, but always considered jointly with other components of an 'integrated framework'.

2.3 *Localized Knowledge Flows*

The third crucial component of such a framework – together with innovative efforts and social filter conditions – comes from the literature on the spatial diffusion of knowledge flows (Storper and Venables, 2004; Sonn and Storper, 2008). The circulation of economically valuable knowledge is made possible by face-to-face contacts that function as highly localized transmission mechanisms and determine the spatial boundedness of knowledge flows. The transmission of highly valuable noncodifiable knowledge calls for repeated human contacts that are only possible within close geographical proximity. As a consequence, the exposure of regional innovative agents to external sources of innovation in close geographical proximity is a persistent source of competitive advantage for the local economy. The possibility to interact face-to-face with other innovative actors – thanks to physical accessibility/geographical centrality with respect to the technological 'core' – improves (*ceteris paribus*) local innovative capabilities. The assessment of the impact of accessibility to extra-regional knowledge on local innovative performance, the analyses of the different knowledge circulation patterns and of their geography are all important components of the comparative analysis of the territorial dynamics of innovation. However, comparative analysis should also account for the interaction of knowledge flows with the underlying absorptive conditions, looking at spatial knowledge flows jointly with the factors conditioning their impact on local innovative performance. In this context, innovation systems can become catalysts for the absorption of localized knowledge flows and their translation into new knowledge. Hence the comparative analysis should be able to detect not only the influence of local innovative efforts on innovative dynamism, but also capture how 'accessibility to extra-regional innovation' in its turn interacts with the endogenous social filter conditions, determining to what extent such knowledge is translated into innovative dynamism at the local and regional level.

2.4 *Global Network*

The 'drivers' discussed earlier are all important factors for the comparative analysis of local innovative conditions. However, the analysis would be incomplete without taking into account a set of additional dimensions (cognitive, organizational, social and institutional proximities) that – together with physical or geographical proximity – make it possible to diffuse and absorb knowledge, shaping the innovative potential of regions and territories (Boschma, 2005).

An additional set of proximities is crucial for the generation of innovation by allowing the emergence of complex innovative network relationships, operating between and across different scales (from local to transnational). What matters for the innovative performance of different territories is the combination of intralocal, extra-local and transnational network connection which 'are not just intra- or intercorporate in nature (as highlighted in Faulconbridge, 2006), but may also encompass other forms of social networks" (Coe and Bunnell, 2003, p. 454). These networks generate a complex pattern of winners and losers with an increasing distance between those enjoying the best balance of the various proximities with the most innovative actors and those at the geographical, cognitive, organizational, social and/or institutional periphery. In developing countries the localization and degree of territorial embeddedness of such 'global' networks is of paramount importance to internal innovative dynamics. Multinational firms (Dunning, 1996, 1998; Cantwell, 2005) and 'lead firms' (Yeung, 2009) engage in different types of spatially specific 'strategic coupling' with local firms, influencing cluster formation and producing heterogeneous patterns of spatial development. From a different perspective, migrants and diasporic communities also play important roles in facilitating innovative activity in developing countries by means of 'extra-local' network connections. Not only individual migrants act as mobile carriers of knowledge[1] but cycles of migration and return between developing 'home' countries and developed 'hosts' have helped develop innovative activity in emerging countries. The social capital and trust embedded in co-ethnic networks is also crucial in assisting location shifts and lowering transaction costs for network members (Rodríguez-Pose and Storper, 2006).

2.5 *Public Policies*

Even if path dependency is very strong in the processes discussed so far, a given course of action is not carved in stone and comparative analyses have to take into account differential evolutionary patterns. External shocks (e.g. in the form of top–down policies) and/or collective action processes (e.g. as bottom–up policies) can change observed trajectories. The systems of innovation perspective, by institutionally embedding the process of innovation, allows us to account for the role of public policies in the comparative analysis of innovation dynamics. The '*a priori*' structure and design of public policies may or may not be supportive of the long-term innovative performance of the regional economy. In addition, the literature on the genesis of local and regional innovation policies also suggests that it is necessary to assess the coherence between the policies' 'explicit' objectives and the 'actual' interventions implemented on the ground, as political economy processes may distort not only their design, but also their implementation [Crescenzi, 2009 for the European Union (EU); Greenbaum and Bondonio, 2004 for the United States (US)]. Given the role of 'power' factors in the design and implementation of public policies, interventions may be the result of the political equilibria reached in the bargaining process between the national governments, the local governments and various pressure groups. Where these processes generate a fundamental mismatch between the local needs of the innovation systems and the policy targets, the evolutionary trajectory of an innovative area might be hampered. This is of great importance in emerging countries where policy stances have also influenced the spatial patterning of economic and innovative activity. Sun (2003) emphasizes, for example, the Chinese government's persistent role in guiding changes to the national innovation system, while Duflo (2010) highlights the importance of internal restrictions on labour and capital mobility – motivated essentially by political considerations – on the development of the Chinese spatial economy. As will be discussed in the next section such a configuration is not necessarily synergic with the needs of its emerging 'knowledge' economy. As a consequence, an effective comparative tool for the analysis of regional innovation needs to incorporate and embed these processes in their dynamic interactions with the key drivers of regional innovative dynamism.

2.6 The 'Integrated Framework' or ' the Base-Line' Scenario for Comparative Analysis

The conceptual framework discussed in this chapter allows us to identify five key factors shaping the geography of innovation in different territorial contexts: innovative activities, systems of innovation (social filter) conditions, geographical factors/accessibility/exposure to knowledge spillovers, international (translocal) linkages and local and regional (innovation) policies. These factors are visualized in Figure 1 where each strand of literature presented in the previous section is translated into the corresponding innovation 'drivers' identified above.

Local innovative activities are the engines of regional economic performance. In quantitative terms they work as inputs in the knowledge production function for the generation of new ideas. However, in a more qualitative perspective, innovative activities can be pursued in different contexts with different roles being played by private firms, research centres and universities. The impact of innovative activities crucially depends upon two other factors: systems of innovation/social filter conditions and geography. In previous paragraphs we discussed how the concept of social filter – the structural socioeconomic preconditions for the development of a well-functioning regional system of innovation – can be adopted as a quantitative proxy for local institutions supportive/detrimental to the process of innovation, making inter-regional and intertemporal comparisons and benchmarking possible. However, from a deductive perspective, the assessment of the social filter conditions can be complemented by qualitative considerations capturing its institutional and relational underpinnings. The same line of reasoning applies to geography: different quantitative proxies (accessibility indices and spatially lagged variables, respectively) have been developed in the literature to capture the impact of geographical distance from economic and innovative activities on local innovative performance. Exposure to knowledge spillovers is an important predictor for the innovative success of any region. Geography is directly linked to innovative activities and socioeconomic conditions in shaping innovation performance. As discussed earlier, innovation dynamics are not only influenced by physical accessibility, but the position of each

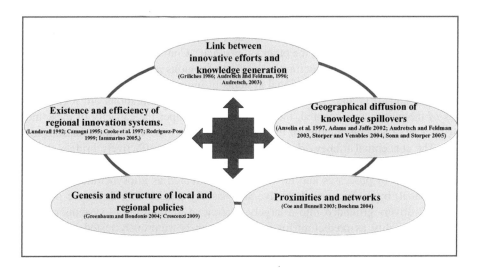

Figure 1. Territorial Drivers of Innovation Dynamics and Streams of Literature Combined in the Integrated Framework.

Source: Adapted from Crescenzi and Rodríguez-Pose (2011).

region in 'global networks' and its exposure to global knowledge flows is also important. The capability of local actors to establish organizational, institutional and social proximity relations with other agents determines the position of the local economy in global networks. Participation in global networks exerts an influence on all the other dimensions mentioned above: it influences the nature and magnitude of local innovative efforts, shapes the local system of innovation and – in particular in emerging countries – impacts upon public policies. Finally, public policies at different levels (from national policies to community-level initiatives), may impinge (directly or indirectly) on local innovative performance.

The comparative analysis of the territorial dynamics of innovation should hence be based on the simultaneous (qualitative and quantitative) assessment of all these five factors and of their reciprocal interactions. The next section will show how these concepts have been applied to both developed and emerging countries, unveiling relevant differences in their geography of innovation.

3. Empirical Evidence on Regional Innovation Through the Lens of an 'Integrated Approach'

The cross-fertilization of linear and nonlinear, quantitative and qualitative approaches to the generation of regional innovative dynamism discussed so far, allows our comparative conceptual framework to reconcile the often contradictory views resulting from the adoption of either an inductive or a deductive approach to innovation dynamics. The relative importance of the various determinants of regional innovation varies significantly when assessed from opposite perspectives. Deductive analyses are designed to capture macro knowledge generation dynamics: they are designed, for example, to assess the aggregate average impact of innovative efforts on the patenting performance of a cross-section of regions, highlighting common and 'general' trends (as in the 'standard' knowledge production function approach). In doing so, these models treat all specific idiosyncratic factors that differentiate one region/RIS from the other as 'residual'. Conversely, inductive analyses tend to focus their attention on the specificities of a set of regions assessing their unique internal dynamics (as in large part of the regional systems of innovation literature), but overlooking inter-regional trade-offs and general trends. Although these limitations are logical consequences of the perspective adopted, they significantly hamper the capacity of these models to provide a more accurate picture of the real world and act as foundations for comparative analysis. The conceptual framework presented in this chapter effectively bridges deductive and inductive approaches by proposing a meso-level perspective based on the inclusion in a macro framework of processes and factors generally treated as idiosyncratic (and confined into the residual) by mainstream deductive analysis. By placing in a deductive perspective development drivers grounded into a largely qualitative literature (e.g. systems of innovation), their generality as predictors for innovation can be rigorously tested and compared across space. As a consequence, key qualitative concepts – traditionally addressed by means of case-study analyses – can be treated in a quantitative framework, emphasizing their 'non-strictly-idiosyncratic' component and identifying the most appropriate proxies.

The integrated approach – applied directly or indirectly to the empirical analysis of regional innovation dynamics – can produce interesting insights on both developed and emerging countries. The cross-fertilization of different theoretical approaches to the analysis of innovation and its economic impact has resulted in the development of empirical models that, in turn, permit to systematically investigate phenomena hitherto 'confined' to the grey areas between different approaches.

3.1 The Territorial Determinants of Innovation in Developed Countries

3.1.1 The European Union

In the case of EU, a large body of literature has indicated that an increase in innovative efforts has a direct impact on regional-level innovative output (Fagerberg et al., 1997; Cheshire and Magrini, 2000; Bilbao-Osorio and Rodríguez-Pose, 2004; Crescenzi, 2005). However, the same literature has made explicit that raising the innovative effort does not necessarily produce the same effects in all regions. This is because a variety of local factors influence this process (Rodríguez-Pose, 1999; Capello and Faggian, 2005; Crescenzi and Rodríguez-Pose, 2011). As shown by the red lines in Figure 2, the literature suggests that the relationship between local innovative efforts and the localized generation of new knowledge is far from linear. Territorial innovation systems, collective learning processes, relational capital and different social filters have been shown to play a crucial role as determinants of the differentiated 'productivity' of innovative efforts in different regions.

The uneven impact of R&D investments in the EU regions is further reinforced by a highly differentiated exposure to extra-regional knowledge flows. The limited physical accessibility of certain territories (i.e. their geographical peripherality) often curbs the potential to successfully translate innovation into regional growth due to both a reduced interconnectedness of the local economy to innovative networks and a lower exposure to knowledge flows (upper right-hand side circle in Figure 2). This is a direct consequence of the strong distance-decay of inter-regional knowledge flows in the EU. Greunz (2003) suggests that in Europe only innovative efforts pursued within a 190 miles (or 306 km) radius have an

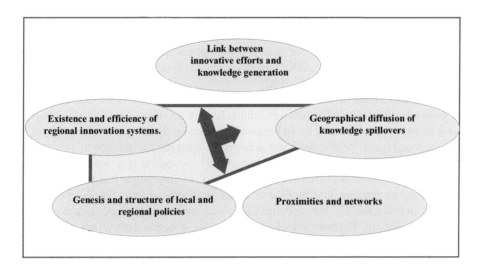

Figure 2. The Territorial Drivers of Innovation Dynamics in the European Union.
Source: Authors' elaboration.

impact on regional patenting activity. Other analyses, despite using different methodologies, reach similar results. Bottazzi and Peri (2003) estimate a maximum radius of 200–300 km for the diffusion of knowledge flows. Moreno *et al.* (2005) leave it at 250 km, whereas for Rodríguez-Pose and Crescenzi (2008) the diffusion of knowledge is bounded to a 180-minute trip-time or 200 km. These empirical estimates of the degree of spatial boundedness of inter-regional knowledge flows point in the direction of the prominent role played by face-to-face interactions and 'temporary' contacts (necessarily constrained by travel-time distance) in the circulation of knowledge among EU regions, where limited labour mobility reduces the probability of long-haul exchanges. In other words, the existing evidence indicates that knowledge flows tend to be driven more by commuting patterns and temporary proximity than by the migration of 'knowledgeable' individuals. The consequence of this is that EU peripheral regions suffer from an intrinsic source of competitive disadvantage, due to the tendency of knowledge to form highly localized pools around innovative centres.

When the evidence outlined earlier is considered in a 'systemic' way, as the integrated approach allows us to do, the inter-relations between the various mechanisms at play are uncovered. As knowledge spillovers are spatially bounded, they create localized pools of knowledge in core areas, where the innovative efforts are also concentrated, leaving only marginal benefits in peripheral areas. However, the impact of such flows crucially depends on a set of localized – largely idiosyncratic but still partially generalizable – meso-level socio-institutional conditions. In this context, territorial-level innovation policies have played a fundamental role in shaping the current territorial dynamics of innovation. The existing literature has shown that the process of economic and political integration and EU policies have profoundly influenced the geography of innovation of European countries and regions (Tsipouri, 2004). In the attempt to counterbalance the uneven spatial distribution of innovative activities – on the basis of territorial equity considerations – the EU has systematically supported R&D activities in lagging regions, both by means of the creation of large public research facilities or by incentivizing the (re)location of R&D intensive firms. The strong policy emphasis on formal R&D has often resulted in a mismatch between the demand of research centres and private firms for highly skilled labour and the scarcity of local supply (Midelfart-Knarvik and Overman, 2002) overlooking the 'systemic' nature of the 'European innovation paradox' (Oughton *et al.*, 2002).

The interlinked drivers of the territorial geography of innovation in Europe are captured by the arrows in Figure 2. What remains relatively underexplored (in both conceptual and empirical terms) by the literature on EU regional innovation dynamics is the role of the fifth pillar: nongeographical 'proximities and networks'. Whereas the impact of the networks generated by both labour (e.g. diasporic communities) and capital (e.g. multinational firms) international/translocal movements on the geography of innovation has been more thoroughly analysed by the literature focused on other geographical areas (as will be discussed later, this is true for the US but also for China and India), for Europe as a whole more research is still needed. Relevant initial insights in this direction come from national-level analyses of the impact of university–industry collaborations (e.g. Ponds *et al.*, 2010, for the Netherlands; D'Este *et al.*, 2012, for the UK). Geographical proximity is an important enabling factor for these forms of knowledge exchange, but the existence of translocal networks is also essential, at least within the borders of the countries considered in these analyses. EU-level evidence shows that networking across regions positively correlates with regional innovative performance (Miguélez and Moreno, 2010). But the research challenge is to explicitly disentangle the impact of a differentiated set of 'proximities' (geographical and nongeographical) on regional innovative performance. Marrocu *et al.* (2011) suggest that, although geographical proximity remains an important factor, technological and cognitive proximity might be even more important conditions for the transmission of knowledge, whereas the role of institutional and organizational proximity seems to be more marginal.

This very dynamic – although still embryonic – strand of literature has still not reached a consensus comparable to that of the other 'pillars' on the relative importance of different nonspatial channels and their impact with respect to the other 'pillars' (such as, e.g. systems of innovation conditions) remains to be explored.

3.1.2 The United States

On the other side of the Atlantic, approaching the territorial dynamism of innovation from an integrated comparative framework leads to a remarkably different picture. Not only the linear link between local R&D investments and innovative output (Anselin *et al.*, 1997; Acs *et al.*, 2002) is stronger than in Europe, but empirical analyses of the spatial diffusion of spillovers have also highlighted a stronger distance decay effect, with knowledge spillovers, in general, not spreading beyond a 80–110 km radius from the metropolitan statistical area (MSA) where they are generated (Jaffe, 1989; Varga, 2000; Ács, 2002). In the US, the generation of innovation usually occurs in relatively self-contained geographical areas that rely on their own R&D inputs and maximize the circulation of knowledge within their boundaries. Higher factor mobility allows for this as it makes knowledge and competencies matching more easily achieved locally (Dosi *et al.*, 2006). Mobility of capital, population and knowledge not only promotes the agglomeration of research activity in specific areas of the country, but also enables the full exploitation of local innovative activities and (informational) synergies. If spatially bound knowledge flows seem to be confined within the functional borders of the US MSAs, the role of 'global' networks and nonspatial proximities

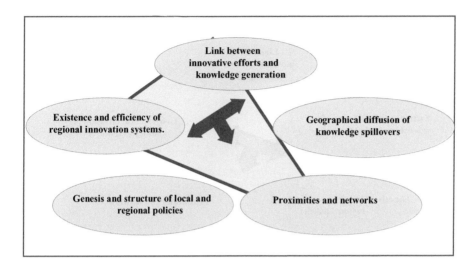

Figure 3. The Territorial Drivers of Innovation Dynamics in the U.S.

Source: Authors' elaboration.

has been shown to be – by a recent, but increasingly consolidated and converging literature – of paramount importance. Bettencourt *et al.* (2007a,b), Fleming *et al.* (2007) and Lobo and Strumsky (2008) provide evidence on the positive impact of extra-local connections of different nature on the local innovative performance of US MSAs. The mobility of knowledgeable individuals across space – not constrained by commuting patterns – makes the complex web of their relations stretch across the entire country while remaining highly localized in specific hotspots.

Although the knowledge circulation mechanisms differ substantially in the two continents, the institutional conditions that support the process of innovation and reinforce local absorptive capabilities are very similar: in the US, as in Europe, having favourable social filter conditions is key to innovation (Crescenzi *et al.*, 2007).

The red arrows in Figure 3 offer a visual summary of the key pillars of the territorial dynamics of innovation in the US through the lens of the integrated approach: the highly localized impact of R&D investments is reinforced by favourable systems of innovation conditions and 'global' networks. Inter-regional spillovers are less important. The spatial impact of innovation policies remains limited: spatial equity considerations rarely enter in the science and technology policy making.

3.2 *The Territorial Determinants of Innovation in Emerging Countries*

When moving into the analysis of emerging countries, not withstanding their increasing importance in the international economic arena, the empirical literature becomes more fragmented. In this context, the integrated framework can offer important insights on possible directions for future research.

The link between formal R&D investments and the generation of innovation is of great practical importance for both China and India, given their current and historic emphasis on

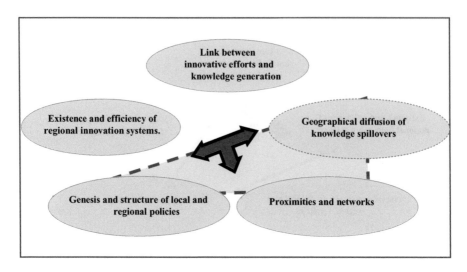

Figure 4. The Territorial Drivers of Innovation Dynamics in China.
Source: Authors' elaboration.

technology-led national growth (Leadbeater and Wilsdon, 2007). Both China and India are investing heavily in 'innovation inputs', such as R&D and human capital, which both feed into and feed from rapid macroeconomic growth (Kjuis and Wang, 2006). A systematic analysis of the geography of these investments suggests that their spatial concentration has increased over time both in China (Sun, 2003) and India (Mitra, 2007). R&D efforts are heavily concentrated in specific 'host spots' in both countries with a special role being played by R&D departments of multinational firms. However, the link between local R&D and innovative output is highly nonlinear in both contexts. The 'productivity' of innovative efforts is much differentiated in space depending on a number of conditioning factors. Figures 4 and 5 highlight – for China and India, respectively – similarities and dissimilarities in terms of these territorial-level conditioning factors.

The role of 'global' networks and nongeographical proximities is vital in the two countries, which have been constantly tapping into the rapidly growing stock of global knowledge through multinational firms and FDI, technology licensing and imported capital goods (Utz and Dahlman, 2005). A number of large-scale quantitative studies suggest that global R&D inflows, technology transfer and export orientation by local firms help improve innovation performance (Liu and Buck, 2007; Ying, 2008; Fu and Gong, 2009; Cheung, 2010). Similarly, qualitative analyses suggest that knowledge diffusion from multinational enterprises (MNEs) has helped technological catch-up (Mu and Lee, 2005), not least through enabling indigenous innovation and locally developed technologies (Von Zedwitz, 2004). Migrants and diasporic communities are also essential in facilitating innovative activity in developing countries as individual migrants act as mobile carriers of knowledge from 'developed' host countries into 'emerging' 'home' economies (Saxenian, 2006). This latter channel tends to have stronger impacts in India, where mobility patterns are freer, than in China, but the situation is evolving rapidly (Parthasarathy, 2004; Taeube, 2004; Saxenian and Sabel, 2008).

The contribution of other territorial-level factors is less 'clear-cut' and generally reflects the fundamentally different role of government intervention in the two countries. In

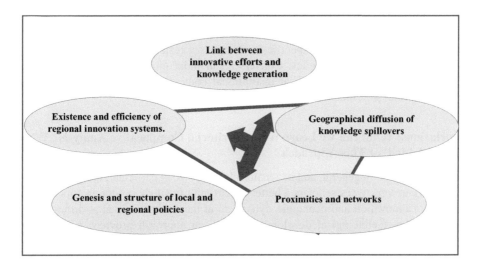

Figure 5. The Territorial Drivers of Innovation Dynamics in India.
Source: Authors' elaboration.

particular, the Chinese experience is relatively unique when compared to all other cases. It is certainly true that governments in both countries are actively developing their domestic innovation capacities. But China has developed a very aggressive strategy based on a rapid increase in R&D expenditure (10–15% until 2020) (Lundin and Schwaag Serger, 2007), whereas India's model focuses on developing skilled human capital, clustering activity in science parks and providing financial instruments such as tax incentives, research grants, concessional loans and venture capital (Mani, 2004). Leadbeater and Wilsdon (2007) draw a contrast between the 'open, cosmopolitan' nature of innovative activity and policy in India, reliant on free factor mobility, and the top–down, 'increasingly techno-nationalist' direction that Chinese leaders are taking (aggressively supporting the clustering of innovative activities in designated areas and leveraging on internal capacity rather than external flows.

This has important implications for the geography of spatially bounded knowledge flows and their localization patterns in the two countries. A number of studies suggest that the spillover–innovation link also operates in developing country contexts, with strong evidence that the spatial concentration of innovative activities boosts efficiency (Scott and Garofoli, 2007; Duranton, 2008; Xu, 2009). However, these effects may be constrained by institutional and political factors generating differentiated dynamics in different countries. Whereas in India connectivity to innovative neighbouring regions seems, as in the EU case, to benefit the local economy, in China this effect has been shown to be negative (dotted line in Figure 4) with major innovative centres 'sucking' resources from their neighbourhood (Crescenzi *et al.*, 2012).

Long-term differences in public policies have also contributed to substantial differences in the systems of innovation conditions of the two countries. The innovation system in China (Schaaper, 2009) is still highly fragmented and not well integrated (Sun, 2003), having a more limited impact on the local productivity of innovative efforts, whereas in India the literature seems to suggest as more directly supportive set of localized systemic institutions (Utz and Dahlman, 2005).

Overall, approaching the territorial dynamics of innovation from an integrated framework indicates that the process of innovation in China appears to be driven by the concentration of substantial R&D resources in specific locations as a result of the interaction of global and (national) state-driven dynamics. Conversely, in India global flows and their impacts are embedded into differentiated local institutional contexts and integrated into localized knowledge-transmission mechanisms.

4. Conclusions: What can we Learn from Territorial Comparative Analysis? What is the 'Value Added' of This Approach?

Assessing innovation in general, and its territorial dynamics, in particular, using an integrated conceptual framework gives scholars a better opportunity to single out the factors that shape the genesis of innovation and economic dynamism at the territorial level at different stages of the process of technological development. Such an approach provides new and more comprehensive ways to gain a better understanding of these processes for leading and lagging regions at the same time. But is there any general lesson that can be learnt from this framework? The systematic review of the key findings of the existing empirical literature on both developed and emerging countries suggests that innovation processes display very differentiated territorial processes in different contexts. A theory-driven framework makes it possible to generalize and compare some key trends, but regional and local innovation-based policies should carefully take into account local specificities possibly leading to the abandonment of 'best-practice' approach to policy transfer. In the same perspective, a systematic analysis of the literature shows that there is no 'optimal' geography of innovation. Hence, it does not make sense to call for an 'Americanization' or 'Europeanization' of the innovation process of countries such as China or India. Instead, public policies should identify the most sustainable models given local conditions and preferences to maximize the potential returns of any innovation policy intervention and its sustainability in time.

Acknowledgments

Financial support by the ESPON 2013 – KIT (European Observation Network of Territorial Development and Cohesion – Knowledge, Innovation and Territory) Project and by the European Research Council under the EU's Seventh Framework Programme (FP7/2007- 2013)/ERC grant agreement n° 269868 is gratefully acknowledged. The research has also benefited from the support of a Leverhulme Trust Major Research Fellowship and is also part of the UK Spatial Economics Research Centre. The authors are solely responsible for any opinions, views or errors contained in the chapter.

Note

1. For example, in the US, ethnic Indian and Chinese immigrant communities have played a significant role in science and technology innovation (Stephan and Levin, 2007), as well as in generating large numbers of spin-outs and startups (Wadhwa et al., 2007).

References

Acs, Z.J. (2002) Innovation and Growth in Cities. Northampton, MA: Edward Elgar.
Acs, Z., Anselin, L. and Varga, A. (2002) Patents and innovation counts as measures of regional production of new knowledge. Research Policy 31: 1069–1085.

Aghion, P. and Howitt, P. (1992) A model of growth through creative destruction. *Econometrica* 60(2): 323–351.

Anselin, L., Varga, A. and Acs, Z. (1997) Local geographic spillovers between university research and high technology innovations. *Journal of Urban Economics* 42: 422–448.

Audretsch, D. B. (2003) Innovation and spatial externalities. *International Regional Science Review* 26(2): 167–174.

Audretsch, D.B. and Feldman, M.P. (1996a) R&D spillovers and the geography of innovation and production. *American Economic Review* 86: 630–640.

Audretsch, D.B. and Feldman, M.P. (1996b) Innovative clusters and the industry life cycle. *Review of Industrial Organization* 11: 253–273.

Bettencourt, L., Lobo, J., Helbing, D., Kühnert, C. and West, G. (2007a) Growth, innovation, scaling, and the pace of life in cities. *Proceedings of the National Academy of Sciences* 104: 7301–7306.

Bettencourt, L., Lobo, J. and Strumsky, D. (2007b) Invention in the city: increasing returns to patenting as a scaling function of metropolitan size. *Research Policy* 36: 107–120.

Bilbao-Osorio, B. and Rodríguez-Pose, A. (2004) From R&D to innovation and economic growth in the EU. *Growth and Change* 35: 434–455.

Boschma R. A. (2005) Competitiveness of regions from an evolutionary perspective. *Regional Studies* 38(9): 1001–1014.

Bottazzi, L. and Peri, G. (2003) Innovation and spillovers in regions: evidence from European patent data. *European Economic Review* 47: 687–710.

Bruche, G. (2009) *A New Geography of Innovation – China and India rising.* New York: Vale Columbia Center, Columbia University.

Camagni, R. (1995) Global network and local milieu: toward a theory of economic space. In G. Conti, E. Malecki and P. Oinas (eds), *The Industrial Enterprise and its Environment: Spatial Perspectives* (pp. 195–216). Aldershot: Avebury.

Camagni, R. and Capello, R. (2003) La città come "milieu" e i "milieux" urbani: teoria e evidenza empirica. In G. Garofoli (ed.) *Impresa e Territorio* (pp. 237–275). Bologna: Il Mulino.

Cantwell, J. (2005) MNCs, local clustering and science-technology relationships. In G. Santangelo (ed.), *Technological Change and Economic Catch-Up: The Role of Science and Multinationals* (pp. 75–94). Cheltenham: Edward Elgar.

Capello, R and Faggian, A. (2005) Collective learning and relational capital in local innovation processes. *Regional Studies* 39(1): 75–87.

Cheshire, P.C. and Magrini, S. (2000) Endogenous processes in European regional growth: convergence and policy. *Growth and Change* 31: 455–479.

Cheung, K. (2010) Spillover effects of FDI via exports on innovation performance of China's high-technology industries. *Journal of Contemporary China* 19(65): 541–557.

Coe, N.M. and Bunnell, T.G. (2003) 'Spatialising' knowledge communities: towards a conceptualisation of transnational innovation networks. *Global Networks* 3(4): 437–456.

Cooke, P. (1997) Regions in a global market: the experiences of Wales and Baden-Wurttemberg. *Review of International Political Economy* 4(2): 349–381.

Crescenzi, R. (2005) Innovation and regional growth in the enlarged Europe: the role of local innovative capabilities, peripherality and education. *Growth and Change* 36: 471–507.

Crescenzi, R. (2009) Undermining the principle of territorial concentration? EU regional policy and the socio-economic disadvantage of European regions. *Regional Studies* 43(1): 111–133.

Crescenzi, R. and Rodríguez-Pose, A. (2009) Systems of innovation and regional growth in the EU: endogenous vs. external innovative efforts and socioeconomic conditions. In U. Fratesi and L. Senn (eds), *Growth and Innovation of Competitive Regions* (pp. 167–192). Springer-Verlag.

Crescenzi, R. and Rodríguez-Pose, A. (2011) *Innovation and Regional Growth in the European Union.* Berlin and New York: Springer-Verlag

Crescenzi, R., Rodríguez-Pose, A. and Storper, M. (2007) The territorial dynamics of innovation: a Europe-United States comparative analysis. *Journal of Economic Geography* 7(6): 673–709.

Crescenzi, R., Rodríguez-Pose, A. and Storper, M. (2012) The territorial dynamics of innovation in China and India. Mimeo.

D'Este, P., Guy, F. and Iammarino, S. (2012) Shaping the formation of university-industry research collaborations: what type of proximity does really matter?. *Journal of Economic Geography*, in press.

Dosi, G., Llerena, P. and Sylos Labini, M. (2006) The relationships between science, technologies and their industrial exploitation: an illustration through the myths and realities of the so-called 'European Paradox'. *Research Policy* 35(10): 1450–1464.

Duflo, E. (2010) Transportation infrastructure and urban growth in China. Presentation to International Growth Centre Conference on Cities and Growth. London, 16 December.

Dunning, J. (1996) The geographical sources of competitiveness in firms: some results of a new survey. *Transnational Corporations* 5(3): 1–21.

Dunning, J. (1998). Location and the multinational enterprise: a neglected factor? *Journal of International Business Studies* 29(1): 45–66.

Duranton, G. (2008). Viewpoint: from cities to productivity and growth in developing countries. *Canadian Journal of Economics/Revue canadienne d'économique* 41: 689–736.

Fagerberg, J. (1988) Why growth rates differ. In G. Dosi, C. Freeman, R. Nelson, G. Silveberg and L. Soete (eds), *Technological Change and Economic Theory*. London: Pinter

Fagerberg, J., Verspagen, B. and Caniels, M. (1997) Technology, growth and unemployment across European Regions. *Regional Studies* 31(5): 457–466.

Faulconbridge, J.R. (2006) Stretching tacit knowledge beyond a local fix? Global spaces of learning in advertising professional service firms. *Journal of Economic Geography* 6: 517–540.

Fleming, L., King, C. and Juda, A. (2007) Small worlds and innovation. *Organization Science* 14(5): 375–393.

Fu, X. and Y. Gong (2009) International and intranational technological spillovers and productivity growth in China. *Asian Economic Papers* 8(2): 1–23.

Gordon, I.R. (2001) Unemployment and spatial labour markets: strong adjustment and persistent concentration. In R. Martin and P. Morrison (eds), *Geographies of Labour Market Inequality*. London: Routledge.

Greenbaum, R.T. and Bondonio, D. (2004) Losing focus: a comparative evaluation of spatially targeted economic revitalisation programmes in the US and the EU. *Regional Studies* 38(3): 319–334.

Greunz, L. (2003) Geographically and technologically mediated knowledge spillovers between European regions. *Annals of Regional Science* 37: 657–680.

Griliches, Z. (1986) Productivity, R&D, and basic research at the firm level in the 1970s. *American Economic Review* 76: 141–154.

Iammarino, S. (2005) An evolutionary integrated view of regional systems of innovation: concepts, measures and historical perspectives. *European Planning Studies* 13(4): 497–519.

Jaffe, A.B. (1989) The real effects of academic research. *American Economic Review* 79(5): 984–1001.

Kuijs, L. and Wang, T. (2006) China's pattern of growth: moving to sustainability and reducing inequality. *China and World Economy* 14(1): 1–14.

Leadbeater, C. and Wilsdon, J. (2007) *The Atlas of Ideas: How Asian innovation can benefit us all*. London: Demos.

Liu, X. and Buck, T. (2007). Innovation performance and channels for international technology spillovers: evidence from Chinese high-tech industries. *Research Policy* 36(3): 355–366.

Lobo J. and Strumsky D. (2008) Metropolitan patenting, inventor agglomeration and social networks: a tale of two effects. *Journal of Urban Economics* 63: 871–884.

Lundin, N. and Schwaag Serger, S. (2007) *Globalization of R&D and China – Empirical Observations and Policy Implications*. Stockholm: Research Institute of Industrial Economics.

Lundvall, B.-A. (1992) *National Systems of Innovation: Towards a Theory of Innovation and Interactive Learning*. London: Pinter.

Lundvall, B.-A., Joseph, K.J., Chaminade, C. and Vang, J. (eds) (2009). *Handbook of Innovation Systems and Developing Countries : Building Domestic Capabilities in a Global Setting*. Edward Elgar: Cheltenham.

Malecki, E. (1997) *Technology and Economic Development: The Dynamics of Local, Regional and National Competitiveness*, 2nd ed. London: Addison Wesley Longman.

Mani, S. (2004). Institutional support for investment in domestic technologies: an analysis of the role of government in India. *Technological Forecasting and Social Change* 71(8): 855–863.

Marrocu, E., Paci, R. and Usai, S. (2011) Proximity, networks and knowledge production in Europe. CRENOS Working Paper, September 2011.

Midelfart-Knarvik, H. and Overman, H.G. (2002) Delocation and European integration: is structural spending justified?. *Economic Policy* 17(35): 322–359.

Miguelez E. and Moreno R. (2010) Research networks and inventors' mobility as drivers of innovation: evidence from Europe. IREA Working Papers 201001, University of Barcelona.

Mitra, R. (2007) *India's Emergence as a Global R&D Center – An Overview of the Indian R&D System and Potential.* Ostersund: Swedish Institute for growth Policy Studies

Moreno, R., Paci, R. and Usai, S. (2005) Spatial spillovers and innovation activity in European regions. *Environment and Planning A* 37: 1793–1812.

Mu, Q. and K., Lee (2005) Knowledge diffusion, market segmentation and technological catch-up: the case of the telecommunication industry in China. *Research Policy* 34(6): 759–783.

Oughton, C., Landabaso, M. and Morgan, K. (2002) The regional innovation paradox: innovation policy and industrial policy. *Journal of Technology Transfer* 27: 97–110.

Padilla-Perez, R., Vang, J. and Chaminade, C. (2009). Regional innovation systems in developing countries: integrating micro and meso-level capabilities. In B.-A. Lundvall, J. Vang, K. J. Joseph, and C. Chaminade (eds), *Handbook of Innovation Systems and Developing Countries.* Cheltenham: Edward Elgar.

Parthasarathy, B. (2004) India's Silicon Valley or Silicon Valley's India? Socially embedding the computer software industry in Bangalore. *International Journal of Urban and Regional Research* 28(3): 664–685.

Ponds, R., van Oort, F. and Frenken, K. (2010) Innovation, spillovers and university-industry collaboration: an extended knowledge production function approach. *Journal of Economic Geography* 10(2): 231–255.

Rodríguez-Pose, A. (1999) Innovation prone and innovation averse societies. Economic performance in Europe. *Growth and Change* 30: 75–105.

Rodríguez-Pose, A. and Crescenzi, R. (2008) R&D, spillovers, innovation systems and the genesis of regional growth in Europe. *Regional Studies* 42(1): 51–67.

Rodríguez-Pose, A. and Storper, M.l. (2006) Better rules or stronger communities? On the social foundations of institutional change and its economic effects. *Economic geography* 82(1): 1–25.

Romer, P.M. (1990) Endogenous technological change. *Journal of Political Economy* 98(5): 97–103.

Saxenian, A.-L. (2006) *The New Argonauts: Regional Advantage in a Global Economy.* Cambridge, MA: Harvard University Press.

Saxenian, A.-L. and Sabel, C. (2008) Venture capital in the 'periphery': the New Argonauts, global search and local institution-building. [Roepke lecture in economic geography]. *Economic Geography*, 84(4): 379–394.

Schaaper, M. (2009) Measuring China's innovation system national specificities and international comparisons. OECD STI Working Paper, January 2009.

Scott, A. and Garofoli, G. (eds) (2007) *Development on the Ground: Clusters, Networks and Regions in Emerging Economies.* Oxford: Routledge.

Scott, A. and Storper, M. (2003) Regions, globalization, development. *Regional Studies* 37: 579–593.

Sonn, J.W. and Storper, M. (2008) The increasing importance of geographical proximity in technological innovation: an analysis of U.S. patent citations, 1975–1997. *Environment and Planning A* 40(5): 1020–1039.

Stephan, P.E. and Levin, S.G. (2007) Foreign scholars in US science: contributions and costs. In R. Ehrenberg and P. Stephan (eds), *Science and the University* (pp. 113–133). Madison, WI: University of Wisconsin Press.

Storper, M. and Venables, A.J. (2004) Buzz: face-to-face contact and the urban economy. *Journal of Economic Geography* 4: 351–370.

Sun, Y. (2003) Geographic patterns of industrial innovation in China during the 1990s. *Tijdschrift voor Economische En Sociale Geografie*, 94(3): 376–389.

Taeube, F. (2004) Proximities and Innovation Evidence From the Indian IT industry in Bangalore. Danish Research Unit for Industrial Economics, Working paper, No. 04–10.

Tsipouri, L. (2004) Innovation for European competitiveness and cohesion: opportunities and difficulties for co-evolution. *Science and Public Policy* 31(6): 465–474.

Utz, A. and Dahlman, C. (2005) *India and the Knowledge Economy: Leveraging Strengths and Opportunities*. Washington, DC: World Bank.

Varga, A. (2000) Local academic knowledge spillovers and the concentration of economic activity. *Journal of Regional Science* 40: 289–309.

Von Zedtwitz, M. (2004) Managing foreign R&D laboratories in China. *R&D Management* 34(4): 439–452.

Wadhwa, V., Saxenian, A., Rissing, B.A., and Gereffi, G. (2007). America's New Immigrant Entrepreneurs: Part I. Duke Science, Technology & Innovation Paper No. 23. Available at http://dx.doi.org/10.2139/ssrn.990152. Accessed on August 28, 2011.

Yeung, H. (2009) Regional development and the competitive dynamics of global production networks: an East Asian perspective. *Regional Studies*, 43(3): 325–351.

Ying, L. (2008) The shape of ideas production function in transition and developing economies: evidence from China. *International Regional Science Review* 31(2): 185–206.

Xu, Z. (2009) Productivity and agglomeration economies in Chinese cities. *Comparative Economic Studies*, 51(3): 284–301.

9

REGIONAL INNOVATION SYSTEMS WITHIN A TRANSITIONAL CONTEXT: EVOLUTIONARY COMPARISON OF THE ELECTRONICS INDUSTRY IN SHENZHEN AND DONGGUAN SINCE THE OPENING OF CHINA

Wenying Fu, Javier Revilla Diez and Daniel Schiller

1. Introduction

In a globalizing world, economic growth is increasingly embedded within complex internationally interdependent networks. Since 1970s, Asian countries have achieved more significant growth rates than other developing countries by being actively involved in global production networks. In this context, threats and opportunities exist simultaneously for the emerging economies. Altenburg (2006) argued that the limited resources in terms of qualified personnel, competitive and diversified firms, and effective institutions in the Asian emerging economies might cut them off from the knowledge-based competition in increasingly return-generated innovation. Park (2003), on the other hand, pointed out that some innovation clusters are emerging in the Asian Pacific Rim, and that successful regional innovation systems (RIS) can be developed through policy initiatives in these clusters.

There are two central elements of RIS. The first one is the willingness and capacity of firms to undertake innovation and interactive learning with other firms and institutions, and the second one is the initiative of policy makers to promote innovation and interactive learning by establishing supportive infrastructure and institutions (Cooke *et al.*, 1997; Howells, 1999; Revilla Diez, 2002; Morgan, 2004; Asheim and Coenen, 2005; Revilla Diez and Berger, 2005). Apart from these two elements, RIS can take different forms (Braczyk *et al.*, 1998). Whereas the RIS in developed regions such as Silicon Valley and Germany's Baden Württemberg region are based on cutting-edge technological innovation, RIS in Asian emerging economies is often based more on external technology and incremental innovation.

Governance mechanisms are considered to be the fundamental infrastructure of RIS, as they are able to facilitate interaction and cooperation. Governance consists of institutions

Innovation, Entrepreneurship, Geography and Growth, First Edition.
Edited by Philip McCann and Les Oxley. Chapters © 2013 The Authors.
Book compilation © 2013 Blackwell Publishing Ltd. Published 2013 by Blackwell Publishing Ltd.

(i.e. the rules of the game) and organizations (i.e. the players of the game) that shape the incentives for economic action. It is thus not limited to governments, but includes privately established and enforced governance mechanisms explicitly. Recently, institutional reform has been found to be the catalyst of rapid industrialization and economic development in many Asian countries (Lundvall *et al.*, 2006; Goldsmith, 2007). In China, the planned economy has been making the transition to a market economy in an incremental fashion, releasing the growth potential that was locked-in by the old, poorly incentivized institutional design. For regional development, Chinese central government has either been directly involved in economic development, such as establishing economic special zones, or has implicitly encouraged the bottom-up development, mainly by allowing more economic developmental autonomy to local governments. Therefore, the uniqueness of China's transitional context must be explicitly taken into account as part of the investigation into the development of RIS in China.

In this chapter, we show how the formation of RIS has unfolded under these two distinct institutional designs and governance modalities to initiate industrialization following the introduction of the opening policy in China. The two cities investigated are Shenzhen and Dongguan, located in the southeast province of Guangdong in China. In Shenzhen, especially in the Special Economic Zone (SEZ), the governance supporting industrialization is rather dirigiste, which is defined as an economic system where the government exerted strong directive influence. It is characterized by a state-oriented involvement of economic development with active strategic policy support. In Dongugan, however, governance that supports industrialization is grassroots, characterized by flexible institutions organized mainly by town and village authorities that are favourable for overseas Chinese investment based on Guanxi (Leung, 1993; Yang, 2010).

The particular regional context of this chapter extends existing concepts that are predominantly applied in Western industrialized regions. The chapter, which is positioned at the interface of innovation economics and economic geography, is intended to provide more generalizable evidence regarding the institutional determinants which help evolve local–global production systems into more coherent RIS.

The remainder of the chapter is organized as follows: Section 2 discusses the theoretical approaches to regional governance modality developed by, amongst others, Cooke *et al.* (1997) and its extended implications within China's transitional context. Section 3 examines the willingness and capacity of firms to undertake innovation and interactive learning in Shenzhen and Dongguan on the basis of a survey of electronics firms in both regions conducted in 2009 for the purposes of this chapter. Section 4 explains the historical and institutional aspects influencing the current divergent innovation patterns in the two cities by reviewing the differing evolutionary patterns of the governance modality in Shenzhen and Dongguan, in both the initial industrialization phase and also in the later transitional phase. This discussion focuses on the path-dependent character of the governance evolution in the two cities and the likely impacts of these different institutional-evolutionary processes on the current regional innovation features. Finally, the chapter concludes by discussing the policy implications derived from the cases in Shenzhen and Dongguan.

2. Evolving Governance and Innovation: Discussion within China's Transitional Context

Due to the transitional context, an evolution of the production system can be observed after the implementation of the opening policy. In China, the production system in the initial industrialization phase is dominated by global corporations with a clustered supply chain of dependent small and medium enterprises (SMEs). The governance is mostly characterized by the formulation of favourable policies such as tax reductions and the support of hard and soft infrastructure for foreign firms' processing functions driven by local government incentives to raise their fiscal income. What is more, since the advent of the opening policy in the late 1970s, the Chinese central government has either been directly involved in economic development, such as by establishing economic special zones, or has implicitly encouraged the bottom-up development, mainly by allowing more economic developmental autonomy to local governments (Xu, 2011). In the initial industrialization phase in China, both grassroots globalized production systems and dirigiste globalized production systems can be distinguished as the two major forms of territorial production systems (Cooke et al., 1997).

In the grassroots globalized production system, the degree of supralocal coordination is low because of the localized nature of organization, and the funding comprises a mix of capital, grants and loans mainly from local banks, local government and possibly the local Chamber of Commerce. On the other hand, in the 'dirigiste' globalized production system, the initiation of industrialization processes is primarily a product of central government policies, leading to a high degree of coordination. Moreover, funding in this type of dirigiste modality is largely centrally determined, although the agencies may have decentralized locations in the regions (Braczyk et al., 1998).

When a specialized regional economy evolves into a more comprehensive innovation system in response to internal and external competitive pressures, the governance of the region should, in theory, co-evolve and adjust the focus of the support to the newly emerging innovation activities. To secure learning and innovation synergies between firms and institutions, governance systems in theory could play an important role in providing access to information, ensuring credibility, coordinating collective actions and even creating a learning atmosphere (Dalum et al., 1992; Amin, 1999; Capello, 1999; Haggard, 2004). Cooke et al. (1997) outline the governance dimension in RIS as follows (Table 1): (1) institutional competence to organize technology transfer and launch science and technology programs; (2) supported infrastructure to enhance the capacity of innovation and to extend the scope of interactive learning and (3) financial and budgetary capacity to reduce innovation-related uncertainty and risk as well as to mobilize innovation-related resources. Yet, the emergence of such complementary features is neither automatic nor inevitable for all regions, and other rather different systems are also often seen to evolve.

From an evolutionary perspective, the initial governance modality in the industrialization phase may therefore have a significant influence on the likelihood of successful transformation from a simple-production-supported governance framework to something of a more sophisticated entrepreneurship and innovation-supported governance system. To be more specific, two aspects of governance are argued to be critical for this evolutionary process, namely the competence of organizations and the institutional advantage (Cooke et al., 1998).

First, the dynamics of the governance evolution towards becoming innovation-supported depend on the competence of the organizations involved. In the initial industrialization phase, when the industrial base is weak, the perspective of resource endowments of related organizations becomes an important baseline for the evolution of governance towards a well-functioning innovation system. In Porter's (1998) competitive model, local endowments such as highly specialized skills and knowledge, institutions, related businesses and demanding customers are emphasized for the construction of a competitive cluster. In a grassroots globalized production system, production capital and know-how tend to depend

Table 1. Governance Content in Production Systems and Innovation Systems.

	Production systems	Innovation systems
Institutional competence	Capacity to design and execute industrial development policies	Capacity to organize technology transfer (local, regional, ...) science and technology programmes
Supported infrastructure	Hard infrastructure such as roads, electricity, ports etc.	Density and quality of infrastructures for innovation such as universities, research institutes, technology transfer agencies, consultants, skill-development and training agencies
	Soft infrastructure such as administrative services to assist the firms	Controled or shared execution of part of strategic infrastructures
Financing and budget	Capacity to impose taxes	Accessibility of capital market for firms
	Autonomy for public spending	High level of financial intermediaries

Source: Adapted from Cooke *et al.* (1997).

heavily on foreign investment. Yet, there is typically only a very limited skill-base in the production system, either from the previous accumulation of knowledge or via assignments from the central government, which would facilitate the absorption of foreign technology. In contrast, the dirigiste globalized production system is able to accumulate the skill and knowledge stock from the old national knowledge system, by benefiting from the relocation of large state-owned firms and research institutes. In short, the original players in the initial industrialization phase in the two different systems often define the capacity of localities to process, absorb and adapt the external technology at early stages in the transition process (Cohen and Levinthal, 1990; Zahra and George, 2002). This in turn may influence the generation of different cumulative development processes in different regions, in which some regions attract a higher level of foreign investment than others, thereby facilitating greater possibilities for learning and competence creation via interactions and technological spillover.

On this point, there are arguments which suggest that the dirigiste governance system outperforms the grassroots governance system in terms of two major institutional advantages. The first aspect is the higher degree of policy coordination in the dirigiste governance, thereby focusing on selected long-term trajectories and developing a level of consensus on desirable futures. The coordinated policy action includes the practice of identifying new strategic industries, creating partnerships between sciences, industry and government and providing incentives for multidisciplinary research along a specific development direction. The second aspect is that the dirigiste approach, which is mostly initiated and governed by national-level agencies with more power, is better able to act as the vanguard of reform and enjoy the privileges of first-mover advantage. The establishment of a stock exchange market is one of the examples of such reforms. It is able to stimulate local technological entrepreneurship and support innovation activities of private firms, giving these places first-mover advantage in developing innovation-related capabilities.

However, these purported advantages both depend on the capacity of the central government in question. It is still a risky option to leave too much of the future of development in the hands of central government authorities with little or no local knowledge for two reasons. First, there are likely to be decision-making mistakes and mis-investment in the selection of key industries for policy priority in situations where little information is collected from the market. Second, soft budget constraints are most likely to occur in state-owned firms, which play an important role in the dirigiste approach, leading to lower efficiency and poorer performance than in private sectors (Qian and Roland, 1998). Therefore, dirigiste modalities must gradually involve more market mechanisms of competition in the transitional process. In addition, the increasing participation of markets fosters entrepreneurial activities which can build on the stock of technological knowledge remaining from the previously dirigiste production systems.

At the same time, the evolutionary process involved in transforming a production system from a grassroots-type governance mode to something akin to an innovation system often faces much more resistance than the dirigiste method. As argued by Easterly (2008), the grassroots approach evolves gradually within the constraint of previous institutions, while the dirigiste approach is able to start with a blank sheet or tear up the old institutional setup. This argument has two implications. First, while the dirigiste governance approach enjoys some institutional advantages, a 'competency trap' can arise in grassroots governance, whereby local limits to the capacity of grassroots organizations to absorb new ideas and develop new trajectories soon become evident (Levitt and March, 1988). Second, vested interests tend to emerge in grassroots governance systems which often oppose any changes that they fear might undermine their current monopoly positions (Boschma, 2004). Such entrenched interests tend to inhibit wider knowledge awareness and militate against any motivations for change (Leonard, 1992). Taken together, these effects create systemic market and policy barriers to the fostering of interactive business innovation processes as new development alternatives unfold elsewhere (Könnölä et al., 2006).

On balance, neither overcentralized systems that leave no autonomy for lower-level policy learning, nor decentralized ones that lack the central governance mechanisms necessary to initiate radical change, will be able to cope with the challenge of industrial upgrading and catching-up (Lundvall et al., 2006). In short, in a transitional context, governance of RIS should involve both a mix of free market power and appropriate central and local government interventions in institutional reforms. Yet, which works better in which context in which region is still to be determined. The comparison of the Shenzhen and Dongguan cases examined here should reveal some different evolutionary patterns of interactive learning and innovation system formation.

3. Innovation Pattern in Shenzhen and Dongguan: Empirical Evidence

In this section, an empirical investigation into the scope and extent of interactive learning and innovation processes in the electronics industry in Shenzhen and Dongguan was conducted to gain insights into the respective RIS. First although, the general regional indicators in both cities are shown in Figure 1 and Table 2. The overall performance and pattern of specialization in the high-tech sector in Shenzhen outperforms that of Dongguan in terms

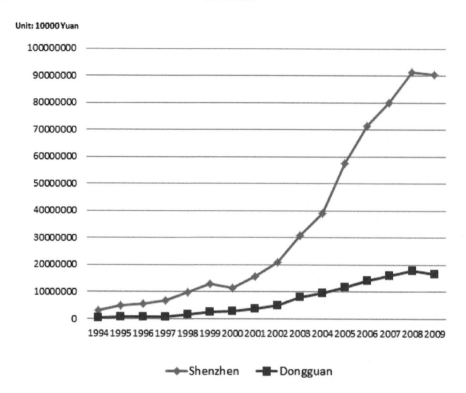

Figure 1. Output Value of the Electronics Industry 1994–2009.
Source: Shenzhen Statistical Yearbooks and Dongguan Statistical Yearbooks.

Table 2. General Indicators in Shenzhen and Dongguan (2009).

	Shenzhen	Dongguan
Population	8 912 300	6 350 000
Gross domestic product (billion Yuan)	820	376
Industrial output value (billion Yuan)	1582	676
Percentage of high-tech manufacturing sector[a]	69%	39%
Employment	6 924 853	5 381 981
Percentage of high-tech manufacturing and service sector[b]	33%	19%
Total R&D expenditure (billion Yuan)	27.97	4.14
Percentage of GDP	3.4%	1.1%
R&D personnel	123 687	18 524
Share of R&D personnel per 1000 employees	17.9	3.4

Sources: Shenzhen Statistical Yearbook 2010, Dongguan Statistical Yearbook 2010 and Second Investigation Report of Guangdong R&D Resources.
[a]High-tech manufacturing sector refers to ordinary equipment, special purpose equipment, transport equipment, electrical equipment and machinery, telecommunications, computer and other electronic equipment (only state-owned firms and firms with over 5 million sales are included).
[b]High-tech manufacturing and service sector includes the high-tech manufacturing sector above and the service sector, that is, information transfer, computer and software services, scientific research, technical services and geographical prospecting.

of industrial output value, employment and R&D. The observation suggests that there are greater innovation and human capital resources in Shenzhen than in Dongguan, as Dongguan is specialized more in the lower value segments of the global value-chains.

3.1 *Survey Design of A Comparative Study*

Comparative study has been argued by many scholars (Staber, 2001; Doloreux, 2004; Asheim and Coenen, 2005; Revilla Diez and Kiese, 2006) as an important means of understanding the function of RIS and capturing hidden variables that are of interest for the construction of the system. Therefore, comparing the evolution of the RIS in Shenzhen and Dongguan, both of which are located in the prosperous Pearl River Delta in the Guangdong province, China, offers an ideal perspective for understanding the specific contents of governance modality that influence the systemic innovation in these region. The empirical data for the research was collected from an electronics firm questionnaire survey in Shenzhen and Dongguan, Guangdong province, China from September until November 2009. The investigation focuses on the electronics industry because of its great dominance and development history in the research area, which enables the inquiry into its evolutionary path.

In total, 312 Shenzhen firms and 281 Dongguan firms were contacted for the purposes of the survey. As in China in general, it is not possible to draw the sample from a comprehensive database so the firms were therefore approached in two ways. Based on several company directories firms were randomly contacted via telephone and mail. As a consequence of the economic crisis, the response rate was rather low. To increase the number of surveyed firms we additionally contacted firms at regional trade fairs in Shenzhen and Donnguan. In total, 167 Shenzhen firms and 177 Dongguan firms filled out the questionnaires, with the response rate in Shenzhen and Dongguan being 54% and 63%, respectively.

In the sample, there are 140 Shenzhen firms and 161 Dongguan firms that undertake product innovation activities. The core innovation questions cover the firms' internal efforts and external interactions during the innovation process. The scope of external interaction covers various business partners, such as parent companies, foreign customers, domestic customers, universities and research institutions and sales agents. In addition, the interaction mode with the partners is identified, that is, interacting with the partners through active search strategies such as the Internet, exhibitions or sales agents, and interacting with partners through the introduction and recommendation of long-term business partners, relatives and friends. Surveyed firms were asked about the importance of each aspect in product innovation activities.

3.2 *Empirical Results of Innovation and Interactive Learning in Shenzhen and Dongguan*

In the econometric analysis, tobit regression was applied to examine the impact of external interactions with other business partners on firms' innovation outcomes. The dependent variable in the regression is the self-evaluation score of the degree of improvement on innovation outcomes (ranging from 0 to 5 with increasing significance of change). Due to the censoring of the valuation towards higher ranks, tobit regression was conducted. Factor analysis was first applied to reduce the number of the independent variables and to simplify the following regression. It was applied to three aspects of innovation processes: sources for new product ideas (NPI), ways of accessing tacit knowledge for new product development (NPTK) and governance (formal or informal) of innovation interaction (NPInteraction). The

Table 3. Independent Variables in Product Innovation Performance Regressions.

	Indicators	Description
Innovation behaviour (factor scores)	NPI_external partners	Interacting with *domestic customers, universities, research institutions and sales agents* to gain innovation ideas
	NPI_internal efforts	Making *internal learning efforts* such as own ideas, license purchasing and reverse engineering
	NPI_parent comp. & foreign	Relying on *parent companies or foreign customers* to gain innovation ideas
	NPTK_active learning	Sending staff *to business partners* for training
	NPTK_passive from customer	Receiving training and know-how from people sent *by domestic and foreign customers*
	NPTK_passive from parent comp.	Receiving training and know-how from people sent *by parent company*
	NPInteraction _informal	Interacting with innovation partners through interaction with *business partners, relatives and friends*
Firm characteristics	Size	Defined according to Chinese firm size standard; 1 as large firms with sales no less 300 million Yuan and no less than 2000 employees, otherwise as small and medium-sized with the value of 0
	Ownership	1 for firms with foreign ownership (wholly owned or partly owned joint venture), 0 for firms with only domestic ownership
	Age	Years since establishment of the firm
Absorptive capacity	Educational level of technical staff	Proportion of technical staff with bachelor degree and above
	Initial technological level of main product	Defined according to International Standard Industrial Classification of all Economic Activities, Rev 3; 1 as producing low-tech products when starting business, 2 as producing medium-tech products when starting business and 3 as producing high-tech products when starting business

derived factors are able to explain over 60% of the variance of the original sample for NPI, 74% for NPTK and 79% for NPInteraction. To avoid multicollinearity, seven independent variables were finally selected, as given in Table 3. The factor scores of each case on each factor are used in the regression model.

   Table 4 provides the descriptive statistics for the variables and tests the variation level between Shenzhen and Dongguan. In the surveyed sample, most of the firms are

Table 4. Descriptive Statistics in Shenzhen and Dongguan.

	Shenzhen				Dongguan				ANOVA	
	Mean	S.D.	Min.	Max.	Mean	S.D.	Min.	Max.	F	Sig.
Firm size	0.06	0.23	0	1	0.11	0.31	0	1	2.255	0.134
Firm ownership	0.28	0.45	0	1	0.47	0.50	0	1	11.95	0.001
Firm age (years)	10.4	7.6	1	57	12.2	7.1	2	51	4.30	0.039
Educational level of technical staff (%)	0.43	0.36	0	1	0.33	0.30	0	1	5.72	0.017
Initial technological level of main product	1.99	0.63	1	3	1.78	0.64	1	3	7.93	0.005
NPI_external partners	0.10	1.05	-2.05	2.53	-0.07	0.96	-2.78	1.69	2.24	0.135
NPI_internal efforts	0.02	0.89	-2.67	1.68	0.11	1.06	-2.61	7.43	0.63	0.427
NPI_parent comp. & foreign	-0.22	0.87	-1.81	2.22	0.27	1.04	-2.89	2.90	19.19	0.000
NPTK_active learning	-0.03	1.01	-2.10	2.57	0.06	0.95	-2.19	2.10	0.68	0.409
NPTK_passive from customer	-0.02	0.94	-1.95	2.08	0.10	1.04	-2.13	2.27	1.03	0.31
NPTK_passive from parent comp.	-0.04	0.98	-1.38	3.28	0.10	1.02	-1.38	3.21	1.40	0.238
NPInteraction informal	-0.14	0.95	-2.52	1.60	0.14	1.03	-2.53	1.60	6.13	0.014

Note: The values of the variables NPI_, NPTK_ and NPInteraction_ are factor scores resulting from a factor analysis. By definition, they have a mean value of 0 and a standard deviation of 1. The observable differences result from the fact that some cases, that were included in the factor analysis, had to be excluded for the tobit regression due to missing values in other variables.

small- and medium sized, with firms' sizes being smaller in Shenzhen than Dongguan. The share of domestically owned firms in Dongguan is less than that in Shenzhen by a significant margin. The human capital levels in Shenzhen are markedly higher in Shenzhen than that in Dongguan according to the share of above bachelor degree technicians, and Shenzhen firms also start with a higher level of production technology than Dongguan. In terms of innovation behaviour, Shenzhen firms turn more to external partners in triggering innovative ideas than Dongguan firms. On the other hand, Dongguan firms rely more on the transfer of tacit knowledge from parent companies and foreign customers, and more frequently use informal relations with friends and business partners.

Table 5 shows the results of the tobit regression on product innovation performance. Three models are run as a comparison, first with the whole model which pools the Shenzhen and Dongguan survey data and then separately the Shenzhen and Dongguan models.

Observing first the variables indicating the behaviour in the various stages of the product innovation process, we see that Shenzhen firms appear to combine their internal absorptive capacity with external knowledge interactions with other partners to trigger innovation outcomes. On the other hand, innovation ideas originating within strict hierarchical organizations, that is, instructions from parent companies and foreign customers, are important for Dongguan firms. As such, interactive learning in Dongguan therefore appears to be largely oriented towards a fairly passive pattern of receiving orders to expand product functions and upgrade product categories from the organizationally proximate partners. On the other hand, interactive relations with external partners are more evident amongst Shenzhen firms in comparison with the Dongguan firms, for whom the role of organizationally proximate partners in promoting innovation is also smaller (0.25 compared to 0.53). In general, firms in Dongguan appear to rely more than Shenzhen firms on the knowledge accumulated within the firm boundary or firm direct partners, rather than on complementary knowledge spillovers and assets outside the firm or the immediate value chain.

There is little evidence of a major role for the level of technology, except for high technology in Dongguan. This observation is consistent with many empirical studies of China based on patent data and formal R&D cooperation (Wang and Lin, 2008; Yu *et al.*, 2011), which have indicated only a very limited role for R&D activities and low-level interfirm knowledge spillovers.

For Shenzhen firms in the sample, there is tentative evidence that older firms have a higher performance in product innovation. This probably reflects the long history of capability accumulation in the region related to innovation activities and greater system openness, which improves the region's knowledge absorptive capacity.

These preliminary survey-based estimates are suggestive of some major differences in the innovation mechanisms operating in the electronics industries of the two neighbouring regions. However, to understand the sources of such differences it is necessary to consider the different historical and institutional features of the regions.

4. Governance in Shenzhen and Dongguan, China: An Evolutionary Overview

In this section, the evolving governance from a production system to an innovation system in Shenzhen and Dongguan is examined, as we seek possible explanations for the different innovation patterns observed earlier. As already outlined, the institutional setups in Shenzhen and Dongguan, which have evolved since China's opening-up policy, correspond

Table 5. Tobit Regression on Innovation Performance.

Independent variables	Product innovation outcome		
	Whole model	Shenzhen model	Dongguan model
Constant	3.56[a]	3.38[a]	3.70[a]
	(0.192)	(0.289)	(0.239)
Educational level of technical staff	0.004[b]	0.005	0.002
	(0.002)	(0.003)	(0.003)
Ownership	−0.30[b]	−0.53[b]	−0.05
	(0.153)	(0.268)	(0.206)
Firm size	0.23	0.32	0.15
	(0.276)	(0.522)	(0.305)
Firm age	0.008	0.03[b]	−0.008
	(0.010)	(0.015)	(0.013)
Initial product type according to technology			
Medium tech versus low tech[c]	0.15	0.08	0.16
	(0.168)	(0.282)	(0.191)
High tech versus low tech[c]	0.37	0.14	0.60[d]
	(0.237)	(0.357)	(0.302)
NPI_external partners	0.31[a]	0.53[a]	0.12
	(0.091)	(0.158)	(0.105)
NPI_internal efforts	0.20[d]	0.39[a]	0.05
	(0.081)	(0.135)	(0.093)
NPI_parent comp. & foreign	0.25[a]	0.21	0.25[d]
	(0.089)	(0.155)	(0.102)
NPTK_active learning	−0.05	−0.28[b]	0.08
	(0.094)	(0.147)	(0.118)
NPTK_passive from customer	−0.07	−0.43[a]	0.16
	(0.087)	(0.135)	(0.103)
NPTK_passive from parent comp.	−0.08	−0.11	−0.12
	(0.082)	(0.133)	(0.098)
NPInteraction_informal	−0.04	0.04	−0.07
	(0.083)	(0.140)	(0.098)
Prob > F	0.0005	0.0006	0.0291
Prob > R2	0.05	0.11	0.07
Number of Observations	240	109	130

Note: Standard errors in parentheses ([a]$p < 0.01$, [b]$p < 0.10$, [d]$p < 0.05$).
[c]Initial product as low-tech as the baseline category.

to the dirigiste and grassroots governance modalities, respectively. The following analysis here is based on evidence available from the 'Shenzhen Electronics Yearbook' (SECC, 2004) and the 'Guangdong Electronics Yearbook' (GECC, 2002). In these two yearbooks, descriptive facts are provided for the developmental path of the electronics industry in Shenzhen and Dongguan. Moreover, an in-depth interview was conducted in late 2007 with the former chair of the Dongguan Electronic Chamber of Commerce (DECC) to gain insights into the industrial development history and changing interests of governments at various levels.

4.1 *Governance Evolution in Shenzhen since the Opening Policy*

Shenzhen was a small, peripheral town before 1978. In 1979, it was selected by the central government as one of the SEZs where the opening policy could be best brought into play, and new reforms were tested for the very first time. The role of the electronics industry was a focus from the very beginning of the special zone development in Shenzhen (GECC, 2002; SECC, 2004). Initial industrialization was driven by the opening-up towards foreign investment, especially from Hong Kong owing to the locational advantage of the region. Shenzhen was then the primary outlet for accommodating the transfer of small-scale and labour-intensive manufacturing facilities from Hong Kong. Meanwhile, a favourable policy for attracting foreign investment was designed to encourage large-scale programmes with longer funding turnover periods, while also aiming to control and limit short-term opportunist behaviour on the part of foreign firms.

4.1.1 *Governance in the Initial Phase of Industrialization in the 1980s*

The central government adopted the strategy of embedding large-scale foreign investment within large domestic firms, including the large state-owned companies directly under the jurisdiction of state ministries and provinces, within renowned universities and research institutes and within military-related plants that were highly specialized in heavy industry. In a sense, this active role of the central government can be described in Xu's (2011) words as 'Centrally Sponsored Local Experiments'. These large joint ventures inherited the primary skill-base of the old national knowledge system from the planned economy and this became the principal technological leader in Shenzhen at that time, rather than the small 'sanlai yibu' factories. They were then able to introduce large-scale production lines building on state-owned assets and scale economies of production, allied with the large endowment of human capital from the state-owned companies which enabled a better absorption of imported technologies (SECC, 2004).

Besides joint ventures with foreign companies, there were also joint ventures between domestic state-owned firms. The alliance amongst these state-owned companies was always accompanied by the tasks of developing a specific leading product technology. In 1986, the Shenzhen Electronics Group Company (later Saige Group), which unifies 117 of the 178 companies in Shenzhen on a voluntary basis, was established under the approval of the Shenzhen City Government. In 1988, the Shenzhen Electronics Group Company arranged the construction of the first specialized electronic parts supply market in China, 'Saige Electronics Supply Market', a milestone in the organization of the electronics industry supply chain in Shenzhen. Within this organizational arrangement, information and production opportunities were more frequently shared amongst member companies (SECC, 2004), and the Saige Electronics Supply Market later served as the breeding ground and incubator of entrepreneurship in Shenzhen.

Meanwhile, network governance was formed in multilevel organizations, encompassing China Central Ministries, the Guangdong province and the Shenzhen City Government, and the industrial park authorities, with the aim of initiating technology transfers, facilitating technological absorption for domestic firms and assisting the business sector in training, quality control and customer searching.

With the support of the coordinated state-led industrial policies and the geographical advantages of proximity to Hong Kong, the electronics industry in Shenzhen has been developing rapidly, relying on processing operation in this period. Nevertheless, the industrial structure in electronics was concentrated in the standard consumer electronics industry (mainly telephones, TV, calculator and radio), a market sector facing saturation and limited space for technological upgrading (SECC, 2004).

4.1.2 *Governance at the Turning Point in the 1990s*

After 1990, the electronics industry in Shenzhen faced rising factor prices and gradually lost the technological advantage in consumer electronics compared to the other regions in China. To achieve a successful upgrading towards high-tech electronics, the Shenzhen City Government strategically identified five industries: PC and software, telecommunication, microelectronics, optical–electro-mechanical integration and new materials. Under the guidance of the selected industries, foreign investment was supported around the five industry fields (SECC, 2004). Moreover, adjusting the organizational competence to initiate the upgrading, the Shenzhen Government implemented two primary measures in terms of financing programmes.

First, firms were offered access to capital markets, with the first capital market being formally opened in Shenzhen in 1992. More recently, the launches of the Small and Medium Enterprise Board (2006) and ChiNet (2009) have made Shenzhen into one of the China's largest clusters of domestic private equity and venture capital investors. Shenzhen's rapid development into one of the most important financial centres in China has greatly supported local entrepreneurship and innovative activities of both small and large private firms. Second, the city government supported the small and medium-sized high-tech private firms with specific funding intermediaries (SECC, 2004), which helped many privately owned technological leaders such as Huawei in Shenzhen.

'In 2002, half of the state-level 909 projects on integrated circuit design were located in Shenzhen and a cluster of integrated circuit design companies was already taking shape, covering the operation of encapsulation, testing, plate making, device providing, scribing and thick film integrating. Most of these were domestic firms such as Guowei, Huawei, Zhongxing, Aisikewei, etc. By the end of 2002, Intel and STMicroelectronics had all followed and established research and design centers for integrated circuits in Shenzhen'. (SECC, 2004)

Owing to Shenzhen's special background as the experimental field for the opening-up policies in China, private firms and the privatization reforms of state-owned companies were encouraged and supported by various levels of government. In 1993, Shenzhen's National People's Congress adopted the 'Stock Limited Corporations Ordinance of Shenzhen Special Zone' and the 'Limited Liability Company Ordinance of Shenzhen Special Zone' with the legislative power of the special zones. Even in small and medium-sized state-owned companies, employee stock ownership was gradually allowed. These conditions gradually allowed the release of the local human capital endowment from the old nationalized research and production system into a market arena. Moreover, the favourable policy treatment in Shenzhen also attracted considerable talent from across the country. The presence of highly qualified migrants who do not own Shenzhen *hukou* also contributed to a high level of entrepreneurial activities in Shenzhen, enabling the exploitation of market opportunities from foreign technology. As a result, many private firms flourished in the 1990s, establishing the base for a wide scope of interactive learning for innovation activities.

4.2 *Governance Evolution in Dongguan since the Opening Policy*

Since the devolution of partial power of fiscal arrangements from the central government to town and village governments, the Dongguan local government has been enthusiastically devoted to economic growth. The industrialization process in Dongguan started in the garment and shoe industries during the 1980s. Compensation trade, that is, the processing of raw materials on clients' demands, the processing and assembling of parts for the clients, all expanded quickly in many villages and towns. The source of orders was mostly Hong Kong owing to the cultural, geographic and linguistic proximity. At that time, there were about 650 000 Dongguanese were settled in Hong Kong. They worked or opened their own factories in Hong Kong, and were therefore the most reliable communicators of business between Hong Kong and their hometown (Interview in Dongguan, September 2007).

4.2.1 *Governance in the Initial Phase of Industrialization in the 1980s*

The Dongguan local government placed great emphasis on encouraging the Hong Kong-Dongguanese to invest in their hometown. In 1981, the office of outward processing and assembly was established to organize this important task. Moreover, the village and town governments also greatly supported the development of the compensation trade by offering cheap land, favourable policies and flexible standards. The distribution of the processing earnings was negotiated between the town and village governments and foreign investors, and mostly under informal frameworks such as verbal agreements (Interview in Dongguan, September 2007). In this way, vested interests were taking shape amongst foreign firms, township and village governments, as well as the peasants who live on the rent of the collectively owned land.

In this process of industrial development, which was based on the grassroots attraction of foreign investment, infrastructure supply was directed to industry-specific and hands-on services. This was provided mainly by the township and village governments, who used their fiscal incomes for constructing factory buildings, roads, electricity and telecommunications, all to improve the investment environment. However, this bottom-up industrialization process gave rise to many small-scale Hong Kong investments in the region, the small scale of which was a result of the fears surrounding the institutional uncertainty. This led to a largely scattered and uncoordinated land-use pattern, which limited or possibly even inhibited many potential agglomeration effects.

4.2.2 *Governance at the Turning Point in the 1990s*

By 1995, the profits of the local garment industry in Dongguan were rapidly shrinking. However, the central government policy regarding the development of electronics industry at the provincial level was focused on the regions of Shenzhen, Guangzhou and Foshan, rather than on Dongguan (GECC, 2002). As such, without the same degree of national institutional backing to enter these industries, Dongguan had to adopt another development

Table 6. Statistics of the Domestic Sector in Shenzhen and Dongguan (2009).

Firm above scale[a]	Shenzhen	Dongguan
Share of domestic firm units	53%	25%
Share of domestic firms' output value	37%	16%
Share of domestic firms' added value	47%	15%

Source: Shenzhen Statistical Yearbook 2010 and Dongguan Statistical Yearbook 2010.
[a]Firms above scale include all state-owned firms and firms with over 5 million in sales.

model, one which built on its existing grassroots-type institutional approach. By the mid 1990s the garment industry firms were increasingly being replaced by new Electronics firms, mainly from Taiwan, along with some of the Shenzhen firms, which were gradually relocating to Dongguan in the middle of the 1990s.

'The profit of the garment industry was shrinking after 1995, and the development of the electronics industry was increasing in pace. At that time, the bosses of medium-sized firms in Taiwan saw the huge profit made by the bosses of small-sized firms investing in Dongguan, and decided to follow and establish plants here. However, the industry is without planning at all because the Dongguan government, especially the town government, would offer land whenever the foreign firms were willing to invest. I remember that many surrounding towns and cities laughed at us because of that, saying 'there are so many stars in the sky in Dongguan but without a moon' (own Interview with DECC Chair Ye in 2007).

This shift, which was attracted by low-cost factors in Dongguan, slowly led to the clustering of not only the Taiwanese firms but also their complex and associated systems of supplier linkages. Delta Electronics, for example, bought 22 small- and medium-sized upstream and downstream Taiwanese firms when investing in Dongguan. Evolving on the basis of the networked production systems brought by these Taiwanese firms since the mid-1990s, the electronics industrial supply chain is now deeply embedded and integrated in Dongguan, and by the beginning of the 21st century, the compensation trade in electronics in Dongguan was deeply established and rooted in the regional production system.

To promote industrial upgrading and to attract large-scale high-tech investments, in 2001 the Dongguan City Government also established the first city-level industrial park, with high entry standards, in 2001. Furthermore, the Dongguan City Government responded to the call from the central and provincial governments to move away from the old low-end processing industries and to attract new high-tech ones. However, this led to great resistance from the township and village governments because they, and also the peasants, rely heavily on the compensation trade associated with processing activities for their major income (Yang, 2010). As such, vested interests had already been firmly shaped from the bottom up, thus creating an inertia for any structural change away from the compensation trade with the lower end of the electronics value-chain (Interview in Dongguan, September 2007).

Due to the weak industrial base in Dongguan before the rapid development, and the lack of overall strategic coordination associated with Dongguan's grassroots and bottom-up approach, the local skilled-labour market and related industrial institutions therefore remained underdeveloped, especially in comparison with the great profits being made via the compensation trade. Indeed, as we see in Table 6, statistics from 2009 show that the domestic sector is much weaker in Dongguan than in Shenzhen. On the basis of the conceptual arguments already discussed and our preliminary survey data outlined earlier, this weaker endogenous development path in Dongguan's business sector allied with its greater dependency on foreign-owned lower-end manufacturing facilities, is expected to impact on the long term development of the RIS in Dongguan.

4.3 *Summary of Governance Differences in Shenzhen and Dongguan*

Shenzhen and Dongguan share many commonalities in the industrializing process. These two cities were both very underdeveloped regions with weak industrial bases before the opening policy was implemented in 1978. The initial industrialization in both cities heavily depended on the combination of foreign investment and a ready supply of low wage rural migrant workers facilitated by the *hukou* regime, which was designed to control labour mobility. Nevertheless, there are two underlying and fundamental differences between the two cities.

The first difference is the locational advantage of Shenzhen, being geographically closer to Hong Kong than Dongguan, which is situated further away between Shenzhen and Guangzhou. This greater proximity, and associated knowledge accessibility that comes with it, has given Shenzhen a slight advantage in accessing transfer of electronics manufacturing and processing facilities from Hong Kong, whereas some less favourable activities, such as the production of garments and shoes, were passed on to Dongguan. Yet, the differences in location cannot account for the major differences in the long-run trajectories of the two adjacent regions. More importantly, it would appear, are the institutional advantages of Shenzhen over Dongguan.

From the above discussion, it can be seen that the development of the electronics industry in Shenzhen was strongly supported from the beginning by the active involvement of state authorities and organizations in a constructive manner, which both reflected and facilitated the emerging relocation trends and needs of the late 1980s global electronics industry to low-cost regions (Luthje, 2004). Shenzhen's position in the vanguard of China's market-oriented reforms gave it a first-mover advantage in developing new innovation-supported institutions, which built on the existing national industrial infrastructure. These changes appear to have facilitated the further establishment and incubation of new local start-up firms and the also the efficient adaptation of existing firms to new and more diversified markets, thereby promoting a virtuous development cycle reflective of a strong RIS. In contrast, the grassroots institutional setup in Dongguan was focused on developing the compensation trade around lower-end processing and assembly activities, in which the monetary gains mainly went to the village and town-level governments, small overseas Chinese investors (mainly Hong Kong and Taiwan) and local peasants, all of which are reflective of a much weaker RIS.

5. Discussion and Conclusion

In this chapter we have compared two city regions in the same province of China which both started the industrialization process at the same time in the wake of the opening policy in the late 1970s, but which exhibited very different institutional systems. It should be remembered that the two cities in this study both started the rapid industrialization process with a poor endowment of local skills and a minimal industrial base, and have developed within a transitional context from a planned economy to a market economy, in which old institutions and organizations have been constantly adjusted and destroyed in the process and replaced by new institutions.

This chapter finds that the dirigiste governance modality in Shenzhen in the initial industrialization phase led to a more mature and developed RIS than the grassroots governance response in Dongguan. Insights from the empirical results show that dirigiste governance in the initial industrialization phase in Shenzhen was more powerful in providing innovation-related resources than the grassroots governance approach of Dongguan.

Grassroots governance in China has been widely applied, because it is cost-efficient for the central government and has actively mobilized the initiative of local governments to develop the economy. Yet, while grassroots governance has been argued to be an important means of mobilizing and promoting local resources and interdependencies (Amin, 2002), the result here suggests that such an approach may also lead to negative lock-in effects. In this particular case, the grassroots approach tended to rely more on the capacity of less competent local authorities, whereas the dirigiste approach had the advantage of more direct support from, and access to, national authorities. Nevertheless, the findings in this chapter should not be viewed as arguments necessarily favouring the central planning method of development over more deregulated market mechanisms. Rather, institutions and institutional reforms are fundamental to the role played by economic geography in innovation and vice-versa, and uncovering these interrelationships is always important for understanding the different development trajectories of regions.

The insights of this chapter suggest that in other regions and other countries undergoing similar transformations, for clusters that develop out of these types of grassroots governance, two lessons can be learned to foster the development of the RIS. First, incentive frameworks should be put in place to avoid any negative lock-in effects associated with local vested interests which inhibit the ability of the region to adjust to the changing market environment. Second, the policy focus should be placed upon enhancing the absorptive capacity of firms and related organizations, such as attracting high quality human capital and encouraging the accumulation and development of technological capabilities within firms.

References

Altenburg, T. (2006) Opportunities for Asian countries to catch up with knowledge-based competition. In B. Lundvall, P. Intarakumnerd and J. Vang (eds), *Asia's Innovation Systems in Transition* (pp. 21–53). Northampton: Edward Elgar.

Amin, A. (1999) An institutionalist perspective on regional economic development. *International journal of urban and regional research* 23: 365–378.

Amin, A. (2002) Spatialities of globalisation. *Environment and Planning A* 34: 385–400.

Asheim, BT. and Coenen, L. (2005) Knowledge bases and regional innovation systems: comparing Nordic clusters. *Research Policy* 34: 1173–1190.

Becker, G.S. and Posner, R.A. (2004) Suicide: an economic approach. Mimeo, Department of Economics, University of Chicago. Available at http://economics.uchicago.edu/download/Suicide_An_Economic_Approach_4.pdf. Accessed on August 29, 2010.

Boschma, R.A. (2004) Competitiveness of regions from an evolutionary perspective. *Regional studies* 38: 1001–1014.

Braczyk, H.J., Cooke, P.N. and Heidenreich, M. (1998) *Regional Innovation Systems: The Role of Governances in a Globalized World*. London: Routledge.

Capello, R. (1999) Spatial transfer of knowledge in high technology milieux: learning versus collective learning processes. *Regional studies* 33: 353–365.

Cohen, W.M. and Levinthal, D.A. (1990) Absorptive capacity – a new perspective on learning and innovation. *Administrative Science Quarterly* 35: 128–152.

Cooke, P., Gomez Uranga, M. and Etxebarria, G. (1997) Regional innovation systems: institutional and organisational dimensions. *Research Policy* 26 475–491.

Cooke, P. (2004) Regional innovation systems: an evolutionary approach. In P. Cooke, M. Heidenreich, and H. J. Braczyk (eds), *Regional Innovation Systems: The Role of Governance in a Globalized World*, 2nd ed. (pp. 1–18). London: Routledge.

Dalum, B., Johnson, B. and Lundvall, B. (1992) *Public Policy in the Learning Economy*. London: Printer.

Doloreux, D. (2004) Regional innovation systems in Canada: a comparative study. *Regional studies* 38: 479–492.

Easterly, W. (2008) Institutions: top down or bottom up? *American Economic Review* 98: 95–99.

GECC (Guangdong Electronic Chamber of Commerce) (2002) Guangdong Electronics Yearbook. Available at http://www.guangdongdz.com/4c_of_c/annual.asp. Accessed on April 18, 2010.

Goldsmith, A.A. (2007) Is governance reform a catalyst for development? *Governance* 20: 165–186.

Haggard, S. (2004) Institutions and growth in East Asia. *Studies in Comparative International Development (SCID)* 38: 53–81.

Howells, J.R.L. (1999) *Regional Systems of Innovation?* Cambridge: Cambridge University Press.

Könnölä, T., Unruh, G.C. and Carrillo-Hermosilla, J. (2006) Prospective voluntary agreements for escaping techno-institutional lock-in. *Ecological Economics* 57: 239–252.

Leonard, D. (1992) Core capabilities and core rigidities: a paradox in managing new product development. *Strategic Management Journal* 13: 111–125.

Leung, C.K. (1993) Personal contacts, subcontracting linkages, and development in the Hong Kong-Zhujiang Delta region. *Annals of the Association of American Geographers* 83: 272–302.

Levitt, B. and March, J.G. (1988) Organizational Learning. *Annual Review of Sociology* 14: 319–340.

Lundvall, B., Intarakumnerd, P. and Vang, J. (2006) *Asia's Innovation Systems in Transition*. Northampton: Edward Elgar.

Luthje, C. (2004) Characteristics of innovating users in a consumer goods field: an empirical study of sport-related product consumers. *Technovation* 24: 683–695.

Morgan, K. (2004) The exaggerated death of geography: learning, proximity and territorial innovation systems. *Journal of Economic Geography* 4: 3–21.

Park, S.O. (2003) Economic spaces in the Pacific Rim: a paradigm shift and new dynamics. *Regional science* 82: 223–247.

Porter, M.E. (1998) Clusters and the new economics of competition. *Harvard Business Review* 6: 77–92.

Qian, Y. and Roland, G. (1998) Federalism and the soft budget constraint. *The American Economic Review* 88: 1143–1162.

Revilla Diez, J. (2002) Metropolitan innovation systems: a comparison between Barcelona, Stockholm, and Vienna. *International regional science review* 25: 63–85.

Revilla Diez, J. and Kiese, M. (2006) Regional innovation potential and innovative networks in Singapore, Penang (Malaysia) and Thailand. *Regional Studies* 40: 1005–1023.

Revilla Diez, J. and Berger, M. (2005) The role of multinational corporations in metropolitan innovation systems – empirical evidence from Europe and South East Asia. *Environment and Planning A* 37: 1813–1835.

Staber, U. (2001) The structure of networks in industrial districts. *International journal of urban and regional research* 25: 537–552.

SECC (Shenzhen Electronic Chamber of Commerce). (2004). Shenzhen Electronics Yearbook. Available at http://www.guangdongdz.com/special_column/sznj/zl02.asp. Accessed on April 18, 2010.

Wang, C.C. and Lin G.C.S. (2008) The growth and spatial distribution of China's ICT industry: new geography of clustering and innovation. *Issues & Studie* 44: 145–192.

Xu. C. (2011) The fundamental institutions of China's reforms and development. *Journal of Economic Literature* 49: (4) 1076–1151.

Yang, C. (2010) Restructuring the export-oriented industrialization in the Pearl River Delta, China: institutional evolution and emerging tension. *Applied Geography* 32: 143–157.

Zhou, Y., Sun, Y., Wei, Y.H.D. and Lin, G.C.S. (2011) De-centering 'spatial fix'-patterns of territorialization and regional technological dynamism of ICT hubs in China. *Journal of Economic Geography* 11: 119–150.

Zahra, S.A. and George, G. (2002) Absorptive capacity: a review, reconceptualization, and extension. *Academy of Management Review* 27: 185–203.

INDEX

Printed and bound by CPI Group (UK) Ltd, Croydon, CR0 4YY

25/03/2025

14647330-0001